THE
MISSION,
THE MEN,
AND ME

THE
MISSION,
THE MEN,
AND ME

LESSONS FROM A

FORMER DELTA FORCE

COMMANDER

PETE BLABER

BERKLEY CALIBER, NEW YORK

THE BERKLEY PUBLISHING GROUP
Published by the Penguin Group
Penguin Group (USA) Inc.
375 Hudson Street, New York, New York 10014, USA
Penguin Group (Canada), 90 Eglinton Avenue East, Suite 700, Toronto, Ontario M4P 2Y3, Canada
(a division of Pearson Penguin Canada Inc.)
Penguin Books Ltd., 80 Strand, London WC2R 0RL, England
Penguin Group Ireland, 25 St. Stephen's Green, Dublin 2, Ireland (a division of Penguin Books Ltd.)
Penguin Group (Australia), 250 Camberwell Road, Camberwell, Victoria 3124, Australia
(a division of Pearson Australia Group Pty. Ltd.)
Penguin Books India Pvt. Ltd., 11 Community Centre, Panchsheel Park, New Delhi—110 017, India
Penguin Group (NZ), 67 Apollo Drive, Rosedale, North Shore 0632, New Zealand
(a division of Pearson New Zealand Ltd.)
Penguin Books (South Africa) (Pty.) Ltd., 24 Sturdee Avenue, Rosebank, Johannesburg 2196,
South Africa

Penguin Books Ltd., Registered Offices: 80 Strand, London WC2R 0RL, England

This book is an original publication of the Berkley Publishing Group.

The publisher has no control over and does not assume any responsibility for author or third-party
websites or their content.

Grateful acknowledgment is made to Sean Naylor for permission to reprint passages from *Not a Good
Day to Die: The Untold Story of Operation Anaconda,* Berkley Caliber Books, 2005. Reprinted by
permission of the author.

First edition: December 2008

Library of Congress Cataloging-in-Publication Data

Blaber, Pete.
    The mission, the men, and me: lessons from a former Delta Force commander / Pete Blaber.
        p.   cm.
    Includes bibliographical references and index.
    ISBN 978-0-425-22372-7
    1. Blaber, Pete.   2. United States. Army—Commando troops—Biography.   3. Terrorism—
Prevention.   I. Title.

    UA34.S64B53 2008
    356'.1670973—dc22   2008019855

PRINTED IN THE UNITED STATES OF AMERICA

10   9   8   7   6   5   4   3

CONTENTS

FOREWORD...IX

INTRODUCTION: 1
The Mission, the Men, and Me

PART 1

1. HOW I GOT HERE: 19
Patterns of Hindsight

2. NATURAL SELECTION: 31
Getting into Delta Force

3. GORILLA WARFARE: 40
Imagine the Unimaginable, Humor Your Imagination

PART 2

4. LEWIS AND CLARK DISCOVER
OSAMA BIN LADEN:.. 63
When in Doubt, Develop the Situation

5. THE EMBASSY BOMBINGS:................................... 86
The Only Failure Is a Failure to Try

6. **THE INFILTRATION OF AL QAEDA:** 94
   Discovering the Art of the Possible

7. **WALKING THE BOB:** 106
   Always Listen to the Guy on the Ground

PART 3

8. **CALM BEFORE THE STORM:** 135
   The Man-Huntin' Project

9. **9/11:** 144
   The Four-Inch Knife Blade

10. **IMAGINE EVERYONE'S POTENTIAL**
    AS THE GUY ON THE GROUND 148

11. **IMAGINE HOW TO SEEK OUT THE GUY**
    ON THE GROUND 164

12. **IMAGINE HOW:** 180
    The Counterfeit Double Agent

PART 4

13. **ON THE GROUND IN AFGHANISTAN:** 201
    Riding the Edge of Chaos

14. **IT'S NOT REALITY UNLESS IT'S SHARED** 203

15. **ORGANIZING FOR COMBAT:** 214
    Dealing with a Natural Disaster

16. **EXPLORING THE FRONTIER:** 220
    Recognizing Enemy Patterns

17. **REALITY CHECK:** 242
    What's Your Recommendation?

18. THE BATTLE BEGINS: 262
    Stay Calm, Think!

19. TAKUR GHAR: 272
    When All the Laughter Died in Sorrow

    NOTES 299

    INDEX 311

FOREWORD

Books written by former government leaders are part of a distinct genre of literature. As any writer will confirm, writing a book is a monumental task—there are no shortcuts to sitting down, day after day, week after week, constantly saturating, incubating, and illuminating, then rewriting. Former government leaders assume the added challenge of ensuring that the content is free from any sensitive information that could aid a sophisticated enemy in harming the United States or its service members. Names, dates, tactics, techniques, and methods all have to be filtered and sanitized to ensure operational security. Therefore, the most important and vexing challenge facing any government official who sets out to write anything for publication, regardless of format, is the need to maintain the operational security of the participants and methods involved. For military and intelligence operatives, this responsibility is spelled out in a formal nondisclosure agreement that each member signs upon entry to their unit, activity, or agency. The agreement generally prohibits unfettered release of the following information:

1. Naming of classified units;
2. Naming of people assigned to classified units;

3. Discussing recent operations and missions that are classified; and

4. Discussing classified tactics, techniques, and procedures.

Disclosure Agreement Safeguards

1. My former unit, Special Forces Operational Detachment—Delta ("Delta") is the same name that geologists use to describe the end of a river that empties into the ocean. It is also the Greek word for difference. The army unofficially considers the name and unit classified. However, "Delta" or "Delta Force" has been so popularized by the Hollywood movie and publication industries that one would be hard pressed to say that these names are not in the public domain. Moreover, my official military records, which are unclassified and available to the public, likewise record the dates and specific jobs I held while assigned to this unit. The reality is that those of us who served there rarely use the term "Delta." Instead, we almost always refer to the organization as "the Unit." Since I am trying to write this book in an accurate, reality-based context, the Unit is the term I most frequently use throughout the book. When I refer to other military or government organizations, activities, or agencies in this book, I do so only in the interest of continuity, and only if another publication or official unclassified government document has already mentioned that organization's participation in the mission at issue.

2. Nicknames, titles, and pseudonyms are used to address this concern. Again, I do this to protect persons, units, activities/agencies and their tactics, techniques, and procedures from compromise or harm by sophisticated enemies of the United States. In the interest of continuity with previous publications, I sometimes refer to certain publicly recognized senior military leaders by their true names. I do this when it's obvious that there is no operational security issue involved. I have otherwise intentionally depersonalized the stories to maintain the anonymity of the individuals involved. So, unless a per-

son is named in a direct quotation from a book or periodical, I refer to that person only by their position (e.g., "commanding general").

Even when military leaders are identified in other open-source documents, such as the bestselling books *Not a Good Day to Die* and *Cobra II*, I only refer to them by their duty position. My intent is not to make judgmental assessments of anyone; rather, it is to extract and share the timeless lessons from the action or mission in the form of guiding principles.

3. All of the operations discussed in this book have been written about in numerous other civilian and government publications. The stories of me and my men in Afghanistan and Iraq are recounted in the two bestsellers listed above. The army expressed no concern with these authors using my true name to recount the events described in those publications. In both cases, the army never sought my permission to use my name or likeness before approving these books for publication and into the public domain.

4. I have used great care to avoid going into context-specific detail concerning any tactics, techniques, and procedures used by any military organization. As described in the opening chapter of this book, the key to success on all battlefields—past, present, and future—has very little to do with electronic whiz-bang gadgets and top-secret technologies; instead, it's all about how you think, how you make decisions, and how you execute those decisions—none of which may be properly considered "classified."

The content of this book is as clear, detailed, and accurate an account of the events and experiences in which I took part as I can provide while maintaining the sanctity of the operational security issues described above.

All of the material contained herein was derived from unclassified publications and sources; nothing written here is intended to confirm or deny, officially or unofficially, any events described, or the views of any individual, government, or agency. The insights in this book are based on my personal perceptions, experiences, and interactions. If a story seems to be missing some level of context-rich detail, the reason is more than likely to protect operational security.

In an effort to protect the nature of specific operations and/or individuals who participated in some of these events, I sometimes had to take liberties with the dates, times, or order of events. Nonetheless, none of the security-instituted adjustments affects the context of the lesson that the story reveals or compromises the persons or agencies that may have been involved.

To ensure continuity of content, I have included some accounts of events in which I was not directly involved. Once again, I only use these accounts to amplify the overarching lesson (e.g., the John Walker Lindh story to demonstrate the utility of developing the situation). In other cases, such as the Battle of Shahi Khot, I include the perspective of some of my men, because without their accounts, the story cannot be accurately or completely told. The details of these accounts come from the aggregation of personal conversations, face-to-face discussions with the principals, after-action discussions, and the many written documents created immediately following each event. All of these documents are unclassified and available to the public. In every case I have attempted to stay true to the facts of the event.

Finally, combat is just like life; no two individuals see it or experience it the same way. This book is my account of what happened. If there are any inaccuracies in the events described herein, the responsibility is mine alone. This book presents my views and does not represent the views of the U.S. Army, the U.S. Department of Defense, or anyone else.

INTRODUCTION:

THE MISSION, THE MEN, AND ME

April 11, 2003

We called ourselves the Wolverines.[1] Our mission was marauding.*
We were five hundred miles behind enemy lines. I commanded the Wolverines. They called me Panther.

The night was moonless and bitter cold. Twelve all-terrain and undercover vehicles stealthily crept across the desert. Driven by heavily armed and heavily bundled Delta operators, the vehicle's fat, knobby tires quietly crunched the frozen sand as they crawled. Just ahead, bathed in the glow of night vision–goggle green, lay the deserted eight-lane highway that fenced Saddam's hometown of Tikrit from the edge of the desert.[2] No Western military force had seen or set foot in this, the most modern and fanatically loyal of Iraqi cities, in more than fifty years. Just one day after the Iraqi regime collapsed,

---

*Inspired by World War II term used to describe three thousand American volunteers of the 5307th Composite Unit (Provisional), aka "Merrill's Marauders," operating behind Japanese lines across Burma, pushing beyond their limits, and fighting pitched battles at every strongpoint. They were led by army officer Frank D. Merrill.

Saddam and his henchmen were officially on the run;[3] the Wolverines were on their scent.

Our destination was underneath the cloverleaf intersection a few hundred meters down the highway. Without any armor protection, the twelve Delta vehicles jockeyed for every available inch of protective cover behind the massive concrete support pillars. Once in position, we relayed the code word to our tanks.

Out of the blackness, five tanks crawled forward. Their hulking hexagonal masses were barely detectable to an attentive ear, and totally invisible to the naked eye. Their destination was the top of the cloverleaf. At the apex of the intersection, they starburst and drove halfway down each of the off-ramps, then shifted into silence. With thermal night sights and guns scanning, they could surveil and secure all four cardinal directions. The fifth tank stayed at the top and maintained an eagle's-eye view of Saddam's backyard below.

With the desert at their backs, the Wolverines were in position.

From the outside looking in, Tikrit appeared like any semimodern town: apartment buildings, gas stations, blinking traffic lights, and cars parked along palm-tree-lined streets. But for one imperceptible detail, nothing was stirring, neither man nor beast. Years of conducting operations in urban environments had taught us that when all is calm in a city, something is usually awry. Watching and waiting behind our guns, we could hear our breath as it froze in front of our faces.

In an instant, the ghostly city roared to life. Enemy muzzle flashes blinked across the urban horizon like flashbulbs at the Super Bowl, except these flashes shot tracers. The tracers instantly coagulated around the tanks. Enemy firing positions were everywhere: apartment buildings, storefronts, and alleys. Pickup trucks with machine guns mounted in their cabs popped in and out of garages, and back and forth around corners like angry cockroaches.

From his vehicle atop the cloverleaf, Bill, my second in command, assessed the situation.[4] One of the most experienced combat commanders in the Unit;[5] he used a purposefully calming tone as he radioed the tanks.

"This is Echo 0-2—backup."

Backing up allowed the tanks to use the elevation of each cloverleaf as protection from the ground-level machine gun fire. As their tracks surged into reverse, the tanks' super-sophisticated fire control systems, thermal-imaging night sights, and ballistic computers digitally collaborated with their 120-millimeter main guns to return fire. Thirty-pound projectiles torched from the tubes. Betrayed by their own muzzle flashes, enemy positions began to disintegrate. Corners of buildings were lopped. Storefronts were in the rear, and angry cockroach pickup trucks were doing fiery backflips. Nevertheless, the cadence of enemy fire did not decrease. Even in wartime while watching for a night attack, most soldiers fall asleep. The enemy we initially engaged consisted only of the men who had been awake and on watch. With each passing minute, additional men awoke from the warmth and slumber of their fetal positions, grabbed their weapons, and joined the fight.

All but one tank driver responded to the order to back up with an affirmative.

"Ahh, Echo 0-2, we got a problem," the missing tank crew finally responded.

"This is Echo 0-2. What's the deal?"

"We must have run over some telephone wire on the way down the ramp, 'cuz now it's completely wrapped around my tracks and I can't back up."

"This is Echo 0-2. Okay, how long till you can get it free?"

"I don't know—we're starting to take a lot of fire," he shouted as his .50-caliber machine gun rhythmically thumped away in the background.

"This is Echo 0-2. Hang in there; I'm sending help."

Before Bill could pass the message, a group of five Delta Force operators moved forward in a half-crouched sprint. At the apex, the five operators split up and joined each of the five tanks to help direct their fire and steady their nerves.

From our hide site a few kilometers out in the desert, I listened intently to the radio transmissions and watched the increasing rate and rapidity of the tracer barrage arcing across the pitch-black sky. I assessed the situation. *If the enemy keeps coming, he'll need help,* I thought. I contacted helicopter gunships loitering in the sky a hundred miles distant, and directed them to fly closer to the highway intersection and prepare to take guidance from Bill and/or his men.[6]

Bill called me first:

"Echo 0-1, this is Echo 0-2. We're taking some pretty heavy fire from all directions. I got one tank potentially stuck on some telephone wire." Bill was still speaking calmly, but every time his hand mike was open, I could hear the roar of the tanks' main guns behind him.[7]

The Doppler-induced *wap-wap* of the attack helicopters whispered from the distance, raised their pitch as they approached, then screamed over our heads and directly into the fight. Five-second chainsaw bursts from their 7.62-millimeter Gatling guns introduced them to the enemy. The battle raged on.

Before the Wolverines drove out of the hide site earlier that evening, I brought them together and addressed the entire force. My intent was to ensure that we weren't becoming victims of our own charade. We needed a shared reality around what we were, what we weren't, and what the mission was that we were trying to accomplish that night.

Tucked behind sand dunes and encircled by nearly impassable desert trenches known as wadis, our hide site contained a tiny cluster of one-story buildings that had once served as the most secret and secure of all Iraqi military bases, like an Iraqi version of Area 51 in the Nevada desert. Completely off the beaten track, and off-limits to all but a few top Iraqi government officials, it was tailor-made to be repurposed as our marauding lair.

We named ourselves the Wolverines, after the teenage gang that took on the invading Soviet army in the famous B movie *Red Dawn*.[8] Like the movie version of the Wolverines, we were using disguises, deception, and diversions to confuse and confound the enemy. Most of us had been undercover numerous times in our careers: as businessmen, as tourists, and even as a bunch of anthropologists on a desert dig. Our approach was to blend in anywhere; it was a way of life. However, none of us had ever attempted what we were now doing in the Iraqi desert during this mission: disguising ourselves as a tank division.

They say you can't judge a book by its cover, but we were hoping the Iraqi military would do just that; sort of a modern-day version of the Trojan horse[9] technique. Except instead of trying to appear nonthreatening to fool the enemy into letting their guard down, as the Greeks used the Trojan horse against the city of Troy, we were trying to appear threatening to make the enemy believe we were the vanguard of a massive tank division. We believed that by conducting hit-and-run operations against the Iraqi military forces defending central Iraq, we could strike fear and panic in their hearts and make them believe we had them surrounded and that their situation was hopeless.

The Wolverines had been wildly successful so far. We had conducted one of the longest ground infiltrations behind enemy lines in the history of modern-day warfare.[10] By combining precision fire with precision maneuver, our small but nimble force was able to achieve effects way out of proportion to our size and the effort we expended.[11] Full enemy brigades had collapsed and fled at the sight and commotion of our marauding attacks. This was the first time in history that a tank unit was attached to a special operations force to conduct special operations missions behind enemy lines. We had destroyed hundreds of Saddam's machines of war—tanks, artillery, rocket launchers, and jets, most of them abandoned by their crews seconds before we drilled them with a technological orgy of laser- and precision-guided munitions.

Our ruse had worked way beyond even our most optimistic expectations.[12] We had accomplished our overall mission of causing Saddam and his top generals to believe the main attack was coming from west of Baghdad, instead of where the entire invasion force was actually attacking from—the south.[13] The Iraqi generals had arrayed their defending forces accordingly; as a result of trying to defend everywhere, they defended nowhere. With the collapse of the Iraqi government, we were the only barrier between Saddam and his last potential escape route out of Iraq. Our counterfeit tank division created the impression that the vast deserts of northwestern Iraq were sealed shut, forcing Saddam and his henchman to go to ground instead of into exile, where they would almost assuredly escape justice. (See Map 1).

The reality behind our ruse was that our Trojan horse was beginning to pull up lame. We had started with ten tanks, delivered to us via C-17s under the cover of night, on an airstrip we scraped onto the desert floor, while blazing across the Mars-like no-man's-land of western Iraq.[14] Hundreds of kilometers of rugged, roadless desert with no logistical support took a toll on the ten.[15] As engines strained and parts snapped, it took ten tanks to make five, and then there was something broken on every one of the five. All were in dire need of maintenance and repair, but there was none to be had.

We had no maintenance personnel, no spare parts, and no way to get them. Not because of some bureaucratic oversight, but because we believed that to succeed at marauding we had to be nimble, and if you want to be nimble, you gotta be quick. Tooth to tail is how the conventional military describes the ratio of combat troops to support troops. Many conventional thinkers describe the perfect ratio as one to nine. Our ratio was one to none. We were 100 percent tooth, with zero tail to slow us down.[16]

Assembled around me as I spoke that evening were about a hundred heavily armed and heavily grizzled warriors. With no access to running water and no resupply, they wore the same clothes and hygienic accoutrements they had donned twenty-four days earlier. Their faces wore the expression of pure, unadulterated courage.

"Remember that we're a small, agile force; we don't have enough combat power or armor protection to take on large Iraqi mechanized forces, or to slug it out with insurgents in an urban area where they can use swarming tactics to cut us to pieces."

I paused while some of the operators murmured. Many of the men in front of me had cut their teeth on the streets of Mogadishu, Somalia. Some of their best friends had been blown to pieces while escorting the ill-fated convoy that had driven haplessly through the streets of Mogadishu to locate a helicopter crash site. They understood with crystal clarity what a swarming enemy can do to vehicles constrained to the tight, chaotic confines of an urban jungle.

"Your mission tonight is to conduct a show of force on the outskirts of Tikrit.[17] We're not trying to seize terrain or destroy an objective; this is an effects-based operation. Our purpose is to make the Tikrit military forces believe they are surrounded by a large U.S. armored formation. But to do that, we can't just hide in the desert; we have to show them the tanks. Approach the outskirts of the city with extreme caution; this is Saddam's hometown, and we know he keeps his best-equipped and most loyal men there to protect it. We want to get close enough to the enemy so they can see us, but we don't want to get decisively engaged. Keep your back to the desert at all times."[18]

"Echo 0-1, this is Echo 0-2. Sit-rep follows."* It was Bill again.

"It's getting pretty hot here. We estimate at least five hundred enemies." He paused. "They got heavy weapons and RPGs." He paused again. "All the roads into the city are barricaded; they have dug-in positions along the streets, bunkers on top of the buildings, and lots of vehicle-mounted antitank weapons. Over."

*Sit-rep is an abbreviation for situation report, a brief report of who, what, when, where, and why.

"What's your recommendation?" I asked him.

"Well, my mission is to conduct a show of force, and we're definitely putting on a show." He paused. "You told me not to get decisively engaged, but even if you didn't tell me that, we're heavily outnumbered and outgunned, and right now I'm in real danger of losing a tank. I recommend we continue to engage and destroy the enemy, but as soon as we free the entangled tank I need to pull back into the desert to prevent from getting overrun."

"Roger; approved. As soon as that tank is free, pull back into the desert and return to our hide site," I told him.

Bill responded, "Roger out."

A split second after Bill signed off, the radio crackled to life again.

"This is Serpent 01. What do you think you are doing?"[19]

It was our commanding general. He was monitoring our radio transmissions from inside his operations center in another country, more than three hundred miles away.[20]

I wasn't really sure about the context of his question, so I quickly summarized our mission and then gave him an update on the current enemy situation.

"Negative, negative, negative. You are not to pull out of that city. I want you to keep moving forward into the city and destroy the enemy," he barked.[21]

From his temperature-controlled operations center, the commanding general saw the battle as a series of color-coded computer icons on a giant flat-screen television. He heard the battle as a series of truncated interrogatives between Bill and me during our intermittent satellite radio transmissions. What he couldn't see was the enemy forces attempting to swarm the cloverleaf, or the robust roadblocks they so deftly constructed on the roads leading into the city. He couldn't feel the biting cold, nor the vulnerability the majority of the Wolverines felt in the unarmored and unprotected vehicles on which they rode. He couldn't hear the sonic crack of the enemy's bullets as they snapped like bullwhips above the men's heads, nor the assessments the men on the ground were making regarding the brutal reality of their current predicament. The commanding general had no context.

A day prior and five hundred miles south, the armored divisions that led the coalition's main attack penetrated Baghdad using the shock and awe of what would from that day forward be referred to in military parlance as a thunder run. They had crushed the enemy resistance by driving a column of armored vehicles through the heart of the city.

More than likely, our commanding general had visions of similar grandeur for our counterfeit armor column.[22] But thunder running wasn't our mission, and my men were only pretending to be part of an armored division. A real armored division has more than three hundred tanks and twice that number of armored support vehicles. We had just five tanks and at least one of them was on life support. More than 150,000 men and vehicles conducted the attack on Baghdad; we were on the edge of Saddam's hometown with fewer than a hundred.

In a respectful yet matter-of-fact tone, I reminded the commanding general what our mission was, and then reiterated the seriousness of the enemy situation. Finally I explained, "I already told Bill to break contact with the enemy and move back into the desert to regroup." The commanding general didn't respond.

A few seconds later my secure satellite phone rang; it was the general's second. He spent a couple of excruciatingly long minutes trying to use Socratic questions to get me to change my mind. I had been patient with the commanding general, but I was in the middle of a mission, and my men's lives were hanging in the balance. Every second I spent appeasing him was a second lost from concentrating on the battle; I couldn't chitchat any longer. I told him the same thing I told the commanding general: "That's not our mission; the situation doesn't warrant it, and I have already ordered the men to pull back."

Around the cloverleaf, the enemy continued to press the fight. High-speed pickup trucks were attempting frontal attacks against the tanks; the enemy was trying to find a kink in our Trojan horse's armor. Most of the helicopter gunships had been hit by small-arms fire and were requesting to pull back.[23] Every man on the cloverleaf was engaging the swarming enemy with whatever weapon he had at his fingertips. Being outnumbered and outgunned was something my guys were uniquely qualified for, and confident that they could handle—at least for a while. It was the radio transmissions between the commanding general and me, broadcast in every vehicle and on every man's headset that were beginning to concern them.

My satellite phone rang one more time; it was the general's second again. An army colonel and a genuinely nice guy, he was caught between a rock and a hard place with his boss.

"Hey, uh, Pete, listen, I think you should, uh, send your guys into the city. If you don't, uh, move through that city, your uh, future as a commander could be affected." The phone went dead.

The three men around me stopped what they were doing and stared at me with wide-eyed trepidation. "What are you gonna do, Panther?" one of them whispered.

Remember the 3Ms, I thought.

The 3Ms is a guiding principle that I learned early in my career, which had provided direction and context for me ever since. In 1985, when I was a brand-new second lieutenant reporting for duty in Korea, my battalion commander, a soft-spoken Vietnam veteran and Marlboro Man lookalike, called me into his office and asked me if I had ever heard of the 3Ms.

"No—sir," I replied sheepishly (I was sure it was something I was supposed to have learned during basic officer training). He sauntered over to the chalkboard and drew three capital Ms, one on top of the other in a column. Then he turned to me and explained.

"The 3Ms are the keys to being successful in life. They stand for the mission, the men, and me." He then drew a line from the top M, through the middle M, down to the bottom M. "They're all connected,"

he continued. "So if you neglect one, you'll screw up the others. The first M stands for the mission; it's the purpose for which you're doing what you're doing. Whether in your personal or professional life, make sure you understand it, and that it makes legal, moral, and ethical sense, then use it to guide all your decisions. The second M stands for the men. Joshua Chamberlain, a Medal of Honor–receiving schoolteacher in the Civil War, once said that 'there are two things an officer must do to lead men: he must care for his men's welfare, and he must show courage.' Welfare of the troops and courage are inextricably linked. When it comes to your men you can't be good at one without being good at the other. Take care of your men's welfare by listening and leading them with sound tactics and techniques that accomplish your mission, and by always having the courage of your convictions to do the right thing by them. The final M stands for me. Me comes last for a reason. You have to take care of yourself, but you should only do so after you have taken care of the mission, and the men. Never put your own personal well-being, or advancement, ahead of the accomplishment of your mission and taking care of your men. . . . "

"Echo 0-1, this is Echo 0-2." Bill's tone was urgent.

"We almost have the tank free, but we gotta move from this position right away or they're going to surround us!" Bill was screaming to hear himself talk over the guttural staccato of the tanks' heavy machine guns. "I'm ready to do whatever you tell me. What do you want me to do?"

"Pull back to the desert as ordered," I told him.

There was no chance for Bill to respond. The enraged voice of the commanding general broke in,

"What did you say? You listen to me, I told you to . . ." Dead silence.

I waited another minute.

"This is Echo 0-1. Say again. Over." I waited a few more seconds and then repeated the call two more times. Still dead silence.

I had no idea what had happened to him, but it really didn't matter. Bill and the rest of the Wolverines were likely already off the cloverleaf, and they weren't taking any more calls after I told them they were cleared to return. I would later learn from a close friend who worked on the commanding general's staff that in the middle of his transmission, the radio system the general was yelling into had short-circuited and thus prevented him from sharing the rest of his response with me and the world. He was so enraged that he threw his radio headset down and stormed off to his quarters.[24]

When the sun came up a few hours later, I walked out into the desert as I did each morning to await the return of the Wolverine marauders. It was the end of yet another twenty-two-hour blur of a combat day. I was standing alone in the desert as the vehicles pulled into the relative safety of our sand dune–encircled hide site. While the men dismounted and began unloading spent ammunition and checking themselves and their vehicles for damage, one of the most senior men in the Unit, Armani, hopped out of the lead vehicle and made a beeline for my location. With hair and clothes completely disheveled, zombielike faraway eyes straining to stay open, and weapons and equipment perfectly maintained and form-fitted to his body, he had the familiar look of a Delta operator returning from an intensive night of combat. I wasn't sure what he was going to say. There was no salutation. Armani simply grabbed my hand, looked me in the eye, and in a voice shouted hoarse from a night of screaming over gunfire, he whispered, "We were hanging on every word of your conversation with the general while we fought last night. We would have been cut to pieces if we'd driven into that city. I just wanted to shake your hand and say thanks."

That simple handshake and the barely audible words of gratitude from a man I completely respected, along with the knowledge that all my men had successfully returned from a dangerous mission, was a defining moment for me that I am as proud of as any event in my entire life. Ironically, I really didn't do anything other than what I was supposed to do. I didn't lead a charge against an enemy machine-gun nest, nor did I execute some Napoleonic cutting-edge operational maneuver; I simply did the right thing. It was the right thing for the mission, it was the right thing for the men, and it was the right thing for me.

There were many lessons from what the audacious men of Task Force Wolverine accomplished during the early days of combat in Iraq. Interviews with captured Iraqi leaders confirmed that Saddam and his generals all believed that our band of a few hundred marauders was the vanguard of the main coalition attack.*25 But the most important lesson I took away from those early days of combat in Iraq, was the primacy of the 3Ms (the Mission, the Men, and Me).

I had used the 3Ms many times in my military career prior to the cloverleaf incident, but that was the first time I had used it to make a split-second life-and-death decision. By refocusing my mind on my mission, my responsibility to my men's welfare, and then putting any thoughts of me completely out of the equation, I was able to recognize and adapt to a hauntingly familiar pattern of modern-day battlefield behavior while it unfolded in front of me (a leader misled by technology and misguided by hubris trying to make life-or-death decisions without the context of the guys on the ground).

One of the unfortunate realities of large organizations such as the military is that the truly meaningful lessons from key events such as the cloverleaf incident, are rarely captured or shared in the historical record. There are many possible reasons for this.26

The first is that the actual event and the lessons it produces may reflect negatively on some or all of the individuals involved, and thus

---

* Saddam was so sure he was surrounded that instead of escaping to the safe sanctuary of Syria, he stayed in Tikrit instead. Eight months later many of the same Wolverines who were on his scent at the cloverleaf sniffed him out of his spider hole and captured him.

are intentionally watered down or cloaked under an arbitrary stamp of secrecy to prevent them from being shared.

In other cases, the key participants, the warriors themselves, are caught up in a cycle of continuous operations and never have adequate time to incubate and illuminate on the real lessons of the events. In the rare cases when the warriors do get time to reflect, write, or share their insights, what they produce is often contaminated by the human psyche's need to achieve importance, or by the administrative policies and political conditions that confront and influence them at the time.

Finally, the lessons themselves are most often misdirected on the dramatic particulars of the tactics and techniques, instead of the patterns of activities and behaviors that were actually responsible for the outcome of the event. For it's not the action—the blinding flash of a concussion grenade, or the stealthy approach of the night vision–clad commando, but the interaction, in the form of the way we think, the way we make decisions, and the way we operationalize our decisions that matter most.

The ultimate goal of this book is to share what I consider to be life-saving and life-changing lessons that I was fortunate enough to learn as a key participant in many of recent history's most impactful events. The single most important lesson I learned, and the plain but powerful foundation that supports the entire book, is that the most effective weapon on any battlefield—whether it be combat, business, or life—is our mind's ability to recognize life's underlying patterns.

Patterns of thinking, patterns of nature, and patterns of history are just a few of the infinite examples of life's underlying patterns that inform the behavior of the complex world that swirls around us. Patterns reveal how the real world works. When recognized, they allow us to understand, adapt, and master the future as it unfolds in front of us.

Although patterns change in every context, the method I learned to recognize the patterns always stayed the same. It was through the use of guiding principles such as the 3Ms.

Using guiding principles to detect patterns is axiomatic. Sailors of antiquity coined the guiding principle "Red sky at night sailor's delight; red sky in morning sailor's warning" to help them recognize and adapt to future weather patterns. The philosopher George Santayana coined the guiding principle "Those who fail to heed the lessons of history are doomed to repeat them," to help all of us recognize that history reveals patterns, and patterns reveal life. Hidden inside both the sailors' and Santayana's guiding principles is an innate lesson with profound implications for all of us: to recognize and adapt to life's underlying patterns, it's the guiding principle you must remember!

With each new battlefield I stepped foot on, and each mission I took part in, I became more and more convinced of the pattern-revealing power of a handful of guiding principles. So I began to write them down on whatever I could find and stash the notes in whatever outfit I happened to be wearing at the time. On the back of hotel stationery and hidden in the lining of my suit jacket in Colombia. Written in alphanumeric code on the inside of my Serbo-Croatian language book while sitting inside a safe house in Bosnia. On the back of a map while being stalked by a grizzly bear in Montana. On a pocket notebook wrapped inside a Ziploc sandwich bag to protect against driving snowstorms in Afghanistan. And in Iraq, while sitting cross-legged in a sandstorm, using infrared ink under the glow of night vision–goggle green. It didn't matter what country I was in, what culture I was interacting with, or what kind of complex situation I was dealing with; the utility of the guiding principles never faltered. I realized that the truly meaningful lessons from all these experiences were the guiding principles.

The power of the guiding principles shared in this book, such as "Always listen to the guy on the ground"; "When in doubt, develop the situation"; and "Don't get treed by a Chihuahua" is that they provide direction and context to both recognize and believe in life's underlying patterns so we can understand, adapt to, and master the future as it unfolds in front of us.

Although the Delta Force culture is one of quiet professionalism that values humility over self-aggrandizement, that same culture also instills an innate sense of responsibility to always strive to make a contribution to the greater good. I believe that the best way to balance this tension is by sharing my experiences and the corresponding lessons learned through this book.

My motivation for writing this book isn't personal or political. Instead, I believe that accurately understanding and sharing lessons from the past is an essential step for gaining insight into and preparing for the future. If properly absorbed, the guiding-principle lessons shared in this book will help ensure that we as individuals and as a nation can learn from our experiences and better prepare ourselves to not only survive, but also to thrive in an uncertain and unpredictable future.

The stories in this book and the guiding-principle lessons they produced belong to all of us.

PART 1

1

HOW I GOT HERE:

PATTERNS OF HINDSIGHT

How do we end up doing what we do in life? How do we become what we become? How did we get where we are today? At some point in our lives, we all ask ourselves these questions. Of course, there's no single, causal explanation or answer, but by looking back through the pattern-revealing lens of hindsight, we can recognize some of the defining activities, experiences, ideas, and opportunities that ultimately shaped our paths. History reveals patterns, and patterns reveal life.

I was born and raised in Oak Park, Illinois. My parents gave birth to nine children. Yes, we were of Irish-Catholic descent (it's the first question most people ask when they hear nine kids).

Built in 1896, the house I grew up in is the same house my mother lives in today. With four boys and five girls, life had its share of unique idiosyncrasies. Food was always scarce. We considered bologna a delicacy, and when there were actually a few slices left, they were usually hidden behind or under something else in the refrigerator—familial Darwinism at work. Although the house had six bedrooms, all four boys slept in the same room. My mother locked us in at night to keep us from going downstairs and raiding the kitchen. To get the extra rations I was sure I needed, I started climbing out the window, crawling across the roof, hanging off the gutters, and dropping to the ground, where I'd then reenter the house through a basement window I had left open before going to bed.

My brothers and sisters would probably say that my greatest talent as a kid was finding things. My parents ran a tight ship. When one of my siblings gained possession of something my parents thought inappropriate, such as my sister's low-cut hip-hugger pants, my older brother's Doors album, or my younger brother's BB gun, my parents confiscated the "offensive" items and stashed them away in the types of places where no one, including my parents, would ever look again. Inevitably my siblings would turn to me for the recovery operation. My process was elementary. The size, shape, and composition of what I was looking for were key. A BB gun required a rifle's length of rigid hiding space volume; a Doors album a long, thin slot; while my sister's pants could be squished away almost anyplace. I'd always imagine where I would hide the object if I were my parents (up high and out of reach from my little brother, odd and unexpected compartments for my sister's stuff, etc). I knew every nook and cranny in the house, so if a dresser or a box in the closet were askew, it was a surefire clue that I was getting hot. Nothing was out of bounds as a hiding place: inside TV sets, behind dresser drawers, on top of the furnace in the basement. I never failed in a finding mission—ever! Helping my brothers and sisters find their stuff was cool, but it wasn't what jazzed me; I thrived on the thrill of the hunt.

I've come to believe that within the heart of every boy lies the seed of a warrior. Even a boy born and raised in a bubble with no exposure to TV or toys will occasionally chew his toast into the shape of a gun, or stealthily roll his bubble across the room to sneak up on his mom. The degree to which the warrior seed grows and flourishes is dependent on the life experiences in which it's nurtured. For me, there was one seminal experience that I first took part in at the age of seven. It wasn't the Boy Scouts. It was "bombing cars."

For me and my friends, bombing cars had nothing to do with trying to scare people or damage their property. Instead, it was our way of imbibing what I have since come to know as "the warrior's cock-tail" (the thrill of the hunt mixed with the thrill of the chase).

To get the best possible chases, the types that would challenge our ability to run, dodge, evade, and outsmart, we were picky. We picked our bombing positions with great care to ensure we always achieved surprise. Houses surrounded by thick evergreen trees or juniper bushes were our favorites. We threw snowballs only at cars driven by men—the younger and the more, the better. Back then, there was a high price to pay if you got caught. You either got the crap kicked out of you and your face washed with snow on the spot, or you were dragged off to the police station and locked up until your parents came to get you—my claim to fame was that I never got caught.

At times, our numbers would swell to upward of fifty kids, some-times heaving more than fifty frozen projectiles; on those days we called it carpet-bombing cars. Before we'd start bombing, I'd gather the younger kids around—most of whom were pretty scared—and share what we called the golden rules of bombing.

"Be prepared. Know how all the gate latches open and shut, and remember who has dogs in their yards. Pull your hat up high so there's nothing blocking your vision and your ability to see what's going on around you.

"When the chase starts, stay flexible. We can run anywhere we want—we're kids, they're not. Change directions a lot: the more you stay out of his sights, the less he'll want to keep chasing you. If the snow is fresh, don't ever hide—your footprints will lead him right on top of you.

"If you can't outrun 'em, you gotta outsmart 'em. If the guy is about to catch you, slow down a bit, then drop to the ground in a ball and he'll trip over you and go flying into the snow. If you get caught, start bawling your eyes out, and tell 'em you were just walking home from school and some older kids told you to start running. If all else fails, just stick with me. I'll make sure you get away."

More than any other activity in my youth, bombing cars was the experience that allowed my warrior seed to grow and thrive, while also arming me with a mind-set full of options as both the hunter and the hunted.

High school was sort of a halcyonic blur for me. I spent most of my time hanging out with my friends, playing sports, or just plain ol' having fun. I ran cross-country and played ice hockey, dual-purpose handrails that kept me out of trouble and in great physical condition. I listened to a lot of Led Zeppelin, and babysat for my neighbors to make my kicking-around money. Although there aren't many things I'd change about my adolescent years, there was one event during my senior year of high school that, if given the opportunity at the time, I definitely would have requested a do-over.

A few months before graduation, a girl who was a neighbor of mine told me that if I were to ask her friend to my prom, her friend would definitely say yes. I was totally psyched. I had yet to attend a single dance in four years of high school, and this would be my last chance. I had had a crush on her friend for a long time, but had never been able to get my nerve up to ask her out on a date. Now, with the threat of rejection greatly minimized, I figured I might just be able to close the deal. While walking home from school that day, I mentally rehearsed the words I'd use when I called her on the phone later that evening. I was the king of dialing six numbers, then hanging up the receiver—this was not going to be easy. Lost in my hypothetical phone conversation, I didn't notice the jacked-up Dodge Charger jump the curb and skid to a stop on the perfectly manicured lawn a few feet away. "Kashmir" by Led Zeppelin was blaring from the Bose in the back. Three of my friends jumped out and surrounded me. They were fired up about something. "Wait until you hear what we got planned for prom night," Billy Pappas, a fuzzy-haired Greek kid who loved to drink beer, announced. *A keg of beer? A live band at the party afterward?* I wondered. Billy didn't wait for my answer. "For all those suckers going to the dance, this is gonna go down as the greatest prank in school history!"

"Wait a minute, Billy. Aren't you going to the prom with your girl-friend?" I asked in disbelief. "No way," he replied. "This will be much more fun!"

"Come on, Pete, we can't pull it off without you," they all chimed in together. I didn't say anything. "Without you we're sure to get caught; we need you, man." Ego has a powerful pull on all humans, but on a male teenager, it's enslaving. As they explained the "plan" to me, I don't remember if it ever seemed like much of a good idea or even like much of a good time, but they acted like they really needed me. I wasn't think-ing in terms of *the* last dance, or *the* girl, who was probably at home that very minute waiting for my call. All I thought about was how much my buddies admired my talents as an escape artist, and how throwing my hat in with them gave me an easy way out of having to step up to the plate to actually dial that seventh number.

The day of the dance, we pooled our dollars and change together and bought a case of beer and a bushel of ripe tomatoes. With the to-matoes and beers divvied up among us, the four of us settled into posi-tion, hidden in a thick tangle of juniper bushes that blanketed the corner house one block down the street from the high school. There we sat for the next two hours, waiting for what the plan predicted would be a parade of buses loaded with prom couples on their way to the dance. We whiled away the hours by guzzling our beer and talking about how stupid all the other guys were for actually going to the prom and missing out on all this "fun." The air lay heavy with the stench of piss and pine. Finally, a single orange school bus rumbled down the street toward our ambush position.

Completely tanked, all four of us lurched out of the bushes hoot-ing and hollering like deranged savages. Each of us heaved five or six tomatoes in a manner completely commensurate with the effects of downing five or six beers. I don't believe a single tomato so much as grazed the bus—I can vouch for all of mine. Standing on the edge of the street in the warm spring twilight of my senior year, I remember staring at a couple who were sitting in the back of the bus, lost in each other's arms, and completely oblivious to me and the tomatoes I had just hurled. Police sirens screamed in the distance; someone had called the cops.

What had I done? I wondered. *I turned aside my last best chance to go to a high school dance for what had to be the lamest prank that I had ever participated in.* Down the street, two of my buddies stood silently, mirror images of me, but not Billy. He was out in the middle of the street in a full-up purple rage, screaming at the top of his lungs, "Screw you, Cindy!" while flipping the bird like a spear at the now distant school bus. That's when it hit me. It all made sense.

The prank was all about revenge against his girlfriend, whom he had broken up with a couple of weeks earlier. To pull off the prank, and—perhaps just as important—to help pay for the beers, he needed me and my buddies.

I'd been duped. *I should have seen it coming.* I could feel the giant *L* forming on my forehead. I felt like a total loser.

"Hey, guys, the cops are coming. Follow me." I turned and sprinted into a nearby alley. Three hours and many miles later, the cops gave up. Thanks to the chase, and the fact that all of us got away, my buddies considered it the greatest prank of all time. Not me. Most of us can remember the name of the person we went to the senior prom with. I can only remember the name of the girl I never asked.

The silver lining of my heartfelt regret was that the incident precipitated a lifelong quest to better understand why I sometimes made such chowderheaded decisions. I never wanted that giant *L* to form on my forehead again. I also had one more mistake to add to my lifelong résumé of mistakes, the curriculum vitae for all wisdom and knowledge.

After high school, I attended Southern Illinois University (SIU), in Carbondale, Illinois. I chose SIU not because of academics, or special curricula, or even because it was in Illinois. I chose SIU, because it was in the middle of the Shawnee National Forest. The 275,000 acres of the Shawnee National Forest lie in the rough, unglaciated wilderness region of southern Illinois between the Ohio and Mississippi rivers. I fell in love with the area on my first visit to the school. Over the next four years, the forest maintained a powerful pull on my scholastic psyche. I spent most weekends hiking with friends into the forest's roughest and least explored recesses. The names of these places—Panthers' Den, Giant City, Trail of Tears, and Devils' Kitchen—were accurate indicators of both their inaccessibility and the wilderness hazards they presented.

In those days, SIU was most famous for its Mardi Gras–like Halloween party. Tens of thousands of students would flock to SIU each year for the festivities. The town encouraged the melee by closing Main Street and allowing the elaborately costumed revelers to party and riot until they literally dropped. The costume was a big deal; you weren't just supposed to wear it, you were expected to *become* it. Pirates, whores, vampires, and gangsters. I noticed that the costume one chose was in many cases, a good indicator of some defining slice of the costume-wearer's personality.

I dressed up as the same thing every year, a commando. I didn't know much about what a commando was. Inside my untainted nonmilitary mind, I perceived a commando as a hybrid of James Bond and a Spartan warrior. My predilection for impersonating a commando had nothing to do with guns or blowing things up—though I definitely thought those were cool, too; rather, it was the intrigue behind the role that completely enraptured me. Specifically, what I considered the tools of the commando trade—disguises, deception, and diversions, all used in the name of outsmarting an adversary. With each successive year that I dressed up and immersed myself in the role, I felt more and more certain that I was finding my path.

During my second year, I went with friends to our school's downtown movie theater to see the twin billing of *The Deer Hunter* and *Apocalypse Now*. I was mesmerized. It wasn't the music, or missiles, or even the moxie that captivated me. Instead, it was the futility of the way we fought the war and the objects of that futility, the brave men who had to do the fighting. The two movies piqued my interest in the

Vietnam War. My newfound curiosity motivated me to do something that all of my academic courses had previously failed to do; I became a regular at the university library.

Sitting at the same table in the rarely visited periodical archives section each night, I spent weeks scouring thick black binders full of old issues of *Life* magazine. I read every Vietnam story, but the pictures had the biggest impact on me. I had lots of questions, so I sought out and talked with some Vietnam veterans who were teaching at the school at the time. They shared many of their perspectives with me, and the more I heard, the more frustrated I became. I was generally frustrated because as hard as it was for me to admit at the time, I realized that my country lost the war. I was specifically frustrated because the more I learned about the decisions made by various leaders during the war, the more I became certain that it was the decisions, not the enemy, that caused us to lose. How could so many seemingly bright, intelligent people in our government have made so many bad decisions? From Kennedy and McNamara through Nixon and Westmoreland, the decisions they made concerning everything from how we got involved to how we actually fought the war completely perplexed me.

I wondered why we didn't create a guerrilla army to fight the Viet Cong instead of spending billions to create a Westernized version of a conventional army that neither fit the culture of the South Vietnamese nor the enemy adversaries they were trying to defeat. When I looked at the combat pictures in *Life*, I wondered why our military forces traveled in such large, lumbering groups instead of splitting up into small teams to give them greater agility. Why did they fly helicopters everywhere, announcing their locations and intentions to the enemy wherever they went? Why didn't they stay in the jungle, instead of going back to their base camps all the time? To defeat the enemy, why didn't we fight like the enemy?

Although it would be many years until I felt comfortable admitting it, I began to grow a deeply seated operational respect for the Viet Cong. They were always light and agile. They carried and wore only what they needed for the mission: a tube of rice, an AK-47, a few maga-zines of ammunition, and loose-fitting, dark pajamas. They seemed to have a whatever-it-takes attitude toward combat operations. They massed only when required, and they usually fought in small groups of as few as two or three men. When things got too hot, they melted back into the jungle to fight again another day. They were nimble.

The American history course I was taking at the time offered a field trip to Gettysburg, Pennsylvania, to tour the famous Civil War battlefield of the same name. Initially I wasn't interested—after all, what could I learn from walking across a bunch of cornfields and talk-ing about a battle and a war that happened more than a hundred years earlier? A few days later, while walking on campus, I ran into one of the Vietnam veterans I had recently befriended. I asked him what he thought about visiting Gettysburg. "If you want to learn about what went wrong in Vietnam," he responded sagely, "you can find the an-swer at Gettysburg." Then he turned around and walked away. That was all he had to say about that. Curious to discover the meaning of his orphic response, I signed up for the trip later that day.

At Gettysburg, our group conducted an interactive tour of the battlefield. Walking across the heavily wooded hills and gently rolling cornfields, our guide explained the tactical significance of each of the major engagements. The most striking was the spot in the middle of the battlefield where the notorious Pickett's Charge took place. General Robert E. Lee, the commanding general of the South, ordered General George Pickett and fifteen thousand of his men to march in a box for-mation across a mile-long stretch of open cornfields and conduct a head-on assault against the front-line forces of the Union Army. The Union forces were ensconced behind a four-foot-high stone wall on top of a panoramic hill. As I stood in the middle of the cornfield and stared up at the hill and the wall, only one thought came to mind: *How could they have done this to their men?* I could not understand how General Lee and his subordinate generals, such as Pickett, could have been so monumentally reckless with the lives of their men. Our tour guide told

us that one of the Southern generals—James Longstreet—seemed to recognize the insanity of the head-on assault when it was first discussed,
but instead of falling on his proverbial sword and doing the right thing
for his boys, he capitulated to the divine exhortations of General Lee.
"It is God's will," Lee continuously reassured his subordinate officers.
Half of the men who started Pickett's notorious suicide charge ended
up killed, or injured. They died for the cause, but they were killed by
their own leaders. Of course, the Southern officers had no corner on
the recklessness market in the Civil War—the Union Army sent their
men to equally unthinkable deaths at Manassas and Fredericksburg,
to name but two.

On the bus ride home from Gettysburg, I wondered why both
sides fought the war the way they fought it. Why did they organize the
way they did—fighting in rank-and-file (box) formations, and always
in the open? Why not just create small teams of men who infiltrate at
night and find openings in the other side's defenses? And why not use
trees and terrain for cover while shooting at the enemy? It all seemed
like common sense to me. Maybe that's what the Vietnam veteran
meant when he told me that Gettysburg would help me understand
what went wrong in Vietnam. The way both wars were fought defied
explanation, because the decisions made around the way they were
fought defied common sense. The pattern of poor operational decision-
making and senseless sacrifice of good men's lives that defined Gettysburg, other Civil War battles, and Vietnam would stay tucked away
in a special corner of my mind throughout my military career, and
remain there to this day.

A few months later, in April 1980, an event occurred that had a
coagulating effect on all of my previous life experiences. While whil-
ing away time between classes in the SIU Student Center, a news flash
interrupted the program on the big-screen TV. The newscaster reported that the United States had just conducted an abortive hostage
rescue mission in the desert of Iran.

In the days that followed, the details of what became known as the Desert One Hostage Rescue Mission were revealed to the nation. Planned and executed under the utmost secrecy, eight helicopters, six C-130 transport planes, and ninety-three Delta Force commandos secretly infiltrated Iran to conduct the hostage rescue mission. The plan was to rendezvous in the middle of the desert at a place called Desert One, fly on helicopters to another point called Desert Two, and then storm the American embassy in Tehran and bring home the U.S. hostages. But Delta Force never made it to Desert Two or Tehran. The mission was aborted after three of the eight helicopters developed mechanical problems on the way to Desert One. The mission ended in disaster when one of the helicopters that did make it to Desert One collided with a transport plane while refueling on the desert floor. Eight American warriors died in the inferno that followed. The hostages would remain in captivity for another eight months.

For the United States, the operation was a monumental failure. Follow-up congressional investigations revealed a surprising level of negligence by the government agencies and military leaders involved. Specifically noted were three major deficiencies: (1) the way the mission was planned and the overly complex plan it produced; (2) the overdependence on the use of ill-equipped helicopters and their ill-trained pilots; (3) and an overemphasis on operational secrecy among military leaders, which prevented them from sharing mission-critical information with each other.[1]

The failed Iranian hostage rescue mission was a Rubicon moment for me. The awareness that brave men had risked and given their lives in an attempt to save fellow Americans caused me to reflect for the first time on my own life. I realized what a great life I actually had, and how fortunate I was to have all the freedoms and opportunities of growing up and living my life in the United States. I also felt equal parts of embarrassment and frustration. Embarrassment that my country had failed such a crucial mission on the world stage and frustration with the way the military planned and executed the mission, which essentially doomed it to failure before it ever got under way.

Once again I asked myself how so many seemingly bright people could make so many bad decisions. I didn't watch the TV news again for almost a month. Instead, I went on a lot of long runs to contemplate what my life was all about, and how I might somehow be able to make a contribution for the greater good. I was, at that point in my college career, an accomplished marathon runner and triathlete. I spent most of my time outside the classroom running, swimming, and biking through the rolling hills and forest trails of southern Illinois. Within a few weeks I knew what I needed to do.

I wanted to pay something back to my country; I wanted to make a contribution. I decided to join the military. Three years later, after completing the requirements for my bachelor's degree and attending graduate school, I signed up to join the army and attend Officer Candidate School. When my recruiter, a senior army noncommissioned officer, asked me what motivated me to join the army, I told him I wanted to make sure that the United States never again failed in an important mission, and to make sure that good men would never again die due to bad decision-making. Although it probably sounded a bit corny at the time, I added "my goal is to save lives, not take lives." He responded by asking me if I was interested in joining the Army Medical Corps. "No," I told him with great officiousness. "I want to join Delta Force."

I wanted to participate in the most sensitive and complex missions our country would face. I wanted to operate as a hybrid of James Bond and a Spartan warrior. I wanted to make a contribution; I joined the military to become an officer in Delta Force.

2

NATURAL SELECTION:[1]

GETTING INTO DELTA FORCE

I had been stuck in the Manzanita vines for more than an hour. Thick as rope and growing to tangled heights of ten to twenty feet, it was like swimming in a sea of a thousand pitchforks. Thrashing, contorting, and sometimes crawling, I simply could not find a way out of the endless maze of vines. Overburdened by the seventy-five-pound rucksack on my back and overhurried by a self-generated time constraint in my head, my subconscious was attempting to build a strong case for hopelessness. *If I don't get out of here soon, I won't have the time or the energy to get to my final point.* I quickly dismissed those thoughts, recalling what one of my mentors had told me before I arrived: "Never, ever give up." I had to find a way out of the vines.

"Stress Phase" is the appropriately named final phase of the Delta Force selection process.[2] Well over half the men who started the course with me many weeks earlier were now gone. At the beginning of this, the final test of the course, we were told to pack a rucksack that weighed at least seventy pounds and prepare for a long-distance movement through the Appalachian Mountains.[3] There was no guidance on how long the movement would be or how long we would be given to complete it.

For me, Stress Phase started at 2:30 A.M. when, in total darkness, I was dropped on a dirt trail in the middle of the mountains (aka nowhere). A Delta cadre member handed me a piece of paper with map coordinates on it and told me to "Find my way to the next rendezvous point (RV), and take all instructions from the cadre."[4] And, oh, yeah, "Don't be late, and don't be light."

The rumor whispered among my fellow selection candidates in the days prior had it that the total length of the movement was forty to fifty miles and that we had to cover the distance in less than seventeen hours or we would fail. I didn't believe it. It just didn't seem realistic that they would make us move that far and that fast, with that amount of weight on our backs after all we had been through already. The previous weeks of the course consisted of a 24/7 series of long-distance land navigation challenges across some of the most austere and arduous terrain in Appalachia. Each day the weight of the rucksacks and the complexity of the terrain increased, while the unspoken time standards to complete the courses were correspondingly decreased.[5] Along the way, most of us had fallen, twisted limbs, and gotten lost more than a few times. The reward for surviving was Stress Phase.

Over the past fifteen hours, I had navigated up, over, and through boulder-choked gorges, densely forested mountains, and bug-infested swamps, while successfully finding my way from one RV to the next. At each RV, the routine was the same. Check in with the cadre, receive new map coordinates, and then head off in search of my next destination. By midafternoon, I was starting to believe the forty- to fifty-mile rumor to be reality, and the reality of the distance, along with the uncertainty about time, was starting to take its toll on me.

Physical and mental endurance were my fortes. For the past three weeks I was certain I had moved as far and as fast as anyone else in the course. But my background as a marathon runner and triathlete were starting to transition from blessing to curse. The same lean and mean physique that had allowed me to survive and thrive to this point was beginning to turn against me: I was wasting away.

The best way to deal with pain is to fool your brain. *It's just around the next bend; I'm almost done; okay, next one for sure,* I coaxed myself. *If I can just escape this never-ending maze of vines and get to the top of the mountain, I can make it to my final point. I have to do something—there's always a way.*

I eyed a nearby birch tree, and decided to take advantage of its natural ladderlike limbs to climb as high as possible and hopefully spot a path that would lead me out of the vines and back on track to my final destination. I quickly mounted the tree and began climbing skyward without thinking to take my rucksack off first. It was a grueling climb. I had to pause after each step to regain my breath. After climbing as high as the girth of the tree would allow—perhaps thirty to forty feet—I slowly sidestepped onto a limb while keeping my left hand on the tree trunk and my right hand on a thin, spindly branch above my head. Out in the distance I spotted what appeared to be a path. I stood on my tiptoes and craned my neck as high as possible to get a better look. That's when it happened. The spindly branch I was using to steady my stance snapped in half, allowing gravity to team up with its friend fatigue and knock my energy-depleted body off balance and plummet like an upside-down turtle back toward where I started. Fully expecting to break my back, I hit the ground hard. I was in shock. Not from the fall, but from the discovery that the same vines I had been battling against for the past hour had suddenly changed sides from adversary to ally and cushioned my impact with the ground.

I checked each of my limbs to ensure that nothing was poking through them. I was okay. *Wait a minute . . . something isn't right. Maybe I hit my head. The ground is moving. Is there something underneath me?* Then that something started screaming.

What the—?

I quickly undid one of my shoulder straps and struggled to turn my head to see what this thing actually was. Walking for fifteen hours with a seventy-five-pound rucksack on your back stiffens every joint in the body; I turned like an arthritic old man, head and upper torso as one. With the peripheral vision of one eye, I spotted a tiny black animal scurry out from under my ruck. *How cool—a baby bear!* Then my spider senses kicked in. Fifty or so feet to my rear, I heard the spastic scream of an enraged animal. It was violently thrashing the vines, and it was getting closer. Turbocharged by a heavy dose of fight-or-flight adrenaline, in one fluid motion I jumped up and bolted. *What kind of screwed-up luck is this? Instead of finding my way out of the vines, I wandered into the middle of a black bear's den—and now I'm gonna get my ass torn apart.*

Holding my rucksack in front of me as a dual-purpose shield and machete, I slashed, pushed, and parted vines, plowing my own path toward anywhere but there. Adrenaline-drained and out of breath, I began to rationalize. *Maybe the bears ran in the other direction.* Then I heard the distinctively immature scream of the cub—it was right behind me. "Get away from me, bear, beat it, get lost!" I was verbally ejaculating anything and everything that my completely frustrated mind could conjure up in the desperate hope that something would deter or distract the little four-legged beacon from continuing its pursuit.

The vines were beginning to thin; I could see the terrain ahead of me again. Off to the right I spotted a trail; it appeared to be going in the general direction of my final point. Another scream from the cub, now perhaps fifty or so feet behind me. A second later the mother screamed back—not a roar, it was more like a high-pitched, blood-curdling affirmation that she was on her way, and she sounded pissed.

"Running for your life" usually connotes covering a lot of ground fast. While I was definitely moving fast—still spastically swinging my rucksack and parting the vines as I went—I wasn't really covering a lot of ground. I guess you could say I was going nowhere fast. *Why hasn't the cub or the mother caught up with me yet?* I wondered. *I'm probably moving faster than I think.*

My mind was racing to create an escape plan. *If I run toward that trail, the bear will easily catch up with me as soon as she breaks free of the vines.* I scanned to the left. *A cliff, not too steep.* The terrain below it looked like it sloped away just enough that if I jumped off at an angle I could land on my feet and roll to cushion the impact. The baby bear wouldn't be able to make the jump, and maybe that would deter the mother from continuing her pursuit. *Trail or cliff? Screw it: I'm going for the cliff. No bear is gonna catch me, I'm gonna jump.* I cut left toward the cliff, angling my approach ever so slightly just before launching myself up and over the bramble bushes that guarded the edge.

It was a magnificent leap, one I could likely never replicate without the motivational stimulus of an angry black bear on my heels. I landed on the slope precisely as I had hoped, at an angle, and feet first. But instead of rolling, my strength-sapped body betrayed me once again. I crumbled like a beanbag and immediately transitioned into a cartwheeling carcass. Arms and legs flailing violently, I rolled end over end. After a couple of hundred feet, I plowed into a medium-sized walnut tree and came to an abrupt stop. Once again, I conducted a quick survey of my limbs. Everything still worked. *What about the bear?* I wondered while maintaining statuelike stillness.

Using the tree as a pivot, I pushed myself up on my knees and slowly scanned upward toward the edge of the cliff. There, slightly occluded by the bramble bush I had so magnificently launched myself over, was baby and mother searching the hillside for my carcass. As so often happens when you stare and focus directly at another living being, the mother abruptly snapped her head in my direction and locked eyes with mine. To my simultaneous horror and shame, I discovered that she—was a pig!

Not a bear, or even a wild boar, but a freaking pig! Dirty and disgusting, it had likely escaped from a local farm. I had run for my life, and jumped off a cliff, all because I had jumped to the conclusion that my life was endangered by a nonexistent bear.

The embarrassment I could handle—I even smiled momentarily. But as I assessed my predicament, the brutal facts of my reality began gut-punching my spirit. My body slumped like a tube of jelly—*I may have just blown my one shot at getting into Delta Force. My map—* *where is my map!* I frantically searched the area around me. No luck. Then I looked downward. Past the tree that arrested my tumble was a sheer drop-off of about five hundred feet. At the bottom was a stream. If my map went past the tree, it was history. There was no going down for me.

Without a map, there was no way to know where I was. For sure, I was woefully off course, and with each passing minute, I was falling way behind schedule. We had been given detailed instructions for what to do if we needed assistance. Those instructions presupposed we were both lost and ready to give up, I was only one of the two. *Stay calm—think!*

Okay, I got caught in the vines because I was trying to get to the top of the mountain. From the top of the mountain, a long ridgeline branched off to the east, like the leg of a crab, directly connecting the mountaintop to my final point. If I can get back to the top of the mountain, then locate that ridgeline, I can follow it like a cookie crumb trail for 3.1 miles to find my final point. I have to get back to the top of the mountain. A lot of ifs for sure, but the only failure is a failure to try.

The afternoon sun was well into its western descent, but there was still enough light for me to pick out a series of small trees and thick bushes to use as anchor points to work my way back to the top of the cliff. Using every bit of body strength I had left, I clawed my way back to the top. Leaping off the edge of the cliff was a regrettable split-second decision that took me more than an hour to correct. It was getting dark, and I still had a long way to go to get to the top of the mountain.

After another thirty minutes of fast-paced meandering, I arrived at what I hoped was the top of the mountain. It was dark now. I had no map and no flashlight. How can you tell you're on top of a tree-covered mountain at night? The topographic definition of a mountaintop describes it as the point where the terrain around you slopes downward in all directions. Hundreds of hours of navigating mountains in the thickly foliaged jungles of Panama had taught me not to depend on visual cues to recognize and identify terrain features. In the jungle you can rarely see more than a few feet in front of you, so even in the light of day you can be standing on the top of a mountain and not see it or recognize it. To compensate for the lack of visual cues, I trained myself to navigate with my feet, to feel instead of see the terrain. The angle of your feet is an amazingly accurate indicator of what type of terrain feature you are standing on. My feet were flat; when I walked a few meters in any direction my feet angled downward. I had found the mountaintop; now, where was that ridgeline?

I had seen the last of the sun when it set, and it was to my right. The ridgeline I needed ran down the eastern side of the mountain. Using slow, soft baby steps, I cautiously probed the eastern side of the mountaintop. Suddenly my feet felt the clear hard-packed flatness of a ridgeline trail. I had found my path.

I checked my watch, I had started walking at 2:30 A.M., it was now 7:00 P.M. I had been moving for 16.5 hours. I had 3.1 mountain miles between me and what I hoped was the finish. If the rumor was correct, I had thirty minutes to do it. As much as I tried to put a positive spin on things, I was almost assuredly over the time limit. It didn't matter; I had never failed a finding mission, and this was not gonna be the first. *Follow the path; it will take me to my destination*, was my mantra; it helped keep my mind off the pain. With arms hanging lifelessly at my sides, I leaned my energy-sapped body forward and broke into a slow zombielike trot. Forty-five minutes later, I saw a light.

I was hallucinating; the light appeared to be a cartoonish apparition of a washing machine. *What is a washing machine doing out here on the trail? It doesn't make sense. Keep moving forward. It's not a washing machine; it's a man with a red penlight. It's one of the Delta cadres.*

"Color and number?" he asked dispassionately. It took me a couple of seconds, but I somehow remembered my coded identification.

"Blue 46," I answered. He wrote something on the clipboard, obviously my time of arrival, but that didn't register with me at the time. "Blue 46, drop your rucksack," he commanded. *Oh well, I gave it my best,* I thought. "Head over to the fire to get warm. There's hot soup and Gatorade waiting for you. Welcome to Delta Force!"

GUIDING-PRINCIPLE LESSON:

Don't Get Treed by a Chihuahua

It's been said that there are no mistakes in life, only lessons. Every mistake is an opportunity to ensure that we never make it again, especially when future consequences can be much more dire. When I saw the little black creature through the corner of my eye, my tired and frustrated mind took a shortcut. I decided it must have been a baby bear with a mother not too far behind. When I heard the spastic scream of the animal in the bushes, I decided it had to be the vicious growl of a mother bear instead of what it actually was—the vicious *oink* of a mother pig. My contextless response was to run for my life and jump off a cliff; I got treed by a chihuahua.

Getting treed by a chihuahua is a metaphor for making decisions without context. Context is the reality of the situation around us. Without context, our minds have a tendency to take shortcuts and recognize patterns that aren't really there; we connect the dots without collecting the dots first. Overreacting, underreacting, and failing to do anything at all are all symptoms of "getting treed." When you first read the words *bombing cars* in the previous chapter, what did you think? Were you treed? A few seconds later, before or after you read the word *snowball*, you likely realized it didn't make sense that a seven-year-old kid would go around blowing up cars, so you climbed back down. Time and common sense work in tandem to bathe our minds with reality-revealing context.

What is common sense? It's knowledge of patterns—both conscious and unconscious. Getting stung by a bee hurts: it's common sense to avoid little black-and-yellow flying objects. We learn by asking questions; when dealing with uncertainty it's common sense to question everything. The act of choosing determines success or failure in our lives; freedom of choice is common sense. I had seen bears run through the wilderness before; I knew that a man cannot outrun a bear. As I ran for my life at a vine-inhibited snail's pace, I wondered why the bears weren't catching up to me. It didn't make sense. The reason the bears weren't catching up to me was because they weren't bears—they were pigs. But that didn't make sense either. I didn't grow up in the Appalachian Mountains, and had no idea that wild man-chasing pigs even existed. So how could I have known it wasn't a bear? Because there was another, more enlightening pattern tugging at the shirttails of my common sense as I fled that day. It was the pattern of being treed by a chihuahua—all those times in my life when I had made chowderheaded decisions without understanding the reality of the situation around me. My common sense was telling me to take time to look, listen, and question everything. Common sense provides context, and context is common sense.

Getting "treed by a chihuahua" during Stress Phase almost cost me entry into Delta Force. The price I alone paid to learn the lesson was nothing more than a few scratches and a bruised ego, but the lesson itself would prove to be priceless. In combat, when leaders make decisions without context, the cost is mission failure, and all too often, the price is paid with the blood of their men. "Don't get treed by a chihuahua!" Before making mission-critical decisions, always ensure that you have context. It's common sense.

3

GORILLA WARFARE:

IMAGINE THE UNIMAGINABLE, HUMOR
YOUR IMAGINATION

North Carolina, Late '90s

As the sun rose on an unseasonably warm November Friday in Fort
Bragg, North Carolina, my body was settling into a comfortable 6:30-
per-mile pace on mile number two of a ten-mile run. Sixty miles of
roller-coaster sand trails bisect the hilly Fort Bragg training area and
serve as access corridors into the otherwise unmolested pine forests
and swamps that define the area. At the Unit, every operator had a
personal responsibility to maintain a rapier level of physical fitness. I
had vowed when I joined the military that I would always strive to be
the fittest man on any battlefield I stepped foot on. I was still confident
in my credibility to make that claim, save for a few of my own fellow
operators in the Unit.

At the very essence of a Delta operator is the ability to think creatively and make adaptive decisions, but to take action on those decisions, we also have to be superbly physically fit. Each of us has to be
both a thinking warrior and an athlete warrior. On this day I was in
touch with both sides. I was running strong and hard and my endorphin-
saturated brain was spawning rapid-fire ideas and insights for future
use. Spastic vibrations against my abdominal wall brought me back to

real time as I recognized my pager's code for a real-world mission. I made an immediate U-turn and headed back toward our compound. As my curiosity intensified, I shifted gears to a 5:30-per-mile pace. There are few things in life more motivating than a mission.

Once inside the compound, I headed to a secure section of the building where one of our intelligence analysts was waiting for me with a packet containing my official orders and a flight itinerary.

"You need to get to Bosnia[1] as quickly as possible; it's a rapidly developing situation," he said.

"Can you tell me what the mission is?" I asked.

He shook his head. "Anything I try to tell you now will almost assuredly be outdated by the time you complete your twenty-two-hour travel itinerary."

I liked his logic. I'd rather be sure I was aboard the next thing flying to Bosnia than sit around talking about information that's skyrocketing on the irrelevancy curve with every passing second. I bolted out of the building and hurried home to grab my prepacked "Bosnia" suitcase.

I'd been to Bosnia four times prior to this operation, including two tours of more than one hundred days in-country. I spoke survival Serbo-Croatian and was well-versed in both the history and the social dynamics of the country. My Bosnia suitcase contained specially selected and purchased East European clothing to help ensure I could blend in with the local populace. It also contained a thirty-day stock of various life-support items for nutrition and hygiene, such as protein powder to maintain muscle mass and hand sanitizer to disinfect all the little critters that were much more likely to render me mission ineffective than a bullet. None of these items was yet available in war-ravaged Bosnia.

I arrived at the tiny Fayetteville, North Carolina, airport and checked my bags to Atlanta, Georgia. Total time elapsed from pager alert to arrival at the Fayetteville airport: two hours.

Bosnia-Herzegovina

For this mission, there were ten Unit members flying into Bosnia. Due to the short notice for making flight reservations, we each flew on separate commercial flights from geographically separate airports on the East Coast to get to Sarajevo. The general mission in Bosnia was to locate and capture individuals known as PIFWCs. Pronounced "piff-wix," PIFWC stands for: Persons Indicted for War Crimes.[2] All had committed crimes against humanity during the Bosnian War, which occurred between 1992 and 1995.[3] The religiously inspired ethnic conflict had historical roots dating all the way back to 1389 and involved three religiously defined factions within Bosnia and Herzegovina: Bosniaks (Muslims), Serbs (Orthodox Christians), and Croatians (Catholic Christians). One of the most devastating symptoms of the deep-rooted animosities among these groups was "ethnic cleansing." According to the United Nations and the International Criminal Tribunal for the former Yugoslavia (ICTY), Bosnian Serb forces perpetrated the majority of ethnic cleansing incidents against the Muslim Bosniaks during the war. The Bosnian Serb government strongly denied these claims, but the 8,300 Bosniak Muslim corpses discovered in mass graves outside the town of Srebrenica proved otherwise. After exhaustive investigations by the UN-sponsored ICTY, many of the high-ranking Serbian political and military leaders who had ordered and/or taken part in ethnic cleansing were officially designated as PIFWCs and placed on the UN's most-wanted list.

The war had ended with the signing of the Dayton Peace Agreement. To ensure all sides abided by the agreement, NATO created SFOR. The United States wasn't the only country involved in SFOR and peacekeeping operations in Bosnia. Nineteen other NATO countries participated at various stages and with various levels of support. For operational purposes, Bosnia was divided into thirds (see Map 2), with the British in the northwest, the Americans in the northeast, and the French in the south. While peacekeeping and nation building were the primary mission of SFOR, every SFOR soldier carried the additional responsibility, if the opportunity allowed, of locating and capturing PIFWCs.

While we were always working in close cooperation with our European allies, one of the main U.S. military objectives was to make contact with and develop intelligence sources who could provide information on the location of the "most wanted" PIFWCs.[4] This required contact with people living in both the Serbian and the Muslim sectors of Bosnia. Complicating our task was that both sides had their own police forces that, as you might expect, were fervently loyal to their own ethnic brethren. Wanted men rarely hide among their enemies, so to locate and capture the predominantly Serbian PIFWCs, we had to build source networks and focus our operational resources on the inhospitable and xenophobic Serb sector.

Once on the ground, our group linked up with twenty of our fellow Unit members who were already developing the situation from a safe house near the Bosnian town of Tuzla.[5] With smoke lazily dancing skyward from its chimney, the safe house was a picturesque stone cottage nestled into the base of a large grassy mountain overlooking the town. As I drove up to the darkened cottage with headlights turned off and night vision goggles turned on, I took a second to appreciate the moment. *This is why I joined Delta—disguises, deception, and diversions*, I thought, smiling with self-actualized satisfaction. After a coded knock on the back door, followed by an exchange of bona fides, we walked inside at exactly 2:00 A.M. Bosnia time. The energy level throughout the house was electric. Although our rule of thumb for international travel was to rest a few hours before preparing for a mission, we did not have that luxury for this mission. *The enemy always has a vote.*

I threw my suitcase in one of the open bedrooms and headed into the dimly lit living room for an update on the situation. To prevent anyone on the outside from seeing inside, the men had taped a specially designed filament to the windows that allowed ambient light to come in but prevented light or activity to be seen from the outside.

Almost thirty men and women from various countries, organizations, and units were assembled in the living room, a truly cosmopolitan gathering.

Our meeting started with a situation update by our intelligence analyst, Glenn. Thirtysomething and with jet-black hair, Glenn was straight out of central casting as a prototypically happy-go-lucky Italian chef. His hallmark was his ability to immerse himself in a situation by locating, combining, and digesting mission-critical information, distilling the key nuggets, then serving it up for sharing with the people who needed it the most: the operators who would carry out the mission.

He began with our raison d'être. The highly detailed information came from one of our intelligence sources, known simply as 4AZ. To protect the anonymity of foreign intelligence sources, the only person who knows the true name of an intelligence source is the individual case officer who handles the source. Everyone else just knows the source by his or her specific alphanumeric designation, in this case 4AZ.[6] 4AZ told his handler that a high-ranking PIFWC would be driving across the Bosnian-Serbian border near the town of Loznica (see Map 3) for secret meetings on the outskirts of Sarajevo. As is often the norm with travel itineraries of wanted men, the meetings were not set for a specific time; rather, they were scheduled to take place during a forty-eight-hour window at a time and place of the PIFWC's choosing. We only had thirty-six hours until his travel window would open.

The PIFWC we would be attempting to capture was one of the most notorious war criminals on the United Nation's most-wanted list. Accusations against him included the murders, sexual assaults, and repeated beatings of numerous Bosnian Croats, Bosnian Muslims, and other non-Serb civilians detained in various detention camps in and around Bosnia.[7] He had full cognizance of the fact that he was both wanted by the United Nations and that he would likely face life in prison if captured. This was an important point to understand, because as any cop in the world will tell you, desperate men are prone to make desperate moves.

Our intelligence source 4AZ also reported that this PIFWC normally traveled with a security detail of four to eight highly trained and highly experienced bodyguards. The PIFWC and his security detail would be driving across the border on a seldom-used rural road that snaked through the mountains. Although the PIFWC was likely using this route to avoid chance run-ins with the many law-enforcement and military organizations that traveled the major highways, the lack of traffic on the mountain road, coupled with his signature late-model multivehicle convoy, would actually make it easier for us. The specificity of the intelligence and the opportunity provided by the rural location led us to believe that this would be the best opportunity we would ever have to capture this individual.

Although we had completely flexible rules of engagement (ROE) for the capture, as a matter of principle our goal was to conduct all capture operations without firing a shot. This particular mission had an additional complication: 4AZ mentioned that the PIFWC might be traveling with his daughter. This meant at least two things. First, whatever concept we came up with to capture the PIFWC would have to depend on nonlethal force to ensure we didn't inadvertently endanger the life of his daughter. Second, to ensure that we didn't initiate an uncontrollable gunfight with PIFWC's security detail, we needed to achieve total surprise.

The Bosnian countryside in this particular area looked very much like the Blue Ridge Mountains near the East Coast of the United States. The medium-sized mountains ranged in size from two to five thousand feet high, and were covered with coniferous trees, and dotted with small, family-owned farms and country homes. In these types of rural communities, everyone knew and looked out for one another. As a result they were always suspicious of outsiders, and/or any out-of-the-ordinary activities.

To understand the on-the-ground reality of the area, two of our

NATO allies prepared to head out to conduct what we referred to as an environmental reconnaissance. It's universally axiomatic that if two men are seen loitering together, or driving through a close-knit community, they stand out, and most people automatically presume they are up to no good. But send a man and a woman out in the same profile and people barely give them a second glance. One of our mantras in the Unit was to blend in anywhere, and I marveled at how effectively this couple had done just that. The male had taken up smoking cheap East European cigarettes and had styled his long brown hair into a greasy and slightly wispy look. He dressed in the uniform of the Balkan male: a black sweater untucked over black polyester pants, topped off with a loose-fitting black leather jacket. The female was dressed as his hot Serbian arm candy. She sported a pea green vinyl jacket and a short gray miniskirt, which appeared to be spray-painted onto her lower torso. Underneath she wore gold-tinted fishnet nylons, and black high heels. She carried a scarf to wear on her head for use when they drove through Muslim-controlled areas where females usually covered their hair. Her hair color made the scarf more than just a nice-to-have cultural accessory. For some reason never understood by any of us, many Bosnian women at that time, dyed their hair a strange metallic red. We sarcastically referred to the color as RNFN, which stood for: red not found in nature. In the finest tradition of making personal sacrifices for the greater good of the team she went out and purchased, then actually dyed her hair with RNFN to complete her montage. I had no doubts that these two would be able to blend in wherever they went without creating any suspicion.

The couple's objective was to collect any and all information on the environment in and around the road on which 4AZ told us the PIFWC would be traveling. To do this they would film the entire route with a covert camera hidden inside the rearview mirror. Our tech people rigged all of our vehicles' glove compartments with mini-laptop computers called Librettos. The Librettos used mapping software called Falconview,[8] which displayed both maps and satellite photos from which we could zoom in to or out of as needed. Cutting-edge technology in the late '90s, but today Moore's Law and Google maps allow us to do the same thing with better resolution for free. Our communication technicians also developed a clandestine antenna that allowed us always-on satellite communications for uploading and downloading data files and messages while on the move. Many of the tactics, techniques, and procedures we developed in Bosnia led to technological and operational breakthroughs that changed the way we conducted clandestine operations around the globe. Aware of the rapidity of operational breakthroughs at the time, many of us referred to Bosnia as a living laboratory.

While we waited for the reconnaissance team to return, one of our teammates, Drago,* schooled us on the cultural dynamics of the capture area. Born and raised in Croatia, he served time in the Croatian Army before immigrating to the United States in his early twenties. Drago still spoke fluent Serbo-Croatian, and had spent the previous day talking to the locals who lived in the area. He confirmed that, like the PIFWC, the vast majority of people near the border crossing were Serbian, and they would not be supportive of any activity by outsiders, especially those trying to capture one of their own. If they noticed strangers on their land, they would almost certainly call the police, who were also closely tied to and supportive of the PIFWCs. The final point that Drago emphasized was that the Serbian police force in the area should be considered both unhelpful, and potentially hostile. If they knew we were operating in the area, they would do everything in their power to impede us, including drawing their weapons and initiating a physical confrontation. Drago's insights underscored that to be successful we would have to infiltrate the xenophobic Serb area without attracting *any* attention. Not only did we need to come up with a

---

*"Drago," not his real name, was killed in action during combat operations in Iraq.

concept that would allow us to achieve surprise, we also would have to do it in as low-key and unobtrusive a manner as possible.

Satisfied that we had a foundational understanding of the area we'd be operating in, we began brainstorming options to actually conduct the capture.

"What about a broken-down vehicle in the middle of the road to make them stop?" asked Bruiser, a stocky ex–football player from upstate New York.

"Example?" someone else asked. "Well," said Bruiser, "if we block the road and cause their vehicle to halt, we can leverage lots of different techniques to disable the vehicle and capture the PIFWC inside." He paused for a second to think, then added, "The downside is that we'll have to find the perfect spot on the road where it's narrow enough that they can't use the shoulder to go around the broken-down vehicle." He paused again. "It also takes a lot of time to set up, so we'll have to have perfect intelligence on when he is actually crossing, and I'm not sure that's realistic. I have no doubt he'll come early or late, but not on time." We never interrupted Bruiser while he talked, because he always provided both the pros and the cons of every option, and it was always beneficial to hear his self-contained, point and counterpoint debates.

Predator weighed in next. Rock-jawed with sandy-colored brown hair, and a tightly muscled frame without an ounce of excess body fat, his physique was perfectly customized for combat-related activities. He could lift his body weight in ways that seemed to defy the laws of gravity. I had once seen him scurry up the side of a nine-story building in Miami in seconds, using a combination of highly refined world-class climbing techniques and a total disregard for his own well-being. On the thinking side, Predator was one of those guys who always came up with points that made me ponder why in the heck I didn't think of them first.

He got up from the couch and began explaining that prior to coming over to Bosnia, he had been experimenting with a new Austrian munition designed to blow open doors from stand-off distances. It wasn't a high-explosive round (meaning it didn't produce any shrapnel); instead it used blast overpressure to force the door open. The round itself was shaped like a giant corndog on a twelve-inch stick.

"It's easy to use," he explained while demonstrating with an actual round in his hands. "You just insert the stick into the barrel of your rifle, cock the rifle, aim, and fire it like an RPG round." Like many of the men in the Unit, Predator was an inveterate tinkerer who seemed to be on a never-ending quest to discover or invent a better mousetrap. When guys such as Predator got a new piece of equipment or technology, they would immediately turn it upside down, flip it on its side, dip it underwater, and then attempt to break it apart and/or modify it. Never accepting anything at face value, they believed that they could find a better use for or improve on everything they touched. No one told Predator to experiment with this munition; he did it because he believed it might make a difference in combat someday.

Predator's tests revealed that with a slight modification to the warhead, the Austrian round produced the same effect as a gigantic concussion grenade. Concussion grenades are used to momentarily stun or disorient people without physically harming them. "In other words," he continued, "if we shoot it at the side door of his vehicle, the blast overpressure will create an intense concussion that will momentarily debilitate everyone inside the vehicle. This'll buy us the precious seconds we need to close in from our hiding place and grab the PIFWC before his security detail can get to their guns and start a shoot-out."

"How do you know for sure that it will really work?" someone asked.

"I tested it on three different vehicles last week," he quickly replied.

"Uh, yeah, but how do you know it will concuss real live humans enough to debilitate them?" I injected.

"Well, a couple of the new guys volunteered to ride in one of the vehicles to see what it would do to a human, and it worked on all of them."

The mental image of that episode gave me pause. It must have brought a pensive look to my face, because everyone in the room was staring at me to see how I was going to react. Although operators were known to push the safety envelope in the name of mission-oriented research, they were rarely, if ever, reckless. The Unit had a matchless safety record, especially given the extreme volatility of what we did day in and day out to prepare for our missions.

When it became obvious that I wasn't going to ask any more questions about the rifle-grenade experiments, Predator continued. "In the tests I conducted, we found that you had to hit the side door panel with a direct hit or the round wasn't effective. Hitting the side door panel of a moving vehicle is a very iffy proposition," he continued. "We found that the target vehicle has to be slowed to twenty miles per hour or below to ensure a high probability of success." This would be a challenge. We all knew that the Bosnians drove like maniacs and that the security detail would probably be traveling closer to sixty miles per hour than twenty. The consensus was that the concussion round seemed like an effective nonlethal technique but only if we could figure out how to get the target vehicle to slow to twenty miles per hour or below.

Tera, our communications specialist, breathed a loud sigh as he set up the laptop computers and satellite antennae for our worldwide communications connectivity. His code name was short for Terabyte, which reflected his monstrous capacity to remember. He and I came into the Unit at the same time, and had been together in Colombia, Somalia, and previous tours in Bosnia. Like many of his counterparts, he could have left the military at any time and been hired at companies such as Cisco, Microsoft, or Google for ten times what he was making in the military. But you can't bring war criminals to justice while you're working at Microsoft, so guys such as Tera stayed.

As Tera connected the final USB cables to the router, he nonchalantly interjected, "I saw a movie once called *Motel Hell* where they got unsuspecting people to stop their vehicles on a dark country road by putting life-size cardboard cutouts of cows in the middle of the road." The comment was so random and so outrageous that after a pregnant pause of contextual bewilderment, everyone in the room reacted with a simultaneous Mount St. Helens–like eruption of laughter. Bruiser blew an entire pressurized mouthful of Diet Coke onto the coffee table in front of him. The fact that many of us were a bit slaphappy from jet lag was likely to blame for much of the craziness, but as professional comedians will tell you, vivid imagery ignites the most intense and longest-lasting laughter.

Motel Hell was a bizarre B movie that instantly attained cultlike status among horror film aficionados; I too had once seen *Motel Hell* while watching late-night TV with some friends. I remembered marveling at the simple genius of the cardboard cow ruse, but until that day in Bosnia, I had never considered operationalizing the concept. As individuals began to compose themselves, something interesting began to happen. A flood of ideas and insights spontaneously began to bubble to the surface. "What if we add a good-looking woman to the broken-down-vehicle concept? Maybe a blonde with a nice figure would be best," someone said. "How about an accident? We could have someone hanging out of a vehicle with blood all over his body." "And the good-looking woman waving her hand for help," said someone else. Both ideas seemed to have potential, so we used each scenario to put ourselves in the minds of the security detail and imagine what they might do.

Most of the individuals in the room had extensive worldwide experience on missions we called protection details. On a protection detail, your sole mission in life is to protect a very important person (VIP), usually in a high-threat country such as Lebanon, Colombia,[9] or Bosnia. Our collective experience on these types of missions allowed us to understand how the PIFWC's security detail would think, decide, and act in response to our actions. When your mission is to protect someone, you have a ruthless optic on the everyday world. Security details don't have time to think about life's day-to-day trivialities. They have to get the person they are protecting from point A to point B as expeditiously and safely as possible. So whether it's an accident or a good-looking woman, security details have no time to debate what to do. There's only one option: keep going! In fact, when your life revolves around detecting threats, you get to a point where every vehicle that is broken down or otherwise blocking your path instigates a higher state of security consciousness in your already very security-conscious mind.

The team's assessment was that neither the blonde nor the bloody scenario would cause an experienced security detail to stop or even to slow down. In fact, most of the men believed that these scenarios would cause the security detail to speed up and begin evasive maneuvers. But the concept of using something bizarre such as cardboard cows to slow the vehicle seemed to bridge our thinking from the nuts and bolts of a vehicular ambush to the task of slowing the vehicle. We were beginning to recognize and refocus our thinking on how to slow the vehicle so we could use nonlethal force to capture the PIFWC without harming his daughter.

Then someone asked Tera why he thought those cardboard cows in the movie were so effective in getting people to stop and get out of their cars. I was about to question why in the hell we were still talking about that crazy movie, but like everyone else in the room, I quelled my urge to "get serious," and listened intently to Tera's response. "Well, I always figured it was a good example of exploiting human nature to accomplish your objective," he explained. "The cardboard cows looked surreal and completely nonthreatening so people were curious to see what they were doing in the middle of the road late at night. It's the same behavior that causes traffic jams on freeways after a fender bender. Every person who passes has to slow down to gawk and try to figure out what happened. The reason they slow down is curiosity. That's how we learn in life, through curiosity. We can't resist its powerful pull—even when it doesn't seem to make sense."

Then Blade, a blond-haired reconnaissance expert and world-class surfer spoke up. "How about a gorilla suit?" The sun was just starting to light the tips of the mountains outside, and once again, the safe house erupted. Bruiser blurted out, "How about a Bozo the clown costume!" "Oh, no that would be too threatening—how about Bugs Bunny, or a French maid's outfit?" someone else added. It took a bit longer this time, but eventually everyone recovered himself. This time the insights that poured forth were all focused on the operational utility of freakishly random costumes.

After a few French maid forays, Bruiser was the first to reflect, "A freaking gorilla suit, that's pure magic. Walk us through it!"

"Well," said Blade with a cautious smile that turned serious as he began to explain, "I'm thinking about these boys driving down this lonely mountain road. They're security-conscious, so they're all probably looking for the usual ambush tricks: broken-down vehicle, fake cops, you know the deal. But if we find a spot on the road that has a sharp hairpin curve, preferably on an uphill grade, simple physics will force them to slow the vehicle down before they make the turn, and when they come around the curve, there's this gorilla walking down the road." He did a good knuckle-dragging ape walk imitation as he continued. "The shock of seeing a freaking gorilla walking down the road, along with their uncontrollable curiosity to understand what the hell it's doing in the middle of Bosnia, may just make them pause a couple of more seconds, which ought to create the perfect conditions for us to fire the rounds and conduct the capture."

Everyone was silent. "Okay," I said, "so let's put ourselves in their shoes again. You're cruising down this lonely rural road—in Bosnia, I might add—and you come around a curve and suddenly you see a large ape walking down the road toward you?"

"I don't know what I would do," said one of our newest team members, who grew up on a sprawling ranch in Wyoming. "A gorilla walking down the road in the middle of the night would be so mind-bogglingly weird that I don't think it would fit any mental model I have. But since it's not really threatening, I gotta go with Tera's point on highway gawkers: I think I would be more curious than anything else. If I were driving, I think I would lean as close to the windshield as possible and then utter those famous last words of many a ruse victim throughout history, 'What in the hell is that?'"

"Exactly," said Predator. "That's the exact moment we'll nail the vehicle with the concussion round, then move in and capture the guy."

We quickly double-clicked our satellite Internet connection and typed "gorilla costumes" into the search engine. Our medic, Sticky, who was one of those *Jeopardy!* champion–like guys who seemed to know something about everything, suddenly opined, "My experience with gorilla costumes has taught me that there are gorilla costumes, and then there are gorilla costumes. For this operation to succeed, we need the Ph.D. of gorilla costumes!"

Without looking up, Bruiser, who was sitting behind the laptop culling through the Google search results replied, "Thank you, Professor von Costume. We were thinking of getting a plastic mask and a fake banana!" Although it was a blinding flash of the obvious, all of us agreed with Professor von Costume's point on the importance of costume quality, so we searched for the most realistic gorilla costume available. After checking on availability of the suit and overnight transoceanic delivery via a combination of commercial and military carriers, we agreed to continue developing the concept in a few hours after some much-needed shut-eye. I went to my room, plopped on the bed, and checked out of the Net.

I woke a few hours later to the obnoxious screeches of one of the scrawniest and scarred-up roosters I had ever seen. Standing defiantly on my bedroom windowsill, while staring straight at me, the war-ravaged rooster didn't seem like he had any intention of shutting the hell up. I grabbed my Glock from under my pillow and sat on the side of the bed for a few seconds to collect my thoughts. *Had we really come up with a concept to use a gorilla costume to capture this guy—or was it all a crazy dream?* The more I thought through the unimaginable concept, the more I could actually imagine it. While staring at the screeching rooster, I jacked the upper slide back on my Glock to make sure a round was chambered. I slid on my shower slippers, then slowly shuffled toward the window, and shot the rooster one final glance before shouting, "The war's over, chill out, dude," which he did. So I shoved the pistol under my shirt and stepped back out to the living room to imagine some more.

Life in a safe house meant we couldn't come and go as we pleased, especially during daylight hours. Any out-of-the-ordinary activity might tip off the locals to our presence and intentions. Therefore, instead of rehearsing the gorilla costume concept on a road with real vehicles, we could only imagine it. It was during our imaginary rehearsals in the living room that morning while grazing on fresh bread and cheese that we confirmed what the cardboard cows revealed to us the night prior: slowing the vehicle was what we in the Unit referred to as the "decisive point" for the capture operation. The definition of decisive point is a point in time or location where the success or failure of your actions will ultimately predicate the success or failure of the entire mission. In other words it wasn't the end-state objective (capturing the PIFWC) that required the priority of our imagination and efforts, it was the enabling objective (slowing the vehicle) that we had to succeed at to give us any shot of achieving mission success.

We also realized something else: given the criticality of slowing the vehicle to the success of our operation; we needed to ensure that we had some type of backup method, or option, in case the gorilla costume didn't work out the way we were expecting it to. The capture team immediately headed back to the drawing board. Within a few hours, they had designed, tinkered with, then developed a tire-puncturing device to slow the vehicle. The device's genius was its simplicity of design: a ten-foot by two-foot rectangular strip of flattened tire rubber studded with hundreds of razor-sharp titanium spikes.* The titanium spikes came off some dastardly contrivance our logistics guys had stashed in their deployment bag of tricks. The rubber mat came from one of our vehicles that they rendered spareless. That night, under the cover of darkness, we tested the spike mat on the dirt road that snaked through the hills behind the safe house. The spikes proved to be wickedly effective. We simply placed the mat off the side of the road and used a thin nylon cord to pull the mat in front of the target vehicle's path. We discovered that the flattening of the tires provided us with a simple, almost foolproof method of ensuring that we slowed the vehicle sufficiently to hit it with the concussion grenade and initiate the capture. On the downside, it definitely wasn't as cool or as funny as the gorilla costume.

The next night, we departed the safe house in a menagerie of five Bosnian vehicles, and headed out to the capture site for the first night of the PIFWC's forty-eight-hour travel window. Blowing snow and rain, which we called "snain," made the forty-mile drive to the capture site take twice as long as expected. Staring at the road ahead of us, with windshield wipers wiping waves of snain back and forth, I imagined how the PIFWC's driver would react to the sight of a large furry thing appearing on the road ahead of him. The lack of visibility made it almost impossible to discern if the thing in the middle of the road was a man, a gorilla, or even a pig. "This weather isn't fit for man nor beast," I begrudgingly concluded. Bruiser, who was sitting in the backseat dressed as a peasant sheep watcher, half-jokingly replied, "We could give the ape an umbrella," but this time the laughter was subdued. The premise of the gorilla suit was to shock the vehicle's

---

*Within a few years, most every police department in America was using the spike mat. Many police departments have now equipped every squad car with one.

driver into slowing his vehicle after he spotted the "freaking gorilla" walking down the road. If the driver couldn't recognize it as a gorilla, he wouldn't be curious, and instead of slowing, he would likely see the gorilla as a threat and either run him over or open fire. We collectively agreed that for opening night there would be no gorilla costume; the spike mat would take center stage.

We stayed in position the entire night. The snain turned to rain and never let up. There was no sign of the PIFWC. Just before sunrise, we peeled out of our positions and headed back to the safe house. At the safe house, Tera approached me with a melancholy look on his face.

"What's up, my man?" I asked.

"Panther," he responded matter-of-factly, "with the weather forecast predicting more of the same 'snain' tonight, and the simplicity and effectiveness of the spike mat, I'm not sure we really need a gorilla costume."

I laughed and told him I was thinking the same thing. Although I loved the gorilla costume concept, the success or failure of our mission depended on our ability to slow the vehicle; and it was hard for the gorilla to compete with the simplicity and wicked effectiveness of the spike mat.

"Let's talk it over with the capture team; we'll leave the decision up to them. It's always good to have options," I reflected as we began preparations for our second and final night at the capture site.

You're probably wondering what actually happened on that lonely mountain road in Bosnia. As mentioned earlier, the enemy always has a vote, and this PIFWC was no different. He changed his plans, as humans so often do, based on personal reasons. He did actually come across the border at a later date, and the weather was cold and clear on the night of his capture. Unfortunately, operational security, and ongoing cases against war criminals by the International Criminal Tribunal in The Hague, preclude me from discussing the specifics of how the mission and the PIFWC went down. Allowing him to get off on a technicality would be unimaginable.

I can tell you this much, though: if you check the right Sasquatch website, you'll find an isolated dot on the site's worldwide map representing one of the only reported sightings of a mythical man-ape creature in the Balkan Mountains of Bosnia.[10]

Imagine that!

Imagine the Unimaginable, Humor Your Imagination

Why is imagination so important? The evolution of man and our ability to dominate the planet is due in large part to our successful ability to imagine. The ability to imagine previously unimaginable uses of fire and water, of animals and plants, and of wood and mud are what saved us from extinction. Imagination allows us to break out of the prison of precedence and free our minds to recognize patterns and options that we've never been able to see before. A free mind is such a beautiful thing because it allows us to say and do things others can't imagine. It's how we discover, it's how we invent, it's how we innovate, and ultimately, it's how we adapt.

I no longer need to "imagine" using a gorilla costume to slow a vehicle for a capture operation because I already imagined it in Bosnia. I can see it. However, as you'll discover in later chapters, there were still other "imaginative" uses for the gorilla costume in my future. So how can we see into the future and imagine the next unimaginable application of fire, or water, of animals and plants, or freakishly random costumes? The answer is funny.

Cognitive science confirms that humor and imagination are indelibly linked.[11] What does the term *Gorilla Warfare* mean to you now? Did a slight smile form on your face? The reason it formed was because you got it. The mind's initial reaction to an imaginative solution is a smile or laughter. This occurs even when the solution itself isn't that funny. We usually smile instead of saying the words *I told you so* because it's a mini "eureka" moment when we're able to make an insightful connection where none previously existed. Next time you solve a riddle, or a Rubik's Cube–like challenge, or discover a new way to use some crazy costume, keep a mirror handy and take note of the smile that naturally forms on your face. Humor is the fertile field where the seeds of imagination are planted, grown, and harvested into imaginative and insightful solutions.

One of the best ways to get to the fertile fields of humor is through outrageousness, and when it comes to making people laugh and developing breakthrough ideas, the more outrageous the better. Outrageous thoughts are barrier busters: they wipe away the vanilla mental models stored in the first layers of our minds and reveal imaginative, out-of-the-box thoughts just below the surface of our consciousness. Inside our blacked-out safe house, the outrageously funny ideas of cardboard cows, clowns, and other costumes sparked our imaginations to discover new ways to slow a vehicle, invent a wickedly effective tire-puncturing device, and come up with innovative options to conduct a capture operation. When it came to finding solutions, we realized that nothing was off-limits. There were no thinking boundaries; there was always a way!

Make no mistake about the importance of humor and imagination in combat. History has proven that it's not the quantity of men or the quality of weapons that make the ultimate difference; it's the ability to out-think and out-imagine the enemy that always has, and always will, determine the ultimate victor. By permitting oneself to laugh at the world, and think outside the boundaries of ordinary, normal thought, brilliant new solutions can arise. As in the case of the gorilla costume, some "wild" ideas turn out to be practical too.

Imagine the Unimaginable, Humor Your Imagination.

PART 2

4

LEWIS AND CLARK DISCOVER OSAMA BIN LADEN:

WHEN IN DOUBT, DEVELOP THE SITUATION

North Carolina, 1998

When I arrived at work, I found a yellow sticky note on my desk with the words *Come see me* scrawled on it. I grabbed my notebook and hurried down the quarter-mile-long marble hallway toward the Unit commander's office. The commander was a big man. At six feet and well over 250 pounds, his cherubic boy-from-Tennessee face made him look much younger than his mid-forties. Obsessed with weaponry, he was always, it seemed, either cleaning a gun or sharpening a knife. When I walked into his office he was doing both. He motioned for me to sit. Without looking up from his desk, he flung a manila folder at me. Spinning like a Frisbee, it landed perfectly in my lap. "Pete, I don't have a lot of time to discuss this with you, but I need you to look at this target folder* and come up with some recommendations on how to capture this guy."

Target folder is the unofficial term used for an actual folder that contains a high-level overview of a person or a place that is of interest for potential future operations.

Cracking open the target folder, I quickly glanced at a map of Afghanistan; then turning the page, found myself staring straight into the icy black eyes of a man named Osama bin Laden (UBL).* "Never heard of this guy," I mumbled, "but I'll get cracking on it right away, boss. When does higher headquarters need this by?" He looked up at me with the sarcastic look he always used when he talked about our higher headquarters. "Right away, of course."

"What does that translate to in actual Julian units?"

"If they knew that we'd all be a lot better off, Pete." I wasn't sure what he meant by that, but this looked like a really cool mission, and I wanted to get started.

"Thanks, sir. Let's hit the range together sometime this week," I replied as I pointed at him while heading out of his office on my way to talk to one of our intelligence analysts.

Dee was a good-looking guy in his early thirties; his ethnic origin appeared to be a mix of African American and Japanese. In all the years I knew him, and in all the long deployments we participated in together, he never once mentioned to me or anyone else that I knew of, whether he was either, and it didn't matter. No one really gave a crap about your background at the Unit; the only thing that mattered was how competent you were. You could be from Venus with antennae protruding from your butt, and no one would think twice as long as you were a solid contributor to the overall mission. Dee was a superb intelligence analyst. He was common-sense smart, and he had a real passion about always ensuring that the Unit operators had everything they needed to allow them to accomplish their missions.

I walked into Dee's office and got right down to business. "What do you know about Afghanistan?"

*Although his full name is often spelled Osama bin Laden, UBL is the transliteration used by the U.S. government. No one inside the government uses OBL. It's always UBL, which is the way I will refer to him throughout this book.

"What do you want to know?" he murmured in his soft-spoken manner.

"How about we start with everything you got," I said.

There was no need to pretend that I was any kind of expert on Afghanistan. My knowledge came from distilled media memories of the Soviet War and, of course, a few documentaries on Discovery Channel. In 1998, UBL and Afghanistan were not even close to being strategic priorities; the U.S. government had its hands full with Iraq, Bosnia, Serbia, and the narco-terrorists in Colombia. Terrorism as a threat was neither understood in a global context nor in terms of its potential for causing massive loss of lives—especially in the United States.

"What do you have there?" Dee asked while looking at my manila target folder.

"I got a mission, Dee, and if you're up for it, you got one, too!"

He smiled and asked, "I heard something was coming down on this. Is this the bin Laden mission?"

"Yep," I uttered while searching through the packet for some kind of mission statement. I located a long paragraph that came from some alphabet soup headquarters at the Pentagon. "Our task is to come up with some recommendations on how to capture him. It looks like he is in the city of Kan-de-har" (See Map 3). Dee was well familiar with the information.

"Yeah, that's correct; he has a house in Kandahar out near the airport. I was just looking at the satellite photos of the compound the other day. Let me put a few target packets together and build some map boards for you. Just give me a couple of hours and meet me in conference room A."

"Sounds good," I replied. I went back to my office and began reading everything inside the target folder, and anything else I could find on Afghanistan and UBL.

Most of the information we had back then was based on information provided by two ex–UBL acquaintances turned informants, both of whom had passed lie-detector tests and had their stories corroborated by other sources.[1] They told us that UBL and Al Qaeda had established a formal military committee that was currently planning operations against U.S. and Western interests worldwide. They were also actively attempting to obtain nuclear material to build a WMD. There were direct links between Al Qaeda and the attacks on U.S. troops in Yemen and Somalia in 1992 and 1993. Al Qaeda also was directly linked to the plot to blow up planes flying between Manila in the Philippines and the United States in 1994 and 1995. In February 1998, UBL, along with other prominent Muslim figures, announced the now-notorious formation of the World Front for Jihad against Jews and Crusaders. They concluded that declaration with a fatwah* that charged every Muslim to obey "God's order to kill the Americans and plunder their money."[2] I was amazed that I hadn't heard any of this information about UBL before. We needed to do something about this guy. *This is why I came to the Unit,* I thought.

A few hours later I walked into the conference room. Dee had transformed the room by assembling an impressive montage of information for our preparation. Two of the walls in the room were made of tackboard, now covered with photos, personal dossiers, and maps. The other two walls were made of whiteboard, which allowed us to sketch operational concepts and to write key facts and assumptions that would need to be addressed as we brainstormed ideas.

I zeroed in on a three-foot-by-three-foot satellite photo labeled "Tarnak Farms (UBL compound)."[3] "How do we know this is where he lives?" I asked.

Dee paged through one of the target folders and responded, "It looks like we have multisource corroboration, to include individuals who have actually visited him there." Multisource usually means you have both signal intelligence (intercepted phone calls) and human in-

---

*Technically defined as a ruling issued by an Islamic scholar. During the '90s UBL issued three fatwahs, calling on Muslims to take up arms against the United States.

telligence (people actually on the ground). Both can be valuable on their own, but when you have them together, it usually means you have something credible. Credibility is everything when it comes to intelligence sources, so you have to know how reliable each of the sources is before you buy into the supposition the source is portraying.

"Visitors, like who?" I asked.

"It looks like a Saudi prince was one of the sources, and the other is an unnamed but reliable group of locals on the ground."[4]

"Okay, find out when the Saudi prince last visited the compound, and find out who the reliable source on the ground refers to." Dee wrote both requests on the whiteboard under the heading "RFI," which stands for requests for information. "How about signal intelligence? Are we listening to his cell phone calls?"[5]

Dee paged through one of his information packets and answered hesitatingly. "I don't know the specifics, but I do know that the cell phone intercepts are the only method we currently have of confirming UBL's location."

"All right, let's find out how often he's talking and how quickly we can get notification when he is talking." Dee nodded in the affirmative while he added the requests to the RFI list. At regular intervals Dee would aggregate the RFIs and input them into various databases to see what information was available on each topic. Incredibly, the multitude of government databases were not and—still are not—linked. Therefore, finding key and essential information is still like a game of go-fish: you have to ask the "right" system or you'll never get the information that may make the difference between mission success and mission failure.[6]

Tarnak Farms was where UBL lived with his family. It was an isolated island of homes conspicuously located in a sea of desert, a few miles outside of Kandahar. The compound consisted of about eighty mud-brick adobe homes, in rows of twenty, which were surrounded by a bleached-white ten-foot-high wall.[7] The nearest man-made structure was the Kandahar airport, about half a mile away, which the United States had funded and built in the mid-1960s.[8]

Dee had spent a significant amount of time studying the compound by comparing time-lapse images. He was able to count the different outfits hanging on clotheslines each day to determine that there were fewer than twenty-five people permanently living in the entire compound.[9]

Throughout the day, a number of operators from different functional areas within the organization joined us and, like me, the complexity and challenges of the mission quickly enamored them. Val was the most experienced operator to join our group. One of the fastest and most accurate pistol shots in the United States, he competed regularly all over the United States in national-level competitions as a civilian. A big man with thick brown hair and a lightning-quick wit, he and I had worked closely together in Somalia and Bosnia. At that time, Val was dating an attractive Swedish girl who also happened to be a practicing nudist. Val, as you might expect, quickly converted to the nudist lifestyle while in the privacy of their home. Soon Val's comfort with nudity began to spill over into his work life. In those days when we traveled for training, our standard operating procedure was to share hotel rooms to ensure that we were good stewards of government money. We had to request a special exception to that policy for Val, because no man wanted to share the tight confines of a hotel room with a practicing nudist.

We spent the rest of the week immersing ourselves in everything we had on Afghanistan and Al Qaeda. We had many questions: How often did UBL stay at Tarnak Farms? How would we know when he was there? Did he have any routines—trips to the market, regularly scheduled meetings, etc? How many bodyguards did he have? How much time did he spend with each of his wives? Was there anywhere we could stage from inside of Afghanistan? If not, how would we get there—and more important, how would we get there in a timely fashion?

Next, we asked for a point of contact in one of the surrounding countries, preferably someone we could contact to ask context-specific questions. The more we stared at the map and information, the more questions we generated, and the more we began to realize how much we didn't know. Val underscored our collective obliviousness when Dee randomly turned to him and asked, "So, Val, how do you think we should capture this guy?"

Val didn't hesitate. "Hold on a second, Dee. Before I answer, I'm going to pull my pants down and do a handstand. Once I'm up, I want you to draw a smiley face on my ass, because the only way I can answer that question is by talking out of my ass!" We all got a kick out of Val's use of vivid imagery. It was humorously imaginative, and he definitely got his point across. Without context-specific knowledge of what was actually happening on the ground, there was no way we could come up with a credible concept to find and capture UBL.

We wrapped things up at 7:30 P.M. on Friday and agreed to reconvene at 8:30 A.M. on Monday morning. I was dog tired. As so often happened during the initial exposure to new missions during my career, I had had a hard time sleeping that entire week. Tossing and turning all night, I just could not stop thinking about the mission, constantly sorting, contemplating, and generating new questions and insights. I knew I couldn't go another week without sleeping, so I stopped by the Unit psychologist's office on my way out of the building. The Unit psychologist (known as "the psyche") plays a prominent role in the Unit. To get in the Unit you first have to pass a barrage of oral and written psychological tests.[10] To stay in the Unit the psyches were always monitoring our performance, but they didn't do it by spying on us; they did it by being there for us. Whether you had a personal problem—such as the death of a family member—or a professional problem—such as you didn't want to be a sniper anymore—you could call or talk in person to one of the psyches at any time, and get some completely nonattributional advice in return.

When I explained my dilemma, the psyche smiled and pulled a

book off the shelf behind his desk. He opened the book to a two-page chart depicting the human brain. "Pete, there's nothing the matter with you; it's all in your mind."

Oh boy, I thought, *here we go.*

He continued, "You need to understand how the human mind works. The mind has three elementary phases it goes through when it's thinking: saturate, incubate, and illuminate. Although they generally occur in order, all three are continuous processes, so your mind is constantly cycling through all three phrases. The saturation phase occurs when the mind is first exposed to something. When you're planning a new mission you're saturating your mind with facts, assumptions, insights, and/or sensory cues—ergo, the saturation phase. The next phase is incubation. This is a critical phase if you ever want to come up with something innovative. The mind needs time to incubate. During this phase the mind subconsciously sorts through all of the inputs and begins to recognize patterns and snap those patterns together to come up with concepts and ideas. This is why you may have heard people say, 'I need to sleep on it' before making a major decision. It's not the sleep per se that they need: it's the time to allow their mind to sort through information and search for patterns. The recognition of patterns that occurs during the incubation phase produces the illumination phase, also known as 'eureka' moments, where your mind begins to translate those patterns and form them into actionable ideas. Saturate, incubate, illuminate—it's how the mind works, and it's probably the main reasons why you have lost so much sleep over the years. The best thing you can do is to keep a pen and paper by your bed. Writing down your thoughts while you're incubating and illuminating should help to temporarily get them off your mind and back to sleep."

"Geez, doc, I was kind of hoping for a few sleeping pills," I replied jokingly. Actually, I was impressed. "It sounds like you've delivered this spiel before."

He turned and put the book back on the shelf. "About a hundred times. This Unit suffers from chronic incubation-induced sleep loss."

"I guess that's a good thing," I replied, "as long as we also suffer from chronic illumination-induced wakefulness, too."

"Go illuminate, my friend," he countered, as he put his hand on my shoulder and walked with me out of the building into the warm pollen-saturated spring air of the North Carolina twilight.

Week 2

When I arrived at the compound early on Monday morning, I found Dee hard at work updating the folders and satellite photos hanging on the walls. Throughout the weekend, the various government databases we had queried had been spitting out answers to our RFIs in the form of reports, documents, articles, and photos. Once everyone else had arrived and grabbed a cup of coffee, Dee began his update.

Known colloquially as "the tribals," there was a group of Afghans working for the U.S. government on the ground in Afghanistan at that time.[11] Although the information we had was sketchy; they were a group of combat-hardened and experienced anti-Soviet mujahideen fighters. Of perhaps greatest import, they were Pashtuns, which is the same tribe that inhabited the areas in which UBL was living and operating. The tribals seemed like they definitely had potential, but without more information about their capabilities and trustworthiness, we had no way of gauging whether they could provide us with any operational assistance. The information on the tribals was compartmented, meaning only a small group of individuals within the U.S. government were allowed access to the information.[12]

We also discovered more information to corroborate that UBL was using Tarnak Farms as his main residence. His wives and at least some of his children were reported to be staying there. UBL also was spending a lot of time in other areas of Afghanistan where his Al Qaeda training camps were located. The two main camps were in the mountainous regions of eastern Afghanistan near the cities of Khowst and Jalalabad (see Maps 3 and 5). He traveled most frequently from his home near Kandahar to the training camp near Khowst. Khowst was the key hub for Al Qaeda in those days due to its relative proximity to the Pakistani border town of Miram Shah, which was the main point of entry for most of the Al Qaeda wannabes from around the globe.

Although the distance between Kandahar and Khowst was less than four hundred miles, it was a twenty-hour trip by car when the weather was good. The road that connected the two towns was a road in name only. Pockmarked with bathtub-sized craters and cracks, and in many places lined on both sides with Soviet-laid minefields, the treacherous journey was an endless series of stop-and-go zigzags that required intense concentration by the driver and extreme patience by the passengers to complete. UBL usually made the excruciatingly long and slow journey, along with his security detail, while traveling in three or four late-model Toyota Land Cruisers.[13] There were all sorts of speculation at that time that for security reasons UBL would sometimes ride in the back of dilapidated pickup trucks, or in decrepit common-man vehicles. We never bought into any of that. UBL was raised with a silver spoon in his mouth, and the privileged very rarely have the discipline to choose the hard right over the easy wrong. And UBL proved to be no different.

Terrorists are by nature paranoid. People who are constantly plotting to kill other people have a tendency to think everyone is just like them, so they naturally think everyone is out to get them; it's one of the reasons why it's so hard to catch a psychopath. UBL's paranoia was inwardly focused. In other words, he believed that the greatest threat to his life came from Al Qaeda insiders. He never shared the details of his travel plans with anyone, including his trusted security detail. As a result, the only intelligence reports that specified UBL's locations were reports generated after he had come and gone.[14]

Intelligence regarding a man's specific location is incredibly perishable. It has a shelf life of hours and sometimes minutes, which usually has evaporated by the time the intelligence gets back to someone who can actually take action on it. The United States did not have any U.S. personnel on the ground inside Afghanistan in the late '90s. So when a human source would report, for example, that he had just seen UBL drive into his compound near Kandahar, it would be days before that report was communicated to a U.S. representative in a nearby country such as Pakistan. UBL was constantly on the move and undoubtedly was using false stories about his travels, because in some cases there were reports of him being in two or more places at once.

The United States had no bases in central Asia at the time, and the distance from the nearest "friendly country" base in the Persian Gulf to Kandahar was approximately a thousand miles. Thus, given the distances from the nearest potential staging bases to the locations where UBL lived and worked, and the minimal time he spent at any of those locations, it would be all but impossible to get a force of any size from anyplace outside of Afghanistan into Afghanistan in time to successfully capture him.

Dee summed it up: "The time-distance reality means we need to put ourselves in a position on the ground where we can take him down when the opportunity arises."

"When you invent your crystal ball and Teleporter, let me know, because I want to be the first to invest," Val replied sarcastically.

Dee didn't blink. "Kidnappers study the patterns of their targets to determine the best place and time to snatch them. They adapt their plans based on their victim's patterns. Even though this guy [UBL] is paranoid, he has some key activity patterns in his lifestyle that we can definitely hone in on." He was pointing to the locations on the map. "His home and family are at Tarnak Farms near Kandahar. His key terrorist camp is in Khowst. There's only one way to get from one location to the other—the long deserted road that runs between them."

Eureka! Traveling from his home in Kandahar to his main terrorist camp in Khowst was an organizational pattern driven by his duty to check up on and give guidance to his subordinates at his terrorist camps. Traveling with his bodyguards in three fully loaded Toyota

Land Cruisers was an operational pattern driven by his real or per-
ceived paranoia. And the amount of time he could hang out in the
austere confines of Tarnak Farms and tolerate his many wives and
kids was a personal pattern, driven by his family relationships and his
own psychology. Tangled all together, the interactions among all these
patterns are what drive the behavior of UBL

"Hey, Panther, snap out of it," Dee mumbled while waving his palm in front of my face.

"Sorry, gents, I was doing the out-of-body thing. You guys nailed it! Once you recognize the patterns that inform the behavior of your enemy, you can adapt to them, and your enemy's toast!"

"Okayyyyy," Val replied with a wry smile, "so let's get a team on the ground in Afghanistan and start making some toast."

The room went pensive.

It was around 1:00 P.M. when one of our staff officers whose job it was to work with our higher headquarters walked into the planning room and announced to all of us that "Higher headquarters has just called and said they want to know where we are with the plan." I looked at Val and subtly shook my head to deter him from injecting his hand-stand metaphor.

"We don't know enough yet," I explained. It felt odd saying those words, almost as if it were an admission of failure or an excuse. I couldn't articulate it to the staff officer at the time, but it just didn't seem right to submit a recommendation at this point in our process for such an important and complex mission.

"They also told me to tell you to make sure you include options to use helicopters and cruise missiles," he added as he walked out of the room. I expected he'd be back real soon. I could almost hear our higher headquarters' indignation when they heard that we hadn't produced a plan for them yet.

The emphasis on helicopters and cruise missiles didn't really sur-prise us; they were becoming the default solution for all missions that required a force to actually spend time on the ground in a hostile country. Unfortunately, we all knew that getting approval to put men on the ground in a hostile environment such as Afghanistan would run head-on into one of the modern-day military's most vexing institutional shortcomings: risk aversion. Risk aversion is a direct by-product of not understanding what's going on around you, and by proxy, another version of "getting treed by a chihuahua." Back then it didn't seem to matter how important the mission was to national security; if there was any risk that a man might be killed or captured during an operation, the operation was deemed not politically worth the risk. Instead of focusing on the opportunity at hand, risk-averse leaders get treed by the potential risk, and fall victim to the greatest operational failure of all: the failure to try.

One of the most unfortunate by-products of risk aversion was, and still is, something we called the footprint paradox. To obviate *any* risk to the small number of men needed to conduct high-risk operations, the upper echelons of the military believed they had to employ massive armadas of helicopters, jets, vehicles, and people to address every possible contingency.

Helicopter-centric planning was and still is the driving force behind the footprint paradox. Heavy-lift helicopters* work well when used for what they were designed and developed for: inserting or extracting men to locations out of sight, sound, and line of fire from the enemy or a target. But they were never designed for the role they played in the '90s and still play today—as all-purpose assault platforms. The Hollywood influence doesn't help. The music and moxie that movies like *Apocalypse Now*, *Blackhawk Down*, and *We Were Soldiers Once and Young* orchestrated to portray helicopter operations as sexy and sophisticated obscures one critical common denominator detail connecting all three stories. The ill-advised use of the helicopter was the

---

*These include the UH-60 and CH-47 models along with all of their specially modified versions.

reason that all the valorous men portrayed in those movies got into the problems that they so heroically had to fight and die to get out of. Hollywood music and cinematography have had a strong influence on the misuse of helicopters in the military, but it was the military's own institutionalization of risk aversion in the '90s that made the helicopter the default solution for attacking almost all high-risk targets.

Coordinating and setting up the type of massive force package needed to support the massive armada of helicopters, headquarters, and humans required contentious diplomatic negotiations, and were all but impossible to hide from the indigenous populace. As a result, the time frame to put the massive footprint in place was measured in weeks. So, in the case of UBL and Afghanistan, not only would we need to know the exact time UBL was going to be at a specific location, we also needed to know it weeks ahead of time so we could get the massive footprint in place without tipping him off that we were coming. When policymakers were briefed on these types of footprint-intensive plans, they quickly shied away from approving them due to the political volatility of staging such a massive force in a foreign country, and the ease with which it could be misinterpreted as an invasion force. Paradoxically, it was the military's insistence on "zero-defect operations" that created the requirement for the massive logistics footprint, which in turn ended up making the operation politically untenable.

The type of risk aversion that drove the footprint paradox seemed especially counterintuitive to us in the Unit. From our perspective, we volunteered for this way of life with full cognizance of the risks that went along with it. We trained our bodies and our minds to a level that gave us supreme confidence in our capability to be successful in any situation, anywhere in the world. The question that high-ranking leaders always seemed to inject in any risk-averse-oriented discussion was, "Is it worth getting a man killed for?" Forty thousand people die on our highways each year, but when you get into your car each morning, do you ask yourself if driving to work is worth getting killed for? The main question that high-level leaders should ask is whether the mission is important to our country. If the answer is yes, then we in the Unit had no issues with laying our lives on the line to accomplish it. Could someone end up getting killed? You bet—we're talking about combat. But we had no intention of ever letting that happen.

"So helicopters are out of the question. What about using cruise missiles?" Dee asked with a pregnant smile on his face.

Val and I had spent many an hour discussing the strengths and limitations of the cruise missile, which, we were convinced, were rarely shared with high-level political leaders before they were forced to decide to use them. Val jumped up and sauntered over to the map again. "The use of cruise missiles is completely dependent on the target. Almost all targets can be broken down into two main categories when assessing their vulnerability to aerial bombs: stationary targets and moving targets. Stationary targets include the obvious—bridges, buildings, and bunkers. Buildings don't change their minds about where they're going to stay for the night, they don't get caught in traffic jams, and they don't get up in the middle of the night to go take a piss. So if you want to destroy an actual building, bridge, or bunker, cruise missiles *are* usually a pretty good option. Moving targets, such as UBL, whether on foot, or in his Land Cruiser, are very rarely static."

"So probably not a cruise missile target?" Dee pondered.

Val paused for a couple of seconds while he collected his thoughts. "Without a guy on the ground, I'd never consider using cruise missiles against a moving target, since there's no flexibility. A cruise missile is on a monorail once it begins its firing sequence—it flies at 880 kilometers per hour, so a thousand-mile distance to the target in Afghanistan would take about one hour and fifty minutes.[15] Lots can happen during that time! With no one on the ground giving a signal that the 'moving target' is actually present and stationary, versus stuck in traffic a mile away, or out on a walk in the hills, you are basically firing blind and hoping to get lucky!" He paused again. "And I know you guys are all converting those kilometers per hour to miles traveled. Save yourself the time, I got that stat from an article in *Popular Science*." I know I was impressed.

"Easy, Poindexter," Dee jokingly murmured just loud enough for everyone to hear.

Val was shaking his head in dismay and looking at the floor.

"Talk to me, Val," I said.

"Panther," he responded, "we can stare at these maps and satellite photos from now until eternity, and we can come up with all kinds of mindless helicopter assault or cruise missile plans, but none of them will have an ice cube's chance in hell of actually getting this dude, unless we can get some people over there on the ground."

"You're right, we have to develop the situation," I added.

"What do you mean by 'develop this situation'?" Dee injected defensively, as if our comments were an indictment of the intelligence portfolio he had prepared for us.

I stood up and moved over to the satellite photos and intelligence reports hanging on the wall and began explaining, "No offense to you, Dee, but these are just pictures and words put together and interpreted by some intelligence analyst in D.C. They're snapshots of reality, frozen in the past. Not a realistic reflection of what's actually happening on the ground right now. What we need is superhigh-resolution SA."

"Explain SA," he asked.

"Situational awareness. It's knowing what's going on around you," Val explained. *Or context dressed in a military uniform*, I witted to myself. "This is Afghanistan, and we're talking about a way of life that is almost incomprehensible to us. Trying to come up with a credible way to get this guy from here in North Carolina is like asking a caveman to put together a rocket ship; the caveman can't do it because he's been living in a cave all his life, and he has no idea what a friggin' rocket ship is." Val and Dee just stood there staring at the satellite photos and maps, but not really staring at anything at all. I continued, "But you know what? If you let that caveman out of his cave, give him enough time to study and play around with those rocket ship parts, and let him talk to a few people who know what a rocket ship is or maybe even how to put one together, the caveman may just be able to figure it out. He needs the time to build up his situational awareness so he can figure it out."

Up until that day I had always been a bit uncomfortable with the military planning process but never could put my finger on what was actually so illogical and dysfunctional about it. The military uses what they call the Military Decision-Making Process (MDMP) to conduct all planning.* All military planners are trained to use the MDMP, from the smallest of small units in the field, to the massive Pentagon staffs that prepare plans for the president's strategic decisions. It's basically a comprehensive, step-by-step doctrinal framework for decision-making and planning. All of the steps are supposed to occur within a ninety-six-hour period. The way it usually works is that upon receipt of a mission, the organization planning the mission sequesters themselves for ninety-six hours and follows the rigidly sequenced step-by-step process. In their race to adhere to the ninety-six-hour standard, planners usually end up prioritizing completion of all the steps in the MDMP process, over the product (a plan that will actually work). As they race to conform with the process, the planners are forced to make mission-critical decisions regarding how they are going to conduct the operation, even though they don't have sufficient information or the situational awareness they need to understand what options are truly available to them. At the end of ninety-six hours, they produce an elaborately detailed plan, which, upon approval of the commander in charge, gets locked in stone in prepara-

---

*The Recognition-Primed Decision Model is a rarely used alternative; but this model is virtually the same, except in step 2, the commander makes all the decisions to "push the process and save time."

tion for execution. What you end up with is a caveman trying to put together a rocket ship, without the time or the situational awareness to figure things out.

In the case of the UBL mission, we had no real situational awareness or context inside our "cave" in North Carolina. Sequestering ourselves for ninety-six hours and following a rigidly structured doctrinal checklist wasn't going to get us any closer to putting that Afghan rocket ship together. Like the caveman, we needed to get out of our cave and build context on the ground in Afghanistan.

The time aspect was especially profound when I reflected on what the Unit psych had shared with me about the way the mind works. Saturate, incubate, and illuminate. Time allows you to saturate your mind with context, so you can incubate and recognize the patterns that produce the "eureka" moments, when insights begin to form into actionable ideas.

This was an epiphany, and I felt a hell of a lot better about our current planning conundrum, but I also had a stark realization that even we, some of the most highly trained and experienced warriors in the world, had no business making recommendations for such an important mission when we didn't understand the on-the-ground context of Afghanistan and UBL. We were experts on how to conduct capture operations for sure, but all we could do was provide a best-guess recommendation to our president, and that's no way to make strategic life-and-death decisions that could change the course of world history.

Week 3

I got a call late Sunday night on the secure phone at my residence and was told that higher headquarters was demanding a plan by noon on Monday so they could brief the commanding general in the afternoon. I skipped my morning workout, and we all met back in the planning room at 6:30 A.M. It was time to start figuring out how we could get a small team on the ground to develop the situation. We looked at all the surrounding countries, specifically Pakistan, Uzbekistan, and Tajikistan. We determined we could get into any of these countries via commercial airlines without drawing a lot of attention. The border between Pakistan and Afghanistan looked especially appealing because from what we were learning, it existed only as a line on a map. On the ground, the border region was just an isolated frontier of rock- and snow-covered mountains.

Dee opened the session by informing us that we still didn't have permission to talk to anyone in any of the surrounding countries' U.S. embassies, so a lot of key questions remained unanswered. Although Dee was clearly used to getting stonewalled, I was sure that if we could just ask the right people, we could get whatever we needed. *There's always a way!* I thought.

I bumped Dee off the computer and opened up a new PowerPoint presentation. In the title space on the first slide I typed "Develop the Situation." For size of force, I listed two to five men. We would cross the Afghanistan-Pakistan border dressed as Pashtun tribesmen, link up with our Afghan allies, then move to a safe house in the Afghan countryside. Our time at the safe house would allow us to build situational awareness, and develop options to capture UBL whenever the opportunity availed itself. We would dress and comport ourselves as Afghans to blend in, and we would bring plenty of money so we could buy things such as food, vehicles, weapons, and, of course, pay the Afghans to assist us. *Wait till they get a load of this option!*

I sent it over to our higher headquarters. Thirty minutes later it came back with a note attached that read, "This will never fly with the CG [commanding general]." Then underneath, as if to underscore why it would never fly, was a list of short questions:

What will you do if you get captured? What will you use for a believable cover story? How can a couple of Americans blend into such a closed, suspicious culture? How will you find your way over the mountains on the border? (It's some of the roughest terrain in the world.) How will you avoid detection on the border? And finally, how will you communicate without satellite radios and a constant resupply of batteries?

Good points all, I realized. "Damn, I wish we could talk to someone on the ground in Pakistan and Afghanistan," I said with frustration. We just couldn't credibly address any of these concerns without some kind of on-the-ground knowledge to back us up.

Val wasn't frustrated; he was furious. "How in the hell do they think Lewis and Clark were able to discover the route to the Pacific Ocean?" None of us wanted to look like an idiot by trying to answer his rhetorical question, so we all just kind of sat there and let him go with it. "They had no idea what they were going to encounter, no maps, no intelligence, nothing, so they did what they knew best: they discovered! Those dudes were gone for three years, but they couldn't take three years of food, water, or equipment with them. And guess what? They weren't able to pick up their satellite radio each night and ask for guidance or request a resupply from headquarters. They learned and figured things out as they went along."

I could see where he was going with the Lewis and Clark analogy, and once again he was spot on. I had just finished reading *Undaunted Courage* by Stephen Ambrose; it was, at the time, my favorite book. Thomas Jefferson knew that he had to take action to figure out what the other half of the continent looked like. He didn't wait for the information to fall into his lap; he put together a corps of discovery, resourced them with whatever they thought they needed, and told them to go west and "make sure they let him know what they discovered as soon as they got back. They didn't spend any time obsessing over what they would have to do at the other end of the country, or what would happen if one of their men were killed or captured; they stayed focused on the situation in front of them and adapted as it unfolded. They got smarter with every mile they traveled, and every Indian tribe they encountered. When they came to a fork in the river, they hedged; they always went with the fork that would allow them to take the most additional forks. There was no timeline, and there was no plan, because Lewis and Clark didn't plan, they prepared."[16]

Everything was snapping together. The Lewis and Clark expedition didn't have a five-hundred-page plan detailing every phase of their journey; they just prepared as best they could, and then developed the situation as they went along. Now we just had to figure out how to translate the Lewis and Clark success story to help us get approval for our plan to infiltrate and develop the situation in Afghanistan. Of course, there was one major difference between then and now: Thomas Jefferson wasn't risk-averse.

Dee tapped on his watch to bring us back to the reality of our current predicament—we had to meet the demands of our higher headquarters and put together some kind of acceptable option. I figured I would meet them halfway and put together a hybrid option that was contingent on having a small team of two to five men on the ground that could build context and then provide real-time information to a small raid force positioned somewhere outside of Afghanistan. So we brainstormed how we could infiltrate the small raid force without using helicopters to get to the target. Our maps showed massive dry lakebeds that pockmarked the desert around Kandahar, within fifty miles of UBL's house at Tarnak Farms.[17] Most of the lakebeds were ten kilometers long and five kilometers wide and as flat as a pool table. We determined that we could land large fixed-wing aircraft (C-130s) on these dry lakebeds in the middle of the night without anyone seeing or hearing us. Once on the ground, the C-130s would regurgitate five to ten all-terrain vehicles, which included three Toyota Land Cruisers similar to the ones UBL used to get around. If the Afghan resistance fighters were available, we would link with them and use them as guides and to augment our force. We would then drive off-road across the desert and set up a hide site; there we would have at least two options that could be modified in any way required based on the situation on the ground. Option A was to drive to UBL's isolated residence at Tarnak Farms. To achieve surprise, we'd send the Land Cruisers in the lead, driving right up to the entrance of the compound or as far as we could go undetected before initiating the raid. Option B was to conduct a roadside ambush of UBL's vehicle convoy while he was traveling from Kandahar to Khowst. This was our preferred option because it provided us lots of flexibility on when and how to execute, and it would ensure, to the highest degree possible, that no innocent civilians would get hurt. *Disguises, deception, and diversions.* These were both highly workable options. I quickly translated the concept into a PowerPoint cartoon, and continued to add details all the way up to the 10:00 A.M. deadline.

At exactly 10:00 A.M., I let our higher headquarters know that I was sending them a hybrid course of action. We called it the Lewis and Clark option, to give it some panache. It took a while to find someone who actually knew what we were working on, but we finally found the lieutenant colonel who had sent it down to us three weeks earlier. He introduced himself and told me how busy he was. "There is lots going on in Bosnia," he said. When I explained why I was calling, he interrupted me and said, "Pete, there's no longer any requirement for inputs from you or your team on that mission."[18]

"But, sir?"

"Pete, there's no longer any requirement for a concept." He sounded a bit irritated. Back then, it wasn't unusual for real-world missions like this one to appear out of nowhere one day, and then fade away a few days later. I wasn't really sure what to think as I hung up the phone. Our concept never went anywhere. I felt a bit like the guy who cups his hand over his mouth to smell his own breath. Was it me? I wondered.

I was frustrated. But my feelings of frustration had nothing to do with foreboding. Instead, I considered this the holy grail of finding missions, and I didn't want our country to fail.

I passed the news on to the team, and without saying a word, the guys just shook their heads in resignation and started taking down the maps and erasing everything on the dry-erase boards. We kept a large folding poster board with a map of Afghanistan on it, and all of the ideas and concepts we developed in manila folders pinned to the sides of the board. Dee kept the UBL board folded up behind his desk. Three years would go by before we would pull it back out and once again direct our focus on Afghanistan and UBL.

THE EMBASSY BOMBINGS:

THE ONLY FAILURE IS A FAILURE TO TRY

Nairobi, Kenya, August 7, 1998 (9:15 A.M.)

Their Al Qaeda supervisor, whom they knew as "Jeff," provided them with a comprehensive step-by-step plan for their mission. The plan included surveillance photos, hand-drawn sketches, maps of the city, and a timeline covering every detail of their mission, including how many seconds the traffic lights along their route stayed red. They were strictly forbidden to deviate from the plan. As they rounded the traffic circle in front of the embassy, they fixed their sights on the rear parking lot entrance a hundred meters to the north of the compound. The truck entered the U.S. Embassy parking lot and immediately accelerated toward the drop-bar gate that led into the underground garage below the embassy compound. Twenty feet in front of the gate, the truck screeched to a stop. The passenger jumped out and ordered the security guard to stand up from his chair and raise the gate. Unimpressed, the guard ignored him. Enraged by the slovenly guard's indifference, the hyped-up passenger quickly became unglued. Things were not going as planned; the passenger panicked and began throwing concussion grenades at the guard, firing his pistol into the air, and screaming expletives. When the guard ran for cover, the driver also panicked, but instead of simply barreling through the gate, he pulled the vehicle up parallel to it, then detonated the explosive device in the back of the truck.[1] Unfortunately, the initial grenade blasts and gunfire had the effect of bringing people in the nearby buildings to their windows just moments before the detonation of the vehicular bomb. This natural human curiosity cost most of them their lives. The explosion sheared off the outside of the U.S. Embassy compound in Nairobi and killed 213 people; only twelve Americans were among the dead. Minutes later a similar situation unfolded at the U.S. Embassy in Tanzania.

Within five hours of the African embassy bombings, the White House situation room was bustling with activity focused on rescuing survivors and sending relief. One floor above, the president and his national security advisers, who consisted of the heads of all the key agencies involved in U.S. foreign policy, began assessing the situation and attempting to piece together what had happened.[2] The discussion quickly focused on the question of who was responsible. Sandy Berger, the president's national security adviser and most trusted confidant, immediately established a tightly compartmented planning process designed to keep all planning secret. Colloquially referred to by its members as the "Small Group," it included the only individuals cleared to know anything about the most sensitive issues connected with planning a response to the embassy bombings. The Small Group consisted of Berger, like the president, a career lawyer and politician; Secretary of State Madeleine Albright, a career Washington, D.C., insider and academic; Secretary of Defense William Cohen, a career politician; CIA director George Tenet, a career congressional staffer; the chairman of the Joint Chiefs of Staff, General Henry Shelton, a career military officer; and National Security Council member Richard Clarke, a career bureaucrat in Washington, D.C.

Week 1 (Post-Embassy Bombings)

Seventy-two hours after the bombing, Kenyan police detained Mohamed Rashed Daoud al Owhali, the Yemeni national who rode in the truck that carried the Nairobi bomb. After he panicked and started shooting at the guard and tossing concussion grenades, he did what most suicide bombers do when given a split second to reflect: he ran away. In his sworn statement, Owhali described the Al Qaeda–affiliated terrorist camps that he attended in Afghanistan to prepare him for the operation. He also underscored that only bad luck and the terrorists' strict adherence to the overly rigid plan that their supervisor Jeff had put together, had prevented the bombing from being much worse.

For the bomb to have achieved maximum damage against its intended target (the American embassy and its staff) it had to detonate in the garage, directly under the embassy. But due to the compartmented nature of Al Qaeda information exchange—the two terrorists were briefed by their superiors on the actual plan only three days before they had to execute it—they were never provided with any latitude for a plan B. When the smallest of details didn't go as planned (the uncooperative guard not responding to their demands), the terrorists weren't able to go with the flow and come up with alternative options (such as simply walking up to and raising the gate themselves after the guard ran for cover). With no options, they had no choices, so they panicked and detonated the bomb prematurely. Perhaps the biggest break in the embassy bombing investigation was the interception of a congratulatory phone call from UBL the day after the bombings.[3] The intercepted phone call and interrogation of the captured member of the bombing team led to the inescapable conclusion that UBL and Al Qaeda were directly responsible.[4]

Sandy Berger made it clear to the Small Group that they needed to develop a plan to respond to the bombings as quickly as possible. With the question of who being firmly established, the Small Group quickly began discussing the what. Specifically, what should be done in response? The Small Group met sporadically during the first week to accommodate the extraordinarily busy administrative schedules of each of the principals, and thus were never able to focus on the situation for more than a few hours at a time. During that first week, General Shelton briefed the group on a plan that he and his staff at the Pentagon developed for a large military raid into Afghanistan.[5] Berger and the Small Group quickly dismissed the concept based on the massive size of the force required, and the time required to assemble the force, which didn't jibe with the group's perceived need to do something quickly. Berger was clearly frustrated with the lack of options and would later reflect: "What we needed most was actionable intelligence on bin Laden's precise location."[6]

Week 2 After the Bombings

On August 17 the Small Group met again. CIA director George Tenet briefed the rest of the group on new intelligence that claimed UBL and a large number of terrorist leaders were going to meet at a camp near Khowst, Afghanistan. Tenet claimed that several hundred would attend. Tenet's PowerPoint presentation showed satellite photos of seventeen medieval-looking buildings carved into the side of a barren ridgeline. Almost immediately after seeing the photos, National Security Council member Richard Clarke leaned over to Tenet and whispered, "You thinking what I'm thinking?" The director of the CIA nodded his head sagaciously, while mouthing the word "yes."[7] They were referring to cruise missiles. Smug with the prospects of good idea ownership, the Small Group saw no reason to consider other options. There wasn't even much debate about the credibility of the intelligence, which was purportedly predicting UBL's location three days in the future. There also was no mention that until this point, no intelligence source had accurately predicted where UBL would be as many as twenty-four hours in advance. The recommendation to the president was to go forward with planning for a cruise missile attack whether there was firm evidence of the presence of UBL and his lieutenants or not.[8]

Although the Small Group possessed a basic grasp of terrorist doctrine, there was a dearth of real-world experience in counterterrorism operations among them, and none of the members possessed even a nanosecond of on-the-ground experience in Afghanistan.[9] The strictly enforced compartmentalized nature of their planning process prevented them from exposure to and interactions with those who understood the nuanced context of UBL, Al Qaeda, and Afghanistan. There were reams of context-specific information available from the CIA's recently established UBL section, but that information also was tightly compartmentalized and was not being shared with either the Small Group or with the other government agencies involved in the planning such as the military and Department of State.[10]

Based primarily on the recommendations of the Small Group, the decision to use cruise missiles to strike what were now being called "the bin Laden camps" near Khowst, Afghanistan, and a pharmaceutical plant in Sudan, was finalized on August 20, 1998.[11] The goal of the operation, officially called Operation Infinite Reach, was to prove that the United States would retaliate against terrorists and those who supported them. Later that night, navy vessels in the Arabian Sea launched scores of cruise missiles at the two targets. In all, seventy-six BGM-109C/D Tomahawk Block III cruise missiles were launched, at an estimated cost of $750,000 apiece, for a total of $57 million.[12] Most of the cruise missiles successfully hit their predesignated targets, and as expected, destroyed the medieval-looking buildings. None of the missiles came close to hitting UBL or any of his top lieutenants, who weren't anywhere near either location at the time the missiles struck the targets.

The cruise missile response wasn't just inefficient and ineffective, it was hugely counterproductive. Afterward, UBL and his key lieutenants realized with great certitude that they were the primary targets of the American military and technological juggernaut. As a result, UBL's inward-facing paranoia went global. After the cruise missile attacks, UBL stopped using his satellite cell phone, which up to that point had provided the only empirical confirmations of his location or intent. He also stopped traveling in his obtrusively conspicuous Toyota Land Cruiser convoy. UBL now knew he was a wanted man, and men who know they're wanted are very hard to capture.

To the Small Group, the plan to use cruise missiles worked fine; it was the intelligence that had failed. They doubled down on prioritizing "actionable intelligence" as the precursor for approving any future operations against UBL. The U.S. intelligence community officially defines the concept of actionable intelligence as "an awareness of information that predicts the location, timing, and intentions of an individual or group." To those of us outside the intelligence community, this definition is more appropriately matched with the term clairvoyance, and common sense tells us that there's no such thing.

Having learned the lesson of the cruise missile myth from the real-world school of hard knocks, the president asked the Small Group if perhaps a commando raid was possible. The compartmentalized nature of the Small Group meant that President Clinton was singularly dependent on the counsel of General Hugh Shelton for all military advice and options. General Shelton informed the president that "without actionable intelligence on bin Laden's exact location, a commando raid's chance of failure is too high." Shelton also told the president that the use of a small commando force was "too Hollywood," then cautioned the president that he would go forward with "boots on the ground" if the president ordered him to do so; however, he had to ensure that the president was completely aware of the "large logistical problems inherent in a military operation such as this one." The secretary of defense, William Cohen, would later tell the 9/11

Commission that "the notion of putting military personnel on the ground without some reasonable certitude that bin Laden was in a particular location would have resulted in the mission's failure and the loss of life in a fruitless effort."[13]

There would be at least two more prime opportunities to capture UBL in the next eighteen months. The intelligence for both operations was deemed credible by both the CIA officers working in the region and the highly trained Afghan tribals working inside Afghanistan.[14] Both opportunities involved options to capture UBL near Tarnak Farms. The Small Group subsequently dismissed both opportunities because they did not regard the intelligence as sufficiently actionable to offset their concerns with the risks involved. Based on the perceived lack of actionable intelligence, the Small Group had concluded that there were no politically acceptable options for attempting capture operations against UBL in Afghanistan. The Small Group believed that unless they were provided with the exact time when UBL would be at a specific location in the future (actionable intelligence), then approving any type of operation to capture UBL was too risky and thus too politically hazardous. The Small Group's obsession with actionable intelligence had turned into an intellectual straitjacket. By narrowly defining the target opportunities to a specific point in time and location, they were in turn making the actionable intelligence requirement theoretically impossible to satisfy.[15] They failed to realize that they had time. They had plenty of time to build better situational awareness and discover the numerous options and opportunities available to capture UBL prior to 9/11. From the first U.S. government planning session following the embassy bombings in August 1998 to the terrorist attacks of September 11, 2001, they had more than three years.

In the end, the Small Group decided that both Afghanistan and Al Qaeda were impenetrable. They had overreacted by firing the cruise missiles; they had underreacted to the two additional prime opportunities to capture UBL near Tarnak Farms; and in the end, they decided to do nothing. By staying "small," secretive, and compartmentalized, they made all their decisions without the reality-revealing benefit of context. The Small Group, and by default, the entire United States government, was treed by a chihuahua.

6

THE INFILTRATION
OF AL QAEDA:

DISCOVERING THE ART OF THE POSSIBLE

December 1998

At a lunch between President Clinton and Pakistani Prime Minister Nawaz Sharif in December 1998, the Pakistani prime minister reflected that "the Americans had wasted their money by launching so many expensive cruise missiles." He went on to say, "They should have sent a few men into Afghanistan with briefcases full of dollars, and they would have gotten the job done."[1]

Infiltrations into known terrorist havens such as Afghanistan, Yemen, Lebanon, and Sudan were deemed to be "far too risky," one knowledgeable individual later explained. "Prior to 9/11 there was no willingness to put Department of Defense personnel in such places. No such request would have been authorized."[2] Unbeknownst to anyone in the administration, at that exact moment the most unlikely of American infiltrators was taking his time to build context, and recognize the patterns and options that would ultimately allow him to produce the holy grail of actionable intelligence: a personal meeting with UBL.

When he left for Yemen, he didn't have a plan. Pressed by his mother for specifics, he told her "he knew what he wanted to do, but had no idea how he would do it." At this point in his life he had made up his mind that he wanted to be part of the Islamic fundamentalist movement. John Walker Lindh was a tall, dark, and gangly seventeen-year-old. He was also, by any measure, a troubled youth. Born in blue-collar Maryland, and transplanted to the unobtrusive opulence of Marin County, California, he was never quite able to find himself. In California he moved from school to school. He suffered from a variety of chronic illnesses, including an embarrassing gastrointestinal disorder in his teenage years that kept him in the bathroom, out of school, and by proxy, away from other kids. Isolated from traditional teenage social networks, movies and the Internet became his social sanctuaries. Surfing through the blogging worlds of rap, hip-hop, UFO-watchers, and CIA wannabes, perhaps it shouldn't come as a surprise that somewhere along the way he hyperlinked into the virtual black hole of Islamic fundamentalism. In short order he was hooked.

Although he knew next to nothing about the Islamic religion or culture, he immersed himself in whatever he could find in the San Francisco area. As it turned out, there was plenty. He began by attending the Mill Valley mosque near his home, where the foreign Islamic network greeted him with open arms. He established contacts with numerous non-U.S. Arabs who were visiting the United States for a variety of reasons, to include, in the case of most of them, no reason at all. Many of these "students of knowledge" extended open invitations for Lindh to visit and study with them in Yemen and Pakistan. As a result, he decided he would travel to Yemen to study a "pure form" of Arabic and to completely immerse himself in the Islamic culture. Based in part on the recommendations of his Arab contacts and supplemented by his own online research, he decided to enroll in the Yemen Language Center in Sana'a, Yemen.

Arriving in Yemen in June 1998* with no idea what to expect, he

---

*All the dates used for John Walker Lindh's journey should be considered approximate; he never wore a watch or carried a cell phone or calendar with him.

adapted his persona based on his own best-guess estimate of how to fit in. Calling himself Suleyman al-Lindh, he dressed in what he believed to be proper Yemeni attire. His clothes were actually those worn by devout Muslims from Pakistan and the Indian subcontinent, which is somewhat akin to walking down the streets of Buffalo in December wearing a Hawaiian shirt. Recognizing the incongruity of his dress, he quickly adjusted his attire to that of the locals. The clothes were the least of his problems. His roommates at the language center were an eclectic cohort of ex-pats from Canada, Northern Ireland, Great Britain, Australia, Indonesia, China, and at least two mysterious men from New York State. He didn't get along with any of them. They nicknamed him Yusuf Islam, in sarcastic reference to the name taken by folk singer Cat Stevens, perhaps the most renowned celebrity convert to Islam. His fellow ex-pats continued to enjoy many of the social accoutrements of the Western way of life—specifically, socializing and sex. Lindh had little patience for these types of secular dalliances. Rather than trying to change the unchangeable, he dropped out of the school and looked elsewhere for a better fit and better options.

He began probing the off-limits sections of the city. Sana'a was a dangerous place, especially for a foreigner without local guides. Tribal kidnappings and other politically motivated killings were common in and around the city. But the American teenager pressed on. He eventually located a Salafi mosque on the edge of town and began attending the all-day prayer sessions. Its bleached-white walls and complete lack of furnishings reflected the sect's strict adherence to the belief that any and all types of comfort items were heresy.[3] The extremist rhetoric and connections Lindh made at this mosque would eventually expose him to the teachings of a fiery political leader, Sheikh al-Zindani, whose ideas closely paralleled those of UBL. The connections Lindh made with al-Zindani followers formed key nodes and pathways he could tap into whenever needed as he continued his journey into the deepest bowels of the Islamic fundamentalist network.

Yet it wasn't the connections he was making in the heart of fundamentalist Islam that would ultimately lead him to his final destination in Afghanistan. That option would avail itself to him upon his return to California in May 1999.

Yemen, May 1999

In May 1999, Lindh was out of money and out of options that would allow him to continue moving forward in his quest. So he did what many teenagers do in this type of predicament: he returned to his parents' home in California to buy time while he figured things out. He spent the next seven months living with his mother in San Francisco. Although frustrated by his geographical and cultural separation from the heart of Islam, it was here, in the placid wine country of northern California, that he would discover the option that would ultimately pave his path into the frontier areas of Pakistan and Afghanistan. In early fall 1999 the Mill Valley mosque hosted a small contingent of traveling missionaries from a group called Tablighi Jama'at. A Pakistani businessman named Khizar Hayat was a member of the group. Hayat and Lindh hit if off immediately. They talked for hours, and before leaving, Hayat invited Lindh to come to his home in the Northwest Frontier Province of Pakistan, to stay with Hayat as his guest. Lindh recognized the invitation as the opportunity he had been waiting for.

February 2000

Just shy of his nineteenth birthday, Lindh returned to Yemen to continue his religious studies at Al-Iman University. The cosmopolitan student body at Al-Iman consisted of five thousand men and women from more than fifty countries, including a sizable contingent from the United States. After seven months of study, Lindh called his friend Hayat in Bannu, Pakistan, to tell him he wanted to take him up on his offer and continue his studies, and his journey, in Pakistan.[4] On October 15 Hayat met Lindh at the Islamabad airport. The two men immediately set out to find the "best fit" madrassa* for Lindh. Lindh rejected all of them, telling Hayat that for now he would rather stay close to Hayat's side in Bannu until he could figure things out.

Bannu is a gateway town into the Northwest Frontier Province (NWFP), one of the last truly nongoverned sociogeographic enclaves of significant size left on the planet. Despite living in one of the most isolated and technologically obsolescent areas of the world, Lindh was able to locate an Internet café in the middle of Bannu, where he began e-mailing his mother every Thursday night. At times Lindh's e-mails to his mother read more like a war correspondent's dispatches from the front. In October 2000, he shared his thoughts on the bombing of the USS *Cole*. At the end of the U.S. presidential election in November 2000, he e-mailed his mother and referred to George W. Bush as "your new president" and added, "I'm glad he's not mine." Although sending a message could sometimes take hours on the overburdened copper wire dial-up connection, Lindh soon became known as something of a computer whiz to the locals. As word of his skills spread, locals began bringing their computers to him for maintenance and repair. Here in the most secure terrorist sanctuary on earth, the inhabitants were handing over their computers, and by default their hard drives, to an enterprising American teenager for maintenance and repair. Lindh was once again plugged into the World Wide Web, and he was communicating.

Within a few months Lindh was able to locate and enroll in a Koranic memorization school a short distance from Hayat's home in Bannu. While listening intently to his fellow students' Pollyannaish stories of the Taliban movement in Afghanistan, Lindh became enthralled by Taliban dogma. Fellow students encouraged him to join the Taliban's

---

*A madrassa is an Islamic religious school. Many of the Taliban were educated in Saudi-financed madrassas in Pakistan that teach Wahhabism, a particularly austere and rigid form of Islam that is rooted in Saudi Arabia.

movement in Afghanistan, and volunteered information on how to contact and enroll in the terrorist training camps near the border city of Peshawar (see Map 3).

In June 2001, Lindh bid his friend and companion Hayat farewell and set out for the main terrorist training camp in Peshawar. When he arrived at the Peshawar camp, the terrorists running the camp told him that it would be difficult for him to work directly with the Afghan Taliban unless he could speak Pashtu, Dari, or Urdu (dialects spoken by the Afghan Taliban). Since Lindh could speak only Arabic, the cadre recommended that he join UBL's Arab Al Qaeda forces instead. Lindh enthusiastically agreed.

A few days later a guide arrived in a small pickup truck to drive Lindh to the Pakistani border town of Torkham (see Map 3). To bypass the perfunctory border checkpoint in the valley below, they left the truck and climbed a zigzagging footpath up and over the sparsely vegetated hills. Once at the top of the mountain they followed the path through the maze of towering rock escarpments that obscured the trail from below. Lindh had never hiked in mountains before. Once across the border, a few kilometers inside Afghanistan, the guide pointed Lindh in the general direction of the nearest Afghan road and instructed him to find his own transportation (a bus or a taxi) to Al Qaeda's headquarters near the Afghanistan capital of Kabul.

With only the clothes on his back, and a small bag containing his Koran and a few personal items, Lindh arrived at Al Qaeda's headquarters outside Kabul the next day. After volunteering his services, he was quickly processed and issued an "assault vest" to carry canteens and AK-47 magazines, of which he had none. After putting the vest on, the Al Qaeda cadre informed him that by accepting the equipment, he was considered an official member of Al Qaeda. Once again, Lindh readily agreed.

From Kabul, Lindh headed south to the Al Farooq terrorist training camp. Al Farooq was just west of Kandahar and UBL's home at Tarnak Farms. The camp was teeming with activity: Saudis, Iraqis,

Pakistanis, and Uzbeks were in attendance. Although the days were long and strenuous, the food rotten and scarce, and living conditions overcrowded and austere, the slightly built Lindh endured, and at times even seemed to thrive.

UBL visited the camp at regular intervals, always surrounded by five heavily armed Yemeni bodyguards. Although UBL appeared sickly to Lindh, he always took time to lecture the recruits on his latest caliphate dogma. At the end of one these diatribes UBL extended an open invitation to any student interested in a personal meeting with him. An option he could not refuse, Lindh once again acquiesced.

After a cursory pat-down by the Yemeni guards, Lindh entered a dilapidated shack on the periphery of the compound. Inside the shack, UBL sat cross-legged in the middle of the dusty floor. Lindh sat directly in front of him. The two began conversing in the universal small talk of commanders and subordinates. "Where are you from?" UBL asked Lindh. "Ireland" was the bizarre response that Lindh blurted out. Not much is known about the rest of the conversation. Did UBL tap into Lindh's on-the-ground knowledge of the West? Did he bounce ideas and concepts for future terrorist operations off the unwitting Lindh? Did UBL mention anything about the impending cataclysm less than sixty days away? Only Lindh and UBL know for sure, but we are sure that the British-tutored UBL, the head of the most treacherous terrorist organization on the planet, accepted the bizarrely shallow cover story of Lindh without challenge. We know this because after the meeting adjourned, both individuals continued uninterrupted toward their dates with destiny.

Just like that, the twenty-year-old Lindh had done it. In less than a month, and without any external support or technology, the American teenager had successfully infiltrated both the "impenetrable" terrorist sanctuary of Afghanistan and the "impenetrable" terrorist cabal of Al Qaeda. Lindh had developed the situation all the way from California to Al Qaeda–occupied Afghanistan, where the holy grail of options—a meeting with UBL—had availed itself to him.

What might have been if an actual U.S. government covert operative had replaced Lindh? The one-on-one meeting with UBL could
have presented numerous additional options. Perhaps the operative
could have chosen the option of simply confirming UBL's presence by
sitting passively through the meeting and siphoning as much information as he could draw out of the unwitting UBL, after which he could
have communicated the truly actionable intelligence to a ready and
waiting capture force poised nearby. On the other hand, the agent
may have decided that the one-on-one meeting presented the ultimate
opportunity to accomplish his overall objective, and seized the moment by using something as simple as a sharp ballpoint pen to change
the course of world history. We can only imagine.

John Walker Lindh's unlikely journey may seem, at first pass, like
one of those one in a million, it could never happen again stories we
attribute to the unlikely confluence of luck and happenstance. But
Lindh was not alone. In the years following September 11, we have
learned that more than a few American-born jihadists were behind
enemy lines and inside Al Qaeda during the same general time
frame.

José Padilla, a pudgy Catholic kid from Chicago with a long history of street crime, followed a path similar to that of John Walker
Lindh. Building context by establishing contacts and discovering options through a mosque in Fort Lauderdale, Florida, Padilla would
eventually seek out, contact, and join Al Qaeda completely on his own.
Padilla's travels took him to Egypt, Saudi Arabia, Afghanistan, and
another supposedly impenetrable country at the time, Iraq. Then there
was Aqil, a troubled Mexican-American youth from San Diego found
in an Afghan training camp fraternizing with one of the men accused
of killing journalist Daniel Pearl. Hiram Torres, also known as Mohamed Salman, graduated first in his New Jersey high school class and
briefly attended Yale before dropping out and heading to Pakistan in
1998. He has not been heard from since. According to *U.S. News and
World Report*, an Algerian government witness claims to have seen

"some black Americans" training at Al Qaeda bases in Sudan and Pakistan. Adam Gahahn, twenty-five, also attended Al Qaeda training camps in Afghanistan and served as an Al Qaeda translator. According to the FBI, he also was associated with senior Al Qaeda lieutenant Abu Zubaida in Pakistan. Last seen near his home in Southern California in 1998, as of 2008 he was still an active member of Al Qaeda, living somewhere in the Northwest Frontier Province.[5]

The first reaction of many when they learn the details of these astounding infiltrations is "you couldn't have planned something like that!" That reaction is as profound as it is exactly right: none of the American "jihadists" could have planned what they ultimately accomplished—not because they couldn't work a plan, but because when it comes to dealing with complexity, traditional planning simply does not work. So how did they succeed where our highly skilled government planners so deftly failed? They used common sense—they developed the situation!

GUIDING-PRINCIPLE LESSON:

When in Doubt, Develop the Situation

Developing the situation is the common-sense approach to dealing with complexity. Both a method and a mind-set, it uses time and our minds to actively build context, so that we can recognize patterns, discover options, and master the future as it unfolds in front of us.

It's the method Lewis and Clark used to discover a path to the Pacific; it's the mind-set John Walker Lindh used to explore Islam; and it was both the method and the mind-set that I and my small team of Delta thinkers used as we searched for a way to find UBL. Understanding what you're looking for is helpful but not required. All that's needed is the motivation to find your path.

Whether you're discovering a continent, exploring new directions in life, or searching for ways to solve complex problems, your thinking, like that of Lewis and Clark, John Walker Lindh, and Delta Force should shift away from traditional planning processes and focus squarely in the direction of developing the situation. Despite the perceived lack of structure involved, the relative advantages of developing the situation over traditional planning are both significant and self-evident. The advantages include, but are not limited to:

1. **Innovation:** discovering innovative options instead of being forced to default to the status quo.
2. **Adaptation:** freedom of choice and flexibility to adapt to uncertainties instead of avoiding them because they weren't part of the plan.
3. **Audacity:** having the audacity to seize opportunities, instead of neglecting them due to risk aversion and fear of the unknown.

Innovation: Developing the situation optimizes our potential to recognize patterns and discover innovative options because it's synergistic with how the human mind thinks and makes decisions. As my Unit psychologist so sagely shared, the human mind works in three elementary phases: saturate, incubate, and illuminate. Time allows us to saturate our mind with context, so we can incubate and spark the eureka moments of illumination that connect the dots, snap together patterns, and discover the options that allow us to find our paths. When we understand that most time constraints in life are self-generated, we understand that we almost always have time to develop the situation, whether in three minutes, three weeks, or three years.

Think of developing the situation as enlightened procrastination. Instead of indecision, going off half-cocked, or doing nothing, we understand that time is an ally that allows us to actively build context and uncover the options hidden from those who create "traditional plans" based on limited information that's frozen in the past—before most options and opportunities have availed themselves. Developing the situation treats life like a movie, not a snapshot.

Adaptation: Happenstance, nature, and human behavior all interact within an environment to constantly alter the situation. No environment is ever static. As the environment around us changes, developing the situation allows us to maintain our most prized freedom: the freedom of choice—to adapt our thinking and decision-making accordingly.

Actively developing the situation on the ground allows us to influence life's underlying patterns as they are emerging, so we can create and explore as many options as needed to find our path. Options beget options; think Lewis and Clark with every Indian tribe and every fork in the river they encountered. Think John Walker Lindh with the acquaintances he made, the schools he enrolled in, and the terror camps he haunted. Think of all the successes you've had in your own life.

Developing the situation provides us with the freedom and flexibility to choose and hedge as many options as possible. Options provide us with choices, and choices allow us to adapt to the naturally unfolding opportunities in front of us instead of being forced to bypass them because they aren't part of the plan. This means we should feel comfortable changing our minds and our methods and, whenever possible, hedging our options. When confronted with obstacles and uncertainties, both Lewis and Clark and John Walker Lindh constantly hedged their options, going backward at times when things weren't working out, to find a better option to enable them to continue on their way. Hedging options allows us to buy time and its offspring—context—by avoiding arbitrary time constraints that lock us into a single choice, such as firing cruise missiles, when we aren't sure what's actually going on around us and we aren't prepared to blindly commit. Remember that the act of choosing determines success or failure in life; freedom of choice is common sense.

Audacity: Audacity isn't taking senseless risks, or being rash; it's a natural byproduct of developing the situation and understanding what's going on around us. Audacity is really just another name for courage of our convictions to take action!

Risk aversion and fear of the unknown are direct symptoms of a lack of context, and are the polar opposites of audacity. The way to deal with a fear of the unknown isn't to avoid it by doing nothing, as our military and presidential planners did after the cruise missile strike in the late '90s. The optimal way to deal with the unknown is to do what Lewis and Clark, and John Walker Lindh did: take action to develop the situation and make the unknown the known.

Whether in combat, business, or your personal life, to master any situation, no matter how complex; learn the lesson of Delta Force, of Lewis and Clark, and even John Walker Lindh: When in doubt, develop the situation!

7

WALKING THE BOB:

ALWAYS LISTEN TO THE GUY ON THE GROUND

February 2001

Beirut, Grenada, Panama, Bogotá, Kuwait, Mogadishu, and Sarajevo—
plenty of hot spots had come and gone in the '80s and '90s; each had
different missions, different enemies, different terrain, and required
different skill sets around tactics, techniques, and procedures. In the
spring of 2001, no one had any idea where the next strategic priority
would be for the United States. I had no doubt that collectively we
were as highly experienced as any special mission unit had ever been.
Nevertheless, one of the most distinctive aspects of the Unit culture is
that we never rest on our laurels. Past success counts for nothing. All
that matters is how well we'll perform on the next real-world mission;
as a result, we were always stretching ourselves to reach higher and
higher states of readiness and proficiency. Once we were able to run
the obstacle course in four minutes, we started working on three.
Once we could hit a target with two shots from 150 meters while running at full speed, we moved back to two hundred meters. Once we
gained proficiency in Serbo-Croatian, we moved on to learning Arabic. And so it went.

In the Unit, we had to prepare for any eventuality—anytime,

anywhere, anyhow. As a commander, I left the individual skill training to my men; they didn't need me or anyone else to tell them what they needed to do to sustain their individual skills or how they should strive to get better. My responsibility was to focus on our collective training, to ensure that, as a group, we best prepared for whatever future missions might come our way. We had some time set aside during the upcoming summer for what we colloquially referred to as environmental training.[1] Environmental training described our philosophy of ensuring that we were prepared to conduct operations in all the major environmental categories, which we defined as cold weather, desert, jungle, and urban. Although the foundational principles such as surprise, speed, and simplicity were similar in all environments, from an operational perspective, conducting a raid in an urban environment is very different from conducting a raid in a jungle, desert, or cold-weather environment. In an urban environment, in a big city, we wore Italian suits with concealed pistols. We'd "hide" in the open without attracting suspicion by just standing in front of a building and pretending to talk on a cell phone while waiting for the right moment to initiate the operation. In a jungle environment we would wear specially patterned camouflage with foliage attached while openly slinging our weapons across our bodies to keep them always ready. Hiding in the jungle was an art form that sometimes required lying deathly still for many hours in mud or swamps while poisonous snakes, frogs, and an assortment of creepy-looking critters crawled over and around our bodies.

Even though we were highly experienced in all four environmental categories, I believed that the four basic categories might be too simplistic. There is an old military maxim that when you try to defend everywhere, you defend nowhere. Applying the same maxim toward preparation for real-world contingencies, I believed there had to be a better way to focus our limited training time on the most likely future mission environments. I asked Predator, who was one of my team leaders at the time, to put together a diverse group of operators and specialists from both inside and outside the Unit, and spend a few weeks thinking about and researching current hot spots around the world. Their objective was to come up with a recommendation on the three or four areas of the world they thought we had the highest probability of deploying to and conducting an operation in. Based on their recommendations, we would attempt to discern what, if any, environmental commonalities they shared, then structure our upcoming environmental training to simulate those same conditions and environments.

After two weeks of immersing himself and the team in the current socioeconomic, political-military, and environmental situation around the planet, Predator came back to me with his recommendations. To determine which countries inferred the highest probability of conducting an operation, he and his team used a common hypothetical scenario, that of a terrorist or revolutionary force gaining control of a WMD, or a high-ranking hostage, and the country asking the United States for assistance in mitigating the situation.[2] His top three most-likely list consisted of Colombia, Kashmir,* and Afghanistan. The common environmental denominator among all three regions jumped out at us like a punch in the nose.

"To get to the bad guys in all three areas, you have to go through the mountains." Predator summed up at the end of the presentation.

No one could remember the last time we conducted any type of collective training in the mountains, which made the thought of doing it even more appealing to me. We knew what we needed to do, so we began exploring how we could do it. We needed to find a location that would closely replicate the common environmental peculiarities of the mountains in Colombia, Kashmir, and Afghanistan. I asked the team

---

*Kashmir refers to an area that includes the Indian-administered regions of Kashmir Valley, Jammu, and Ladakh, and the Pakistani-administered regions of Northern Areas and Asad Kashmir.

to ensure that the location they recommended was as difficult to operate in and as unforgiving as possible.

"If it's easy to move through and operate in, then the president can get anyone to conduct the mission!"

Using maps, almanacs, and the Internet, we searched for mountain wilderness areas the world over. Nepal, New Zealand, and Alaska all came close, but the corner of the world we chose to cavort in was the Bob Marshall Wilderness Area in Montana. The Bob Marshall has it all: rugged peaks, alpine lakes, cascading waterfalls, and grassy meadows spread throughout towering coniferous forests and massive river valleys. The Bob Marshall is one of the most fully preserved mountain ecosystems in the world. The total landmass is 1,535,352 acres. Most locals simply refer to the area as "the Bob." As directed by the Wilderness Act of 1964, "No roads, structures, vehicles" or other mechanical contrivances are allowed inside. The size and scenery are one of a kind, but the Bob offered us something else that no other wilderness area in the world had: grizzly bears.

The U.S. Forest Service claims that the Bob is home to the largest concentration of grizzly bears south of Kodiak, Alaska. The grizzly bear is an original resident of the Bob. In much the same way that we would study, understand, and respect the local populace of any foreign country we operated in, we took the same perspective toward the grizzly bear. The best way to show respect to a grizzly is to avoid it at all cost. With a sense of smell a hundred times greater than that of a dog, a grizzly will flee when it detects a large group of humans approaching, but dense brush, heavy winds, and grizzly cubs can all increase the potential for human-bear confrontations. The grizzly provided us with a tangible reminder of the import of knowing what's going on around us at all times, while also requiring us to exercise strict tactical discipline in camp and during movement. Not only was the Bob a great fit in terms of mountainous terrain, but also, if we could move a hundred miles through the mountains without being detected by a grizzly and its supersensitive olfactory sense, we felt like we'd be well prepared to infiltrate unnoticed past Al Qaeda in Afghanistan, or the FARC guerrillas of Colombia.

A few days later I flew to Kalispell, Montana, with a small team to conduct what we called a pre-mission site survey. First we visited the National Forest Service offices that managed the Bob. Even though these were public lands, they were clearly the local Forest Service's backyard. We just wanted to let them know we'd be cutting through.

Although we were eager to lay eyes on the terrain in and around the Bob, we also wanted to spend as much time as possible talking to the locals and picking their brains on anything and everything they knew about the area. The mom-and-pop restaurants in rural Montana are great places to meet people. Not just "Hi, how ya doin' " in rural Montana; when people introduce themselves to you, they actually engage you in real conversations. We never told anyone we were from Delta Force, or the real reason we were so interested in one of the most unforgiving wilderness areas in the world, but we never lied, either; we just steered the conversation away from both topics, by using ambiguity or conversational diversions. While eating lunch in a diner a few miles from the eastern border of the Bob, we asked our waiter a few questions and soon found ourselves engaged in a free-flowing give-and-take discussion involving the entire diner, with cooks, customers, and custodians all chiming in. Talking out loud to the entire diner, I explained to them that we were preparing to come back out in June and walk a hundred miles across the length of the wilderness. Most hemmed and harrumphed with skepticism regarding our ability to walk across the entire length of the Bob without local guides or pack animals to carry our supplies. They were even more skeptical about our desire to cross the Continental Divide in June.* "June is too

---

*Continental Divide or Great Divide is the name given to the North American portion of the mountainous ridge that separates the watersheds that drain into the Pacific Ocean from those river systems that drain into the Atlantic Ocean.

early. The snow is too deep. There's only a handful of passes that a human can use to cross the Continental Divide, and they're completely covered in snow until early July when the snow melts enough to allow for navigation and traction on the high-altitude ledges." Earlier that day, the Forest Rangers put it more bluntly "The passes aren't navigable until early July; don't even try it. You need to wait for the snow to melt or you'll walk off of a cliff."

The man at the table next to us didn't make any attempt to hide the fact that he had something he wanted to add. When he couldn't contain himself any longer, he put his fork down, pulled the napkin off his shirt, turned in his chair and asked, "Mind if I throw in my two cents?" Dressed in a dark red flannel shirt and heavily faded blue jeans, he introduced himself as Walter and proudly announced that he was sixty, though he looked as fit as and well preserved as most forty-year-olds.

"Don't pay too much heed to the skeptics," he whispered matter-of-factly. "Every year a few backpackers get lost and die around them passes, so they just want to make sure you boys understand how dangerous it is." He grinned, looked around the restaurant, and then continued, "I've been through the passes in spring before; it ain't easy, but it can be done." Then he reminded us why it's so important to respect the emotional intelligence of everyone you come in contact with. "I've been awatchin' you boys since you first pulled in here. You ain't no normal backpackers. Most backpackers snack on fruit and nuts and move around real slow; they're nice enough folks, but they don't really care about gettin' anywhere in particular. You boys, on the other hand, you look like meat-eaters to me." (I looked around the table and noticed we were all eating burgers, but that's not what he meant.) "You move with a purpose, and you're asking people their opinions 'cause you care about what you're gonna be doin', and you know this's the best information you can get. I reckon you boys are military and you got reasons for goin' up in them crazy mountains."

Talk about pattern recognition. So much for our cover, I thought.

"Well, sir, you guessed right, we are in the military, but it usually takes one to recognize one, and we've been watching you, too. Someone as fit and observant as you are, I'm guessing you're a Vietnam vet." A tobacco-stained toothy grin spread across his face like a puddle of water while he reached across the table to shake my hand. "Special Forces, '66 to '68." I shook his wiry yet powerful callus-encrusted paw and replied, "From all of us, thank you for your service; it's a real honor to meet you." After thanking us profusely for thanking him, he turned serious again and asked why we were so hell-bent on crossing the Continental Divide before the snow melted. I leaned in close to him and whispered, "Same reason you went to the jungles of Panama before you went to Vietnam." His eyes twinkled while he subtly shook his head in silent affirmation. " 'Nuff said, what can I do to help you boys out?" he asked. I cut right to the chase. "What would you say is the most important advice or equipment for getting over the passes before the snow melts?" He didn't hesitate. "Take snowshoes with you; the snow is still deep in June, and it will be soft and heavy underneath with a hard crust on the surface. Without snowshoes it's like trying to walk on top of a giant apple pie." He paused, and I made a mental note to order a piece of pie for dessert so I could better understand his metaphor. "The snowshoes will keep you from post-holing* and getting stuck every time you take a step. They were lifesavers for me when I was up there last spring." All of us stopped eating, yanked out our pens and notebooks from our cargo pockets, and scribbled this new packing list item down for purchase. Walter spent the rest of the meal telling us about life in Montana—he loved it—and how much he missed the good old days in the military. When we told him the tentative dates for our journey, he gave us his phone number and invited us to his ranch for a steak dinner. After an hour or so, he stood up, bid us good luck, shook all of our hands, and then ambled out the door to

---

*The type of hole dug in the ground to secure a fence post.

his Chevy pickup truck. Someone said what we were all thinking: "What a great dude, let's get some pie."

Before we departed for a long car ride to the edge of the Bob, we headed to the back of the restaurant to hit the head. On the wall of the hallway leading to the men's room were two faded eight-by-ten pictures. I recognized the thin black frames as government issue. One picture was of a handsome young man in a white T-shirt standing in front of a billowing wall of intensely green jungle that needed no location caption. The other picture framed a citation for the Silver Star, the third highest award for valor in the military. Walter's name was on the citation.

After laying eyes on the exterior of the Bob we headed back to North Carolina to make final preparations for what we were now referring to as the long walk. Despite the doubts from all but Walter that we could make it over the passes, there was no hubris behind our decision to do it anyway. We simply understood the reality of real-world events: they happen when they happen without consideration for snow depth, or temperature, or the increased complexities they infer. If a real-world mission required us to infiltrate up and over wilderness mountains, we would have to figure out a way to do it. *There's always a way!*

One of the keys to survival in the wilderness is quality preparation. If you fail to prepare, you prepare to fail. To prepare for the Bob, we once again drew inspiration from the Lewis and Clark expedition, which had actually passed through the northern sections of the Bob during its journey in 1805. The three main areas of our focus were the terrain, the weather, and the supplies we would need to survive.

We spent many hours studying maps of the area to familiarize ourselves with the terrain we'd be passing over and through. We identified primary and alternate routes from our start point to our finish points—no easy task when you're talking about a hundred miles of mountain wilderness. Understanding time/distance estimates is critical in the mountains. If you try to predict exact distances for each day of travel, and then attempt to rigidly adhere to those predictions, your team could end up being forced to move at night—an extremely dangerous proposition in grizzly country. Most credible backpacking guides will tell you that experienced hikers can generally cover ten to twelve miles per day in the mountains. We prepared for ten to twenty miles per day, with an understanding that weather, terrain, and the unexpected would all result in our moving tenish miles on some days, and twentyish miles on others.

The point-A-to-point-B route we decided on would require us to walk and climb somewhere between eighty to a hundred total miles depending on river and snow levels. We would navigate up and over four mountain ranges, the highest of which was on the Continental Divide at just over nine thousand feet.

Weather was the biggest wild card. Not only would it affect our time/distance estimates, but also it was the driving factor behind our packing loads and the weight we'd have to carry. The previous year it had snowed in the Bob in late July. In June temperatures normally dip into the thirties and forties at night. The potential for the deadly onset of hypothermia is high anytime you get cold-wet in the wilderness, so we had to ensure we had clothing that would allow us to both stay warm, and stay dry. Unlike Lewis and Clark, we had access to the very best lightweight thermo-regulating clothing that science and money could offer. I packed a wardrobe full of Polartec fleece: hat, gloves, jacket, and pants. Made with the specially treated water-repellent fibers, the fleece offers more warmth for its weight than wool. I also brought along a poncho and a pair of ultrathin Gore-Tex pants that would allow me to stay dry while moving in rain or snow.

Once we stepped foot into the Bob, what each man carried on his back is what each man would have to sustain himself for five to seven days. As such, we tailored the weight and size of everything we'd be carrying in an attempt to come within a pound or two of forty pounds, the time-tested ideal weight for an average-size man to carry. I had only violated the forty-pound guidance a few times in my long-distance backpacking career, but the pain I sustained was more than enough to convince me that the forty-pound standard is right on target.

The Unit offered us a wide variety of backpacks to meet almost any mission requirement. Stored in a building that could easily pass as a private REI retail outlet, we could pick or choose almost any brand or model. Most backpacks weigh four to six pounds empty. My choice was a backpack made by a company called Kelty. The quintessential long-range mountain pack, it uses carbon-fiber levitators to support the loads, and is made with a nearly indestructible space-age material called spectra fabric. Weighing 1.8 pounds empty, it's also the lightest backpack ever made. At a cost of six hundred dollars, the Kelty was also the most expensive, but its weight is well worth its price. I would use every ounce of weight savings for extra food.

When you finally break to set up camp after a long day of moving through the mountains, the need for food completely consumes the human animal. My criteria for food came down to this: it had to have enough calories to meet my energy requirements, it had to be lightweight and compact, but most of all it had to taste really good. My tried-and-tested solution was to pack a combination of Mountain House freeze-dried meals for breakfasts and dinners in camp, and heaps of high-calorie trail mix—heavily laced with M&Ms to continuously graze on while moving throughout the day. I gauged the amounts I brought on a six-thousand-calorie-a-day requirement. I never skimped on food. Whether on a real-world mission or on an otherworldly backpacking trip, if you are hungry, all you think about is how hungry you are.

Most of the locals and guides we talked to recommended carrying a firearm to protect against marauding bears. Some also recommended Cayenne pepper–based bear spray as an acceptable alternative. I chose a Smith & Wesson .44 Magnum, that when combined with specially made 265-grain full-metal jacket bullets, appropriately earned its nickname—the hand-cannon. I based my decision on practicality and peace of mind. I had no intention of ever shooting a bear unless the bear was clearly in the no-turning-back attack mode. If a grizzly bear is bold enough to venture into a well-disciplined campsite at night, there is clearly something wrong with the bear. The bear may be sick, injured, or demented, and it's almost assuredly going to do whatever it takes to eat something or someone in the camp. A revolver is one of the most dependable guns ever made. It will shoot when it's wet, when it's full of mud, when it's freezing cold, and after it tumbles down a rocky cliff. A can of pepper spray, on the other hand, is a can, and is extremely vulnerable to each of the environmental contingencies mentioned above. In theory, pepper spray seems like it should work, but empirical proof of its efficacy is very thin. I did not want to go out of this world frantically pressing down on a spray-can nozzle hoping the effects would kick in while an insane grizzly munched away on my head. If a grizz was gonna eat me, I was gonna be his last supper.

Initially, not everyone in our group agreed. At one of our early preparation meetings, a couple of the guys dismissed the need for a hand-cannon, arguing that it made no sense to carry the extra weight of a large pistol and bullets. The chance of ever even seeing a grizzly is so small, they exhorted, that it made much more sense to save weight and carry a can of pepper spray, which weighs only a few ounces. The heated debate went back and forth for a few minutes until Predator interrupted with the clincher, "It's not just for bear protection," he let on. "We're going to be out in the middle of nowhere. Have you ever seen the movie *Deliverance*?" Everyone ended up packing a pistol after thinking through that scenario.

A few real-world contingency missions delayed the dates when we originally wanted to conduct the hike, and unfortunately, the new dates meant that some of the men were not able to join us. Ironically, the only time we could now fit the hike in was during our planned leave (vacation) period. The choice came down to this: leave or long walk? It was a no-brainer. We cancelled our vacation plans, signed out on leave, then flew west to Kalispell, Montana, the gateway to the Bob.

After checking into the local Holiday Inn and enjoying the traditional "last supper" of steak and beer at a local restaurant, we got together in one of the hotel rooms for our final coordination meeting. We divided ourselves into teams of four to five men. Each team had a different start point, and a different route through the Bob. Two of our logistics people would coordinate and execute all "backside" support for the trip. They would drive each team to their start point, and then pick up each team at their designated finish point over a hundred miles and five to seven days later.

Everyone was excited, but I also detected a slight air of apprehension among a few of the guys. Once some of them actually laid eyes on the terrain surrounding the Bob, it began to sink in that they were about to walk off the edge of the grid and into one of the most austere and hostile wilderness settings on the planet. Although the actual boundaries of the Bob are roughly a hundred miles by fifty miles, the forests and national parks that cocoon those boundaries make the distances from the interior of the Bob to civilization (roads or houses) roughly twice those numbers. If anything was to go wrong while we were in the interior of the Bob, we could be twenty-five to two hundred miles from the nearest road or vehicle. If someone broke an ankle or blew out a knee, the other team members would have to make a stretcher out of branches and twine and carry the wounded individual out of the wilderness. Every team carried a first-aid bag that mirrored the bags we carried in combat. Many of us were used to severing the umbilical cord to civilization and hanging it out there for the mission—rural Colombia came to mind—but for some of our newer guys, this was definitely pushing them out of their comfort zone, which was exactly why we chose to conduct our environmental training in the Bob.

During our meeting our logistics guys handed out the supplies they had picked up for us at a local hunting store that day: fishing lures, unscented mosquito repellent, sunscreen, water purification tablets, and fancily wrapped energy bars. I wanted to bring every one of these nice-to-have sundry items with me, but my backpack weighed exactly forty pounds; something would have to give.

At the end of the meeting, we each went back to our individual hotel rooms to make final adjustments to our equipment and settle in for our final night of mattress-assisted sleep. Once in my room, I went right to my backpack. *How can I make room for all this new stuff?* After months of thinking and preparing for the trek, I was borderline obsessive-compulsive about the weight of my pack. I looked at everything: food and clothes were definitely off-limits. *Hmmm, do I really need these snowshoes? I can't eat 'em, they can't keep me warm, and how bad can it be in the passes? Walking on a piecrust might be difficult for Walter—after all, he is sixty years old—but with my superior fitness, I should be able to gut it out.* I pulled the snowshoes off my pack, then shoved all the new sundry items into one of the outside pockets. Not completely satisfied, I squeezed out half of the small tube of Bacitracin (ointment for cuts) in my first-aid kit, saving maybe another gram of additional weight. My pack was as light as it could possibly get. I was ready to walk. Without taking my eyes off my pack, I backed into bed and faded into a state of fretful sleep. *The snowshoes were made of titanium and weighed less than two pounds. What did Walter say was the most important advice or equipment for getting over the passes before the snow melts? If we don't get over the pass, we don't accomplish our mission!*

I shot up out of bed. *You friggin' idiot, the snowshoes may not be edible, but taking them gives me options for what is sure to be the most difficult and dangerous portion of our trek. The mission is to accomplish the mission, not to do it as comfortably as possible.* I reattached my snowshoes, pulled out the sundry items, and laughed at my foolishly juicy rationalization while shaking my head and staring at the bedside clock. It was 3:00 A.M. Wake-up time was 4:30 A.M. for the long drive to the trailhead; I kept a close eye on my backpack and the clock for the rest of the night.

My team consisted of five men: Kap, Roy, Casanova, Stu, and me. Once dropped off at the trailhead, we were all business. There was no pomp and no hesitation. Each man hoisted his backpack over his shoulder and onto his back; cinched down the shoulder straps as tightly as his biceps could pull them; buckled the thick waiststrap; then without uttering a word, began moving south down the trail toward the interior of the Bob. We started slowly, but gradually picked up steam to a pace that could have easily qualified as a slow trot. On the first day of any long-range movement it's easy to get lured onto the wrong side of the tortoise vs. the hare debate. Every mile you put behind you today is one more mile you won't have in front of you tomorrow is the thought process. The illogic of speed is intoxicating; to keep it from going toxic, we used the 50/10 technique. The 50/10 technique breaks every hour into fifty minutes of walking and ten minutes of resting. It's designed to ensure regular monitoring, and maintenance of the feet, and to prevent the bane of all backpackers and soldiers—the blister. The ten-minute rest period each hour ensures each person has time to check, massage, and elevate his feet. When friction hot spots begin to form on the feet, the ten-minute break allows you to address the hot spots with Band-Aids or new socks before the hot spots turn into the pleasure-ending penance of a blister. The bonus aspect of the ten-minute rest period for me was that it served as a mini-sanctuary, always just a few minutes up ahead, where I'd have the opportunity to stop, relax, and smell the proverbial roses, while reveling in the visual grandeur of one of the last great remnants of primeval America.

Our objective for the first day was a place called Schaefer Meadows. The map depicted Schaefer Meadows as a large, open meadow where three creeks joined and dumped into the middle fork of the Flathead River. We figured the most expeditious route to get there was to follow the river until we bumped into the three creeks. Warmer-than-normal June temperatures created heavier-than-expected snowmelt, which resulted in the river running much higher and faster than we had anticipated. Our original route had us crossing back and forth across the normally placid knee-deep river, which now roared white at well over six feet deep. Less than ten miles into our hundred-mile movement, without anyone saying a word, we changed course. Instead of crossing back and forth across the raging river, we would do what orienteering aficionados call handrailing: we'd use the river as a hand-rail, and conduct the entire first day's movement on the north side of the river.

We started walking at seven in the morning; nine hours later we es-timated that we had meandered eighteen brush-beating, skin-scratching, energy-depleting riverbank miles. At four in the afternoon we rounded what seemed like the thousandth bend in the Flathead River. Peeking as we rounded the bend, we were optimistic that we would finally lay eyes on our destination. We were not disappointed. In front of us lay the open expanse of a pristine subalpine meadow, spangled yellow from end to end with gently swaying spring wildflowers. Gazing across the meadow, we were surprised to see a well-maintained log cabin that, judging by the horse parked in front, appeared occupied. Just as I pulled out my map to double-check the location, the cabin door swung open and out ran a blond-haired woman gleefully screeching at the top of her lungs, "Backpackers!"

As she rapidly closed the distance across the spangled meadow, blond ponytail bucking up and down behind her head, we stood frozen in a herd-of-deer-in-headlights trance. "Welcome, backpackers," she hailed as she arrived, while vigorously pumping each of our sweat-sopped and swollen paws. "My name is Sue. I'm the forest ranger for the Schaefer Meadows station. You're the first backpackers I've ever seen out here," she gleamed. No one responded. We just stared. Her golden-blond hair, blue-green eyes, and tan-clean complexion com-bined to give her an outdoorsy natural beauty, but it was her gregari-ous self-confidence and happy-go-lucky demeanor that made her naturally gorgeous. "Come in, come in, it's so great to see people," she repeated as she started walking back to the cabin in her ultra-drab one-size-fits-all National Park Service uniform that she wore with such pride. As we walked with her toward the cabin, I made a mental note to file the scenario away for potential future use. Here were five heavily armed and heavily grizzled Delta operators completely disarmed by the charm and effervescent exhortations of an attractive, self-assured blond forest ranger in the middle of the wilderness.

We followed her up the steps onto the porch and inside the cabin like a litter of puppies. After sitting each of us down around a lacquered picnic table, she immediately began chopping fresh oranges into quarters and passing them around the table. We devoured them. She pulled a cookie jar full of chocolate chip cookies off the countertop and implored us to eat as many as we liked. We destroyed them. Once we digested our astonishingly pleasant predicament, we actually began to converse.

"Where are you from? How long do they make you stay out here alone like this? Have you ever been married?" Casanova didn't get his nickname from some random or arbitrary event as some of the guys in the Unit did; his nickname was well-earned, self-explanatory, and still relevant. A good-looking guy who purported to be some infinitesimal fraction of an obscure American Indian tribe, he had a hairdresserlike proclivity for conversing with women. He was suavely attempting to develop the situation for his personal special mission. But for every leading interrogative with which Casanova probed, Roy and I countered with questions about the environment. "Have you been down Dolly Varden Creek lately?" "How deep is the snow on Pentagon Mountain?" "How about on Spotted Bear Pass?" Maybe it was the fact that we still had well over eighty miles of never-before-seen river valleys and mountains in front of us, or maybe it was the what-if-she-were-your-little-sister syndrome. I'm not exactly sure. Whatever the case, while Roy and I were thinking how lucky we were to run into a friendly forest ranger full of on-the-ground insights, Casanova seemed singularly focused on how running into a friendly forest ranger might allow him to get lucky.

Roy spread out his map on the picnic table, showed her our planned route, then asked her what she thought and whether she had any suggestions. She was politely circumspect in choosing her answers. "That's probably the route I would have come up with if I had never been out here before, but let me show you some other options you might want to consider for getting to your destination." Stu had spent a lot of time back at the Unit calculating the time/distance variables for our "planned" route. A forty-three-year-old steely-eyed Italian with jet-black hair and a body-builder physique, Stu looked like a cartoon caricature of a superhero. His specialty was languages; he could speak at least five fluently. As Ranger Sue discussed her recommended changes to our routes, Stu began to pace around the room and wipe his palm across his face. When Roy began tracing her newly recommended route on his map, I thought Stu was going to blow out one of his signature forehead veins. Years before most of us arrived in the Unit, there was an unspoken philosophy that unless someone had put one foot in front of the other in the Appalachian mountains (Delta Selection), they weren't qualified to override someone who had. The last vestiges of that philosophy lived on in a handful of old-timers like Stu. To Stu, she was too young, too female, and too inexperienced to override what he had already decided was best for the team. To the rest of us, that antiquated philosophy simply didn't make sense. As it turned out, she was one of the last people to cross the passes before the heavy snows sealed them shut in late September. She knew the lay of the land like the back of her hand.

"Do you think we can get over the passes?" I asked her.

The room went quiet, and she used the pregnant pause to perfection while she looked thoughtfully at each of us, then smiled and declared, "Normally I'd say no; the snow is still ten to twenty feet deep in some places, there's no trail to follow or terrain to read, and you'll be post-holing with every step you take. But judging by your fitness levels, equipment, and experience, I definitely think you guys can make it." Casanova smiled suavely; he almost assuredly considered Sue's comment as a positive affirmation that she thought he had a nice body.

Sue's insightful inputs went beyond just the mechanics of distance and direction. "Don't walk along the west side of the creek, it won't be worth your while: all you'll see is pine trees. If you walk on the east side you'll have unfettered views of the cliffs that line the west side of the creek; there are usually lots of bighorn sheep out grazing during this time of the year—"

"What about bears?" Casanova interrupted. The rest of us smirked; this was the first time he came up for air to ask a question that actually had something to do with our trek.

She answered cautiously, "I see you guys are armed, which is smart; as long as you maintain good camp discipline you shouldn't have any problem. One whiff of the five of you and any bear in her right mind will hightail it in the opposite direction way before you get a chance to see her." *We must really smell like shit,* I thought as I attempted a nonchalant whiff of my right armpit.

"You need to be especially cautious on switchback trails going up the mountain on this side of the pass," she added with emphasis, while pointing to a spot on the map called Switchback Pass.

"That's where the spring sun melts the deep snow first and uncovers the berry bushes. The bears are still thin at this time of year and they're on an unrelenting quest to find the tastiest and freshest berries." She continued, "If you don't pay extra close attention on the switchback trail, you could easily surprise a bear that's preoccupied with feeding. since you'll be downhill from her, it will make you seem smaller and much more vulnerable to attack." We told her we were planning to take Spotted Bear Pass, which was farther south than Switchback.

"Well, I think you guys can get through either of those passes," she replied.

"Hey, thanks, that's really good info," I said as I started to fold up my map. We had been talking for more than two hours, and we needed to set up our camp before it got dark. Roy and I stood to cue the others. I shook her hand and thanked her profusely, while Casanova covertly copied his cell-phone number along with "call me" on a napkin and left in on the counter.

We set up our camp about half a mile downriver from Ranger Sue's cabin at a spot where the meadow collided with the river. The meadow provided a soft and smooth moss-covered surface on which we could erect our two-person tents. The temperature plunged into the high thirties. We built a small fire; then each of us pulled up a rock or a log to sit on and do what people have been doing around fires since the dawn of time: gaze dreamily at the hypnotic dance of orange and blue flames while discussing the events of the day behind and what to expect of the day ahead. Inevitably, the conversation always looped back to Ranger Sue. We didn't stay up long; we were all dog tired. Usually it's hard to fall asleep the first night in the wilderness. The uneven, rock-covered ground limits position options, and it takes time to adjust one's senses to the natural commotion of the nocturnal wilderness. Luckily, I fell asleep right away, waking only once when I thought I heard Casanova getting up to stoke the fire.

The next day we followed Ranger Sue's advice and walked along the east side of Dolly Varden Creek while marveling at the massifs and massive limestone cliffs that rimmed our valley-bottom route. Bald eagles and bighorn sheep dotted our day. While the rest of us savored the scenic splendor, Stu stewed. Intrigued by his seething silence, I asked him if something was bothering him. He didn't answer; he was boiling. One of the most highly educated and worldly individuals I had ever worked with, he surprised all of us that he just could not get over our wholesale dumping of his planned route. The fact that we took Ranger Sue's advice over his was too much for him to swallow. Stu's ego had usurped his common sense. With each passing mile, as it became more and more obvious that his route would have taken us twice as long and revealed half the scenic splendor as Sue's, Stu slowly began to simmer down. By 4:00 P.M., after covering more than twenty magnificent miles, we decided to stop for the day to set up camp. Stu and I went off to forage for firewood. While foraging, he uttered his first words of the day, "I saw four bald eagles today; that was really a great route." *Time and common sense strike again,* I thought.

While sitting around the fire that night, our iridium satellite phone rang. We carried the iridium phone so the Unit could always reach us in case of an alert. When it rang, we all perked up with the same thought: *a mission.* The caller on the other end said only one word—it was a code word followed by Roy's and my names. Translation: Roy and I needed to get back to the Unit as quickly as possible. Without saying a word, we unfolded our maps, turned on our headlamps, and began assessing our options. It didn't take long to recognize what we needed to do. If Roy and I crossed the Continental Divide at Switchback Pass instead of at Spotted Bear Pass, we could shave forty miles (or two to three day's travel) off the route, and if things went smoothly, we could get back to North Carolina in less than seventy-two hours.

To ensure that we could use every available second of daylight for movement, we woke up before sunrise and began packing our gear. We were a tad shy of thirty miles and one Continental Divide away from our pickup point. After chugging down a piping hot cup of joe, Roy and I shook hands with the rest of the team and headed off on our own toward Switchback Pass.

Switchback is a colloquial term for the natural zigzag pattern used to move up or down a steep grade. It's the pattern animals use to walk up or down steep slopes, and it's the time-tested physics-based pattern used to design and construct mountain roads the world over. The switchback trail leading up to Switchback Pass was the longest and steepest switchback that either Roy or I had ever encountered. Pausing at the base and gazing skyward, it reminded me of something I'd once seen in a Dr. Seuss book.

The majority of the three-hour trek up the never-ending switchback went by in a monotonous blur. We plodded upward at a steady step pace while the temperature climbed to an unseasonably balmy seventy-five degrees. The weight of our packs, combined with the thin air and the dehydrating heat, began to sap us of our strength and breath. I was suffering from severe crocodile bite on both shoulders, while Roy battled double blisters on both his feet. We were in a perpetual state of fidgeting to find relief. Then we froze.

The birds that had been chirping away a few seconds before went mute. Most outdoorsmen recognize this antipattern as an alarm: a predator is nearby. I strained to hear, see, or smell anything out of the ordinary. A subtle procession of pebbles tumbled down the mountain from the trail a few switchbacks above. Roy and I simultaneously swung toward the movement while unbuckling the retention snaps on our holsters. Ranger Sue's admonition was still fresh on our minds; we weren't thinking we might have surprised a bighorn sheep. Rapidly scanning the mountain above us by reversing the path of the tumbling pebbles, a hundred feet above we spotted the massive hindquarters of a grizzly lumbering up and away toward the snow-covered alpine sanctuary near the peak. What a magnificent sight. The grizzly slowed as she approached the tree line, and then glanced back over her shoulder while shaking her head in what appeared to be angry disgust. We had seen a grizzly in the best of all sighting scenarios—running away in the opposite direction from us. Spotting the grizzly was a wonderful thing—every outdoorsman yearns to see one in the wild—but the elation of the moment quickly evaporated when it dawned on us that the grizzly was not equally elated to see us. Those berries weren't just nice-to-have sundry items to her; they were life-sustaining. We had just come between her and her berries. To the grizzly, we were trespassing.

Following standard antigrizzly protocol, we stayed where we were for a few more minutes, and then began talking loudly and moving upward along the trail with extreme caution. We wanted to make sure there wasn't a hidden animal carcass stashed out of view that might cause the grizzly to come charging back to protect it from us.

After another hour of zigzagging and looking over our shoulders, we finally arrived at the top of the mountain. The most common reason why hikers get lost and perish at high altitude is that the tops of most high-altitude mountains consist of byzantine series of outcroppings, corridors, creekbeds and other strange terrain features that can befuddle even the most experienced navigators. To navigate effectively in mountainous terrain you have to be able to read terrain. The term *reading terrain* describes the ability to match the terrain you see in front of you with the terrain depicted on the map. Both Roy and I considered ourselves experts at reading terrain. But to read something, you have to be able to see it, and all the terrain on top of this mountain was ensconced in twenty-foot-deep snow.

"Let's rock and roll," Roy uttered, as we stepped off the boulder and sunk down to our waists in the snow. Warrior pride isn't easily dissuaded; we tried a few more steps. No change—with each step our legs would sink three to four feet deep, and then require a strength-sapping struggle to pull them free. We were post-holing through the piecrust. Screw this! We turned around and did a half-walk, half-breaststroke back to the boulder shore. This was why we brought the snowshoes, I gladly admitted to myself as we began slipping our boots into the bindings. Just as I was putting my second snowshoe on, we heard the unmistakably throaty growl of a grizzly bear (given the altitude and the terrain, I was almost positive it wasn't a pig).

"What the hell was that about?' Roy whispered.

"Not really sure," I whispered back, "but let's get moving."

With the titanium snowshoes on our feet, we pranced across the piecrusted surface like astronauts walking across the moon. This is what Alaskans call the great counterintuitive axiom of the north: with the right equipment, it is easier to move in the mountains in the winter than in the summer. The hard crust over the deep snow allowed us to move directly across the uneven boulder-strewn terrain below it. The normally treacherous-to-cross high-mountain streams and ravines were completely covered in snow, so instead of having to search for a fjord to cross safely and dryly, we were able to walk on top and over them while staying directly on our line of march.

Within a couple of hours, and just before we lost the sun, Roy and I passed over and through the top of the Continental Divide. After taking a few "happy snaps" to record the moment, we paused to look behind us at the mile-long maze of snow-covered terrain we had just traversed. We felt good about ourselves and about what we had just accomplished. But while staring at the snowshoe prints that traced our path, we realized we couldn't have made that path without Walter's sage advice, nor would we have had the opportunity to wear his advice if it weren't for Ranger Sue's sagacious "watch out for grizzlies while walking on the switchback" advice.

I pulled out my acetate-covered map and used a stubby grease pencil to write the words *Always listen to the guy on the ground* across the top. With the sun disappearing fast, we rapidly descended the east side of the divide, aided by the law of gravity and a noticeably receding snowpack. Within minutes we came upon a magnificent hundred-foot iced-over waterfall, its motionless exterior betrayed by the roar of a jet engine revving at full throttle underneath. Darkness settled in. There was no need to move any farther; the base of the waterfall would make a fine campsite for our last night in the Bob. After building a small fire, we cracked open a flask of Knob Creek Kentucky Whiskey that Roy had saved for just such a moment. We passed, sipped, and savored a few shots while laughing about who had won more of the "which way to go" debates that had punctuated the entire day. The light from the full moon made the snowcapped peaks and the pine-forested valley below us glow like an Ansel Adams picture. Although neither of us ever mentioned the grizzly bear, it was never far from our minds that night. We stayed up most of the night sipping whiskey, stoking the roaring fire, and talking about life.

The next day we walked twenty-two miles to our designated rendezvous point, where one of our support guys was waiting in an SUV with tickets and a recommendation for the quickest way to get back to North Carolina.

Over the next three days, all of the other teams made it up and over the passes, experiencing trials and tribulations similar to the ones

Roy and I had encountered. There was even another grizzly bear encounter. It would turn out to be some of the most valuable training any of us had ever experienced.

Always Listen to the Guy on the Ground

We spent a lot of time preparing for our journey through the Bob. We studied the history of the area, we studied the terrain and weather patterns, we studied the animals—especially the grizzly—and we applied the intellectual rigor of scientists to our selection of food, clothing, and survival equipment. But the most profound insight we took away from the Bob came from our interactions with Walter and Ranger Sue. When it comes to understanding what's going on around you, there's no better external source of reality-revealing context than to always listen to the guy on the ground.

"Guy on the ground" is a metaphor for the people who are actually interacting with the environment. Whether on the front lines, the front office, or in an isolated forest ranger outpost in Montana, they're your best external source for understanding the reality of the situation on the ground. Listening is just that—listening—it doesn't mean abdicating responsibility or doing everything the individual(s) says, although you might—it only implies that you listen to him or her as one of your primary inputs.

The type of knowledge that makes guys on the ground like Walter and Ranger Sue so valuable is called tacit knowledge. Tacit knowledge is contextualized knowledge of people, places, ideas, and experiences. It involves knowing how to obtain desired endstates, knowing what to do to obtain them, and knowing when and where to act on them. It's knowledge in practice that's developed from direct experience and action, and usually is shared only through highly interactive conversation, storytelling, and shared experience. Like the orphic advice from the Vietnam veteran I befriended in college: "If you want to learn about what went wrong in Vietnam, you can find the answer at Gettysburg."

Tacit knowledge is a web of networked and multidimensional knowledge; as such, it is also difficult to articulate or write. (Imagine trying to teach someone how to swim over the telephone or e-mail.) Thus you usually need to do two things to access it: you have to seek out and make face-to-face contact with the source, and/or you have to ask context-specific questions to uncover it. "Walter, what would you say is the most important technique or equipment for getting over the passes?" "Ranger Sue, do you think we can make it over the passes in current conditions? What about bears?"

If someone has enabling information that can contribute to accomplishing our goals, we must be willing to add their talents and their skills to our own, no matter how different that person is from us. Even if it implies that everything we planned or thought we knew was incorrect. To do this we must be capable of divorcing ourselves from our emotions. Pride and hubris are two of the most common derailers of a person's common sense. Despite the obvious lifesaving utility of Ranger Sue's advice, Stu had a hard time getting over our wholesale dumping of his planned route. To Stu it was a de facto admission that a young, blond, noncombat-tested female was better qualified to provide mission-critical advice to our group than he was. For leaders, this is one of the key virtues of internalizing this guiding principle. It allows us to recognize that it's okay for our initial thought process and decision to be wrong. In fact, until we get on-the-ground input, we should expect that most of what we think we know will likely turn out to be incorrect or incomplete. This mind-set allows us to maintain our most prized freedom, the freedom of choice to change our minds and liberate our thinking from the common-sense-blocking emotions of pride and hubris.

Whether the president of the most powerful country in the world, or a member of a team moving through the Montana wilderness, the lesson is the same: to make optimal decisions you have to have context, and the best external source of reality-revealing context is to always listen to the guy on the ground. It's common sense!

PART 3

The operative assumption today is that someone, somewhere, has key information or a better idea; and the operative compulsion should be to find out who has that information/idea, learn it, and put it into action—fast!

—JACK WELCH

8

CALM BEFORE THE STORM:

THE MAN-HUNTIN' PROJECT

June–August 2001

With some middle-of-the-night-assistance from the Unit travel agent, Roy and I used planes, brains, automobiles, and good ol' shoe leather express to get from the border of the Bob back to North Carolina in just a bit under twelve hours. Lewis and Clark would have been impressed. As was always the case at the Unit, the only expectation I had when I got back was to expect the unexpected. And in that regard, this mission did not disappoint.

It turned out that I was called back to participate in a collaborative effort between the U.S. military and civilian defense contractors. Where the idea came from I was never told, but the unstated objective was to see if we could figure out a way to improve the process for finding solutions to the military's most difficult-to-solve operational needs. Although I must admit I was bit perplexed at first about having been yanked out of the Bob, and almost getting munched by a bear in the process, the more I thought about the potential of the project, the more excited I got about participating.

Historically, this type of solution-focused collaboration between the military and civilian defense contractors has generated some evolutionary and revolutionary results. It was during a collaborative effort to improve military radar systems around 1946 that an enterprising scientist noticed that the candy bar in his pocket had melted while he tested a new vacuum tube. After placing some popcorn kernels near the same tube, he watched with a eureka sparkle in his eye as the kernels swelled, popped, then gave birth to the idea of the microwave oven.[1] When military and civilian scientists needed a solution to make the sharing of information between computer systems at various defense-sponsored universities more convenient, they collaborated to develop the mother of all military inventions; what the Pentagon officially dubbed the "Intergalactic Network," but is now known worldwide as the Internet. When the military needed a device to help its ships and planes safely navigate around the globe, it was a collaborative effort between scientists in the air force, navy, and a leading defense contractor that led to the invention of the GPS navigation system that is almost ubiquitous today in our cars, airplanes, and cell phones.[2]

All three defense contractors I'd be working with had research facilities spread around the outskirts of the Greater Los Angeles area. Only a few hours after setting down my backpack and locking my hand-cannon in my weapons locker at the Unit, I headed back to the airport to catch a plane to Los Angeles. I was accompanied by a savvy acquisitions officer who had spent most of his career as a fighter pilot until he experienced a life-flashing incident during an engine flameout while flying a night-training mission over the desert southwest. He landed his plane, hung up his flight suit, and changed career paths to become a defense acquisitions officer. Our itinerary had us spending one full day with each company. Each company had put together a cross-functional team of engineers and scientists they referred to as project design teams. Each of the three design teams consisted of various types of engineers—design, electrical, aeronautical. You name it, they had degrees for it. Our day-long agendas were set up as open-ended sessions that would first expose unmet operational needs, and then focus on collaboratively brainstorming potential solutions.

This was the first time I had ever directly interacted with defense contractors, and they immediately impressed me with their dedication and passion. "We live to discover and develop ways to keep you guys safe and help you to accomplish your missions," they told me repeatedly. I noticed that everyone was going out of their way to thank me for participating. They seemed almost uncomfortably appreciative of my presence and input—so much so that during our lunch break on the first day, I asked a fiftysomething engineer named Stan why my presence was such a big deal. Stan was a Vietnam veteran who had worked for the company for more than twenty years. Along the way he had participated in numerous breakthrough projects, including the development of stealth technology. Stan didn't need time to mull over his answer. "Oh, you wouldn't believe how bad it's gotten since they initiated the defense acquisition reforms. We're not allowed to contact guys like you to get feedback anymore, so we end up developing technologies that aren't what you guys really need." His frustration progressed to anger. "Instead of calling someone like you for advice when we run into a design issue, we end up guessing what the technology should do and how it should perform. Without feedback from the guys who are going to use our stuff, we end up wasting government money instead of saving it, and it takes us twice as long to get a project right."

Enacted in 1994, the intent of the defense acquisition reforms was to prevent the unwarranted influence of the defense industry on the military's weapons and technology acquisition. The cause célèbre for enacting the reforms was the notorious six-hundred-dollar toilet seat. The six-hundred-dollar toilet seat was supposed to be prima facie for what happens when the military and the defense industry collude with each other for reasons of self-interest instead of national security. The supposedly overpriced toilet seat became the rallying cry around which Congress and some media outlets allied to ensure that the government would never again get ripped off by licentious defense contractors. The problem was, as Stan explained, "neither the politicians nor the media ever checked the facts around why the toilet seat actually cost six hundred dollars." The legend of the notorious toilet seat surfaced when twenty navy planes had to be rebuilt to extend their service life in the late '80s. The onboard toilets on the planes required a uniquely shaped fiberglass form (toilet seat) that also had to satisfy strict military design specifications for vibration resistance, fire retardance, weight, and even durability. Unfortunately, the type of toilet seat you purchase at the local hardware store didn't check any of those boxes. Additionally, the molds for the seats had to be specially made because the production process for these particular seats had been closed down for more than two decades. So when you understand what was actually required to design and manufacture the six-hundred-dollar toilet, you begin to recognize why it actually cost six hundred dollars.

But no one bothered to seek out, ask questions of, and listen to the few people (such as Stan) who could explain why the toilet seat cost so much. Congress responded by passing legislation that minimized interactions between the defense contractors whose job is to discover and develop new technologies and equipment, and the operational side of the military—who they are supposed to be developing it for. Thus the unintended consequence of the defense acquisition reforms was, and still is, the inability of the military to rapidly translate and communicate key operational needs and gaps to the people who are in business to figure out how to close those gaps. Although this type of restriction may not seem so detrimental when thinking in terms of developing toilet seats, imagine the potentially life-threatening consequences when developing mission-critical items such as gas masks, weapons, and armor protection for vehicles.

Stan told me that I was the first military representative they had talked to in the past year who possessed current real-world operational experience. What they usually got were what he described as "individuals with one foot in the retirement grave" who may or may not have had combat experience in the past but whose relevance had usually vanished with the crumbling of the Berlin Wall.

As our project progressed and I spent time with each of the three design teams, I realized that their mental models of what defined "modern-day warfare" were vastly different from mine. When most of them described their version of warfare in 2001, they described scenarios in terms of Desert Storm and Kosovo—and solutions in terms of bombs and bombers. They were always asking if a faster jet fighter or a bigger tank would help us fill current real-world gaps.

Going into the session I wasn't sure what kinds of breakthrough technologies we really needed, but the more I talked about recent real-world events, the more I started to realize just how much warfare had both changed, and concomitantly, just how much it had stayed the same.

I realized that during my combat career, from 1989 to the present day (2001), almost every major strategic operation conducted by the United States had either started out, or ended up, focusing on locating and capturing a specific individual, rather than defeating a country's military or seizing expansive swaths of terrain. Manuel Noriega in 1989, the Colombian drug cartel kingpins in 1992 and 93, Mohamed Farrah Aideed in Somalia in 1993, and the PIFWCs in Bosnia from 1995 to the present. In retrospect, I also realized that it was Saddam Hussein, not the entire Iraqi military, who was (or should have been) the object of our military efforts in the 1991 Gulf War. It hit me that *the history of modern-day warfare is the history of man-hunting!*

As I discussed this revelation with Stan and his design team, Stan illuminated that this method of thinking and its resultant operational focus could have been, and perhaps should have been, the true military objective of almost every major U.S. military action over the past sixty years.

"What might have been," he asked the group, "if we could have located and captured Adolf Hitler prior to '41, or Kim Il Sung in the early '50s? And think about the 'nonwars' and the genocide we might have prevented." He paused and added, "Idi Amin in Uganda, or Pol

Pot, the butcher of Cambodia who ordered the murder of two million of his own people in the late '70s."

The room came alive with chatter. A handsome woman in her early forties stood up and began pacing the floor; then she piggybacked, "What we need is to develop a way to identify, track, and locate specific people." She was standing across the room, but locked eyes with me as she asked, "What if you could do this from outer space?" The room went quiet and everyone looked at me. I thought about it for a few seconds, and then responded, "That would work as long as I had a cool-looking space suit."

"Very funny." She smiled as she walked to the whiteboard and drew a satellite hovering over the earth. "What if we could figure out a way to use a satellite to detect a person's genetic code?"

"How would we do that?" Sam queried.

"Did you know that humans exfoliate skin from their bodies 24/7?" she asked rhetorically. "We actually leave an 'invisible to the naked eye' trail of skin behind us everywhere we go!" she added. The room erupted in sidebar rumblings. *I wonder if the satellite could detect someone's genetic code while he or she was wearing a gorilla suit.*

"What's so funny?" Stan asked me.

"I was just thinking about some wild way I might be able to disguise my skin exfoliation and prevent the satellite from detecting me."

Eureka! The insight that something as simple as a gorilla suit might defeat the skin exfoliate detector on a satellite, brought me back down to earth. We weren't talking about an all-purpose technological panacea for finding people; the reality and complexity of life virtually guarantee there never will be one. Instead, these types of capabilities should be looked at as part of an overall system. A buffet of capabilities that could be used in combination with our guys working the situation on the ground to assist in the vexing challenge of locating a wanted man.

After three days of anything-goes, free-thinking sessions, we had come up with lots of out-of-the-box ideas, many with significant potential to make breakthrough contributions to current real-world operational challenges: clandestine communications devices: inert human tracking chips; DNA detection devices on satellites; and, of course, all kinds of weird flying machines and weapons systems.

All of the design teams requested that we come back out for another session in two weeks. They specifically requested that we bring back a few "real-world-mission scenarios" to help them better understand the context of current real-world challenges. While my counterpart, the acquisitions officer, called back to our higher headquarters and passed on the request, I thought about the Lewis and Clark scenario that my team had developed back at Fort Bragg in 1998. It represented both a current real-world scenario and our most intractable and unsolved operational challenge: how to infiltrate Afghanistan to find UBL.

When I got back to the Unit, I opened the Lewis and Clark file for the first time in three years and reacquainted myself with the concept. I wondered if we had made any progress in finding UBL; I hadn't heard anything about him since the embassy bombings. Maybe he wasn't a clear and present danger anymore.

As soon as I finished reviewing the slides, I sent the presentation to our higher headquarters so they could decide whether to approve it for sharing with the civilian defense contractors. Within a couple of days it was declassified and approved to be shown in its entirety to all three companies.

In late August, I flew back out to Southern California to conduct the mission-scenario briefings. I didn't make any changes to the concept after it was declassified; it still had the original four phases we put together in 1998. Phase I: send in a couple of guys (Lewis and Clark) to link up with some trusted Afghans and begin developing the situation on the ground. Phase II: when the situation warranted it, land transport planes on one of the massive dry lakebeds in the middle of the night and unload additional men and vehicles to link with our guys on the ground. Phase III: move to a desert hide site and prepare to locate and track UBL. Phase IV: based on the situation on the ground, conduct an operation to capture him.

After showing the Lewis and Clark concept to the design teams, I was deluged with questions and comments that honed right in on the decisive point: the ability to pinpoint UBL's location and then track his movements. Without knowing it, the defense contractors had identified finding the man (UBL) as being the biggest operational challenge we faced. "Why don't you send some people to live and work in Afghanistan so you have a continual presence in country?" "Why don't you watch the people who live and work with UBL?" "Why don't you guys just hire some Afghans and ask them what you should do?" Their questions were perfect surrogates for the three best sources of context: time, common sense, and always listening to the guy on the ground. I was impressed. I wrote every one of their questions down.

On the final day, we met with the lead engineers from each company who unanimously requested that our collaborative relationship continue. One of them, a regal-looking white-haired man with a newscaster's face, summed it up for all of them: "If we could schedule regular interactions like this one, we're confident that we can discover and develop more innovative technologies to help you guys solve your most vexing operational challenges. And in the process, do it much more efficiently and effectively for the American taxpayer." I wholeheartedly agreed and pledged to go back and provide the same feedback to key leaders in the military.

While driving through the verdant Santa Monica Mountains on my way back to the airport, I reflected on the potential of the concepts we had just discussed. Specifically, how valuable it would be to have a buffet of technologies to find and capture dangerous individuals anywhere on the globe. If we could fully develop this Orwellian capability, it could underpin our strategy for global security for the next fifty years, in much the same way that nuclear weapons formed the foundation of our defense strategy for the past fifty. In theory, we could reverse the magnetic poles of warfare—to strike at the individual causing the problem, rather than the force and the people under his or her command, a potentially revolutionary and evolutionary form of warfare. We spend billions of dollars on bombs and bombers to destroy men and machines, when the reality is that more often than not, it all comes down to finding and locating individuals—man-hunting. We need to combine our best minds and best organizations in a collaborative fashion, in much the same way we did to develop the atomic bomb, except instead of calling it the Manhattan Project, we should call the modern-day version, the Manhuntin' Project.

As I pondered the potential of the Manhuntin' Project for the future, I was oblivious to the real-world events snapping together at that exact moment, just two weeks shy of 9/11. It would be years before I fully understood the irony of it all.

We had scheduled the next collaborative brainstorming session with the defense contractors for the last week of September 2001. That meeting would never happen.

9

9/11:

THE FOUR-INCH KNIFE BLADE

When 9/11 occurred, I was following a mock terrorist around the streets of Budapest, Hungary, as part of a training exercise. After receiving a cell phone call from one of our intelligence analysts telling me that an aircraft had crashed into the World Trade Center, I pretended to let the terrorist I was following slip away, and hurried back to my hotel room to check it out. I arrived just in time to turn on BBC and watch the second plane hit the North Tower and, ultimately, both of the towers crumbling.

Like a lot of Americans, I immediately commiserated with my comrades about whether we could have or should have imagined something like this happening and perhaps prevented it. One of my closest friends had been traveling in the United States on another commercial flight that day, and I was able to reach him by phone late that evening. After discussing the media reports that described the terrorists passing uncontested through security with blades and box cutters in their carry-on luggage, my friend related to me how he had also passed through security earlier that morning with a pocketknife attached to his keychain. He reminded me that the four-inch knife blade on his pocketknife was within the maximum allowable length that the FAA permitted passengers to carry on board commercial aircraft. "What a difference a day makes!" he lamented. *It takes time and context to recognize patterns.* Prior to 9/11, it had never struck any of us as odd that the FAA allowed passengers to carry four-inch knife blades on board commercial aircraft. Today it is almost unimaginable!

Perhaps we didn't think it odd that the FAA allowed four-inch knife blades on board aircraft at the time, because most of us thought of a measly four-inch knife blade as an all-purpose handyman's tool or, in extremis, as a last-ditch instrument for wilderness survival. Like the cardboard cows and gorilla suit, most of us had never imagined "the art of the possible" regarding a four-inch knife blade on an aircraft. The terrorists, on the other hand, thought of that same four-inch knife blade as a powerful instrument for terror and coercion. By initiating each hijacking with the slitting of their first victims' throats, the terrorists were able to shock everyone else on the plane into a temporary state of submission, which bought the terrorists the mission-critical minutes they needed to organize, gain control of the aircraft, and turn the planes toward their targets.

This got me to thinking that one of the only ways we can ever hope to see these types of "unimaginable" events unfolding before they occur is to look at the world around us through the minds and eyes of others.

There were plenty of facts and events (now known as dots) that occurred prior to 9/11 that, if connected, might have allowed us to understand and adapt to what was unfolding before it actually happened. Flight schools, terrorist watch lists, meetings, and cell-phone calls, but to collect dots you have to recognize them first. Even when recognized, dots don't always add up the same way to different people with different backgrounds, and different life experiences, so the key patterns they reveal can be missed entirely. In the case of 9/11, for example, most of us had a mental model of how an airplane hijacking was supposed to unfold. We also had a mental model of what a weapon of mass destruction was. A hijacked plane entailed an emergency landing and a protracted negotiation for the hostages in exchange for something of value to the hijackers, which usually included their safe passage or escape. A weapon of mass destruction was a military weapon that was either dropped from a plane or launched as a rocket. These mental models were based on our interpretations of numerous incidents, or dots that coalesced over the course of our lifetimes. But the terrorists who masterminded 9/11 were able to imagine the unimaginable with regard to what a hijacked airplane could do when fully loaded with fuel and flown into a high-rise building in a large city, because they also were able to imagine and accept the fact that they would be killing themselves in the process.

How many of us had ever sat around thinking, "Wouldn't a great way to get attention and kill innocent people be to hijack a bunch of planes filled with fuel and fly them into buildings?" We have very little in common with the kind of person who thinks about hijacking airplanes and flying them into buildings to kill innocent people and themselves along with them. That is not us. It's not that we don't have the mental capacity to imagine something like that; it's actually pretty simple. Rather, we have boundaries called values that prevent us from thinking that way. Psychotic terrorists do not.

Therefore, to recognize and connect the dots and make the unimaginable imaginable, we need contact with and input from people who think the same way terrorists do. To find the kinds of people with the type of on-the-ground knowledge that can enable us to understand and connect the dots, we have to imagine how to seek out and listen to them. It's very rarely the self-styled expert or the academician, though both can make positive contributions to our knowledge base. Rather, it's the person who has walked the specific ground, lived the specific lifestyle, and possesses a specific psychosocial mind-set whom we need. Very rarely are they cut from the same cloth as you and I, so we usually need to go outside our social networks to find them.

The archetypal example is portrayed in the 1991 movie *Silence of the Lambs*, where Jodie Foster, who plays a junior FBI agent, seeks out, listens to, and acts on information from a psychotic murderer named Hannibal Lecter. Despite the fact that Hannibal Lecter was serving a life sentence in prison while the murders took place, Jodie Foster's character understood that Lecter had the same mind-set and many of the same life experiences as the killer she was trying to capture. *Silence of the Lambs* was just a movie, but if we in the United States had had someone like Hannibal Lecter who had the same mind-set and many of the same life experiences as the terrorists that masterminded 9/11, we surely would have tapped into his knowledge base, wouldn't we?

10

IMAGINE EVERYONE'S POTENTIAL AS THE GUY ON THE GROUND

October 2001, Desert Island, Persian Gulf[1]

In early October, just a few weeks after 9/11, the military decided to set up a massive staging base on a remote desert island in the Persian Gulf to prepare for combat operations in Afghanistan.[2] Fifty or so of my fellow Unit members and I were among the first to land on the barren desert island. As the tail ramp lowered and I stepped off the back of the aircraft, my senses were greeted by the unmistakable furnace blast of Middle Eastern desert heat. I slid my ballistic Oakleys down onto my face and stared out at a sea of murky brown sand that stretched from horizon to horizon. *Ah, yes—back in the middle of nowhere!* We were told that this was the "hidden airfield" we would be using to set up our base of operations. Rob was one of the operations officers who worked for me at the time. A Special Forces veteran and also a borderline savant, he sauntered up next to me and only half-jokingly posited that we could have flown circles over the United States for the past twenty-three hours and just as easily been standing in the middle of the desert in Arizona and never known it. But this desert had no cactuses, and one of the big things you learn about the U.S. government when you've worked in its most secretive organizations for a few years is this: The U.S. government is incapable of a planning a complex conspiracy—past, present, or future. The reason: when it comes to dealing with complexity, traditional planning (aka the kind the government uses) simply does not work. "Sorry, Rob," I deadpanned, "I know Arizona, and this, my friend, is no Arizona."

For some of the newer members in the Unit, it was the first time they had ever witnessed the awesome capability of America's Special Operations logistics forces to pre-position massive amounts of men, equipment, and supplies in a short time.[3] It reminded me of watching fast-motion photography of an ant colony building its nest. As soon as the sun went down and visibility dropped to zero, giant cargo planes, flying without lights, came screeching out of the night sky in perfectly synched intervals of ten minutes. As the wheels touched down, the roaring turbocharged engines changed pitch and braked the behemoth flying machines with physics-defying precision. Each cargo plane would then turn off the main runway without a second to spare before another plane, waiting empty at the opposite end of the runway, would release its brakes, accelerate to full power, and go roaring past in the opposite direction to take off and make room for the next plane to land a few minutes later. With Hollywood special effects–like orderliness, this cycle went on all night long. Once the giant planes were in their parking spot, they'd drop their tail ramps and regurgitate their cargo to the ravenous tongues of tandem two-ton forklifts driven by young men who deftly handled the machines like they were Porsches. The entire choreography was done impervious to the naked eye—to be part of it, you had to have night-vision goggles strapped to your head and a real-world mission to inspire your heart. One wrong turn or second of inattentiveness by any of the actors involved, and a hundred things could kill any of them in a hundred really ugly ways.

A small city grew like a weed in front of our mission-focused eyes. Hundreds of brand-spanking-new prefabricated tents, each with its own temperature control ventilation unit, were snapped together to create row after row of living areas to sleep in by day, and plan and prepare for combat in by night. Shower tents and Porta Potties were positioned at distances that always seemed to be too far away to walk to in the middle of the night. The area in which all the planning would take place was called the Joint Operations Center, or JOC.[4] The JOC was a sprawling tent compound made up of a byzantine series of more than a hundred specially designed connecting tents that could only have been designed by someone who had spent far too many years working at the Pentagon. I believe the configuration was that of a spoked wheel, but I'm not really sure; I just followed signs to get to wherever I needed to go.

Within twenty-four hours of our plane touching down, we were watching BBC on seventy-two-inch plasma flat-screen TVs. Massive generators created a harmonic resonance of white noise while cooling the hundreds of laptop computers sending and receiving data with their counterparts throughout our own private version of the World Wide Web. Satellite dishes, servers, supplies and accoutrements were all in place to provide everything needed for the planning process. This was to become the mother of all footprints; there were thousands of men and women in place. It was a who's who in the special operations community, with a sprinkling of who-the-hell-are-they? thrown in for good measure. There was just one thing missing: we had no situational awareness of Afghanistan, Al Qaeda, or UBL.

While the footprint was metamorphosing, the pressure was building in D.C. for the military to actually "do something." "There just aren't any targets in Afghanistan" became the standard DOD response when the civilian leadership in D.C. asked for updates.[5] Just as the intelligence community had done in the late '90s, the military was committing the mental model error of thinking about targets in Afghanistan as physical structures—terrorist training camps, military barracks, and UBL's house (all of which were now empty)—instead of thinking in terms of the location of individual leaders. History was repeating itself. In actuality our military mission *wasn't* about destroying structures, defeating an army, or taking control of large swaths of terrain; it was about hunting down men.

I should point out something that struck me as odd at the time. At no time during the first few weeks after 9/11 were my comrades and I in the Unit given the mission to find, follow, and capture UBL and his key associates. Rather, our unofficial mission, in those first critical months after 9/11, was like the rest of the military, to find targets to bomb or attack. Satellite photos were scrutinized; old intelligence reports were dusted off; and in the end, two targets were chosen by someone or someones in our higher headquarters.[6]

When an intelligence officer first presented "the targets" to us in a briefing, he nonchalantly added that there wasn't any enemy on either target. I looked around the room expecting to hear a thundering murmur and a collective look of complete befuddlement. Instead, there was thundering silence. As Bob Woodward would later describe the two targets in his book *Bush at War*, one was an empty airfield in the middle of the desert, and the other was the long-abandoned home of Taliban leader Mullah Omar.[7]

Val leaned over to me and whispered, "You gotta be shittin'me. If we're going to risk our men's lives getting to a target, it ought to be worth something when we get there."

The intelligence officer then described the military intelligence community's version of the enemy situation in southern Afghanistan.

"There is a ring of fire around Kandahar [see Map 3]," he said with great officiousness. "It consists of concentric circles of rockets, handheld missile launchers, and antiaircraft guns." He pointed to the satellite photos that showed tanks and antiaircraft guns on the outskirts of the city, each with a little PowerPoint arrow describing its official nomenclature. "And the enemy is very proficient at using them." He made some kind of comparison between Kandahar and Hanoi. He then described the enemy without differentiating among the Afghan people, the hard-core Taliban, and the foreign Al Qaeda. I wasn't sure what to think about the briefing, but Val summed it up eloquently in his own special way when he posited, "Does this guy know how to do a handstand?"

Although I was puzzled by the mission against what appeared to be empty targets, my faith in the institution of the military assuaged my initial concerns. I genuinely believed that time and common sense would reveal information, insights, and ideas that would refocus our efforts toward finding UBL and other Al Qaeda and Taliban leaders who were all still at large inside Afghanistan. I figured that these targets were just an opening best guess by our higher headquarters, and that once they got more information they would surely focus on the actual enemy.

As time played out, we began to recognize that common sense was an uncommon virtue in our higher headquarters at that time. As we were about to discover, our commanding general actually believed that the most important objectives in the early stages of the operation were *psychological*. In other words, he believed that if we raided empty targets in Afghanistan and filmed the raids for the world to see (he always said CNN), we would have some kind of morale-breaking effect on the enemy. We were told he had written a couple of papers on the uses of the media and psychological operations in wartime. He believed in his theories. It was his reality. My fellow Unit members and I, on the other hand, believed that it was futile to conduct psychological operations on psychos! Think about it—would the type of person who volunteers to sacrifice his own life in a suicide mission, just to get to a place where he can have his way with seventy-two virgins, *really* back down due to "moral distress" inflicted by a CNN video clip of bombings on targets he knows are empty? I was thinking no.

Over the next couple of days, it became oppressively clear that the military decision-making process had already calcified around the two targets. With political pressure mounting, and deadlines for action rapidly approaching, the total collective thought power of the military turned to basing rights, fuel storage capabilities, time-distance limitations of aircraft, and the logistical conundrum around continuing to transport megatons of equipment and people to keep all of us supplied with food, water, and fuel in the middle of nowhere. It was now all about obsessing over the details. There was no give-and-take, no "let's develop the situation and figure this thing out." Instead of being purveyors of the "art of war," we had regressed to "painting by numbers."

Of course, there was only one way to get to the empty targets and back to our island base on the same night. We would have to cram as many men as possible into large, lumbering, heavy-lift CH-47 helicopters, and fly for eight hours to the empty targets outside of Kandahar. We'd then search for any intelligence that might just happen to be lying around, get back in our helicopters, and fly back to our tents. The entire mission would be filmed by military cameramen. Despite the fact that there was no enemy threat on either target, the threats from accidents and happenstance were immense. This would be the longest wartime helicopter mission in history—a thousand miles each way. Getting to the target would put massive stress on both the pilots and the mechanical integrity of the helicopters. Landing on the target also would be dicey because any enemy within ten miles would know exactly what was happening and would flock to the area to take a couple of potshots at the slow-moving "flying mobile homes" as they attempted to land and take off. We were concerned, and we had lots of questions. But when the intelligence officer finished the briefing and asked for questions, all that was discussed was the logistics concerning how to get the film downloaded, edited, and back to the United States for use on the nightly news.

For my comrades and me in the Unit, we were beginning to understand a stark new reality concerning our role in the global war against terrorists. Instead of rolling up our sleeves, immersing ourselves in a mission, and developing out-of-the-box concepts and ideas for our country's most sensitive missions, we now found ourselves on the receiving end of the massive military decision-making hierarchy, whose hierarchical tendrils stretched six thousand miles back across the ocean, to Florida and Washington, D.C. On past missions these types of distances would have prevented the constant real-time involvement from faraway leaders and staff officers, but the Afghanistan campaign marked the beginning of a new command and control dynamic that would change the way the U.S. military thinks about, makes decisions about, and executes tactics and strategies in wartime. The technology is known by three letters: VTC.

VTC stands for video teleconference. The navy originally developed and refined VTC technology to allow officers to communicate more effectively between ships at sea. The army began using the technology in the mid-'90s while in Bosnia. In those early days of planning on the desert island, we spent at least five hours every day sitting around darkened conference tents, huddled together like thought lemmings watching staff officers around the globe read from PowerPoint slides and then pontificate on anything and everything they felt like talking about. Thirty to fifty leaders at a time were forced to listen to senior officers lecture on what each thought someone one step above them thought we should do next. There was no real collaborative give-and-take involved—which, if allowed, might actually make the technology useful. Instead the VTC protocol was for everyone to sit around stoically, and the only one who was allowed to talk was the commanding general of our higher headquarters. It was the antithesis of the collaborative free-think sessions we conducted in our safe houses in Bosnia.

The main selling point of the VTC was and still is that it *increases* situational awareness.[8] But it's a false sense of situational awareness. To the generals in Tampa, Florida, staring at a flat-screen television in their headquarters buildings, our commanding general appeared to be the guy on the ground. They constantly deferred to him for all decisions concerning the enemy, the weather, and the terrain in Afghanistan. He was right there, wasn't he? Although we were five thousand miles closer to Afghanistan than the staff in Tampa, we were still almost a thousand miles away from the enemy-occupied ground. Even worse, we were cocooned inside air-conditioned tents in the middle of the desert, on an island. Distance-negating technologies such as the VTC require a significant warning asterisk to the guy-on-the-ground guiding principle. The acid test for guy-on-the-ground relevance is whether the individual possesses tacit knowledge, which is developed from direct experience and action in the actual environment. When it comes to tacit knowledge, it is generally true that the closer the person is to the environment, the more likely he or she is to possess tacit knowledge. However, when it comes to tacit knowledge, the word *close* does not solely connote distance. Close is a holistic concept that entails interaction, understanding, knowledge, and experience. Geographic proximity to the target does not the guy-on-the-ground make. The only information we could access on the island came through the satellite-linked cables hooked to our secure computers and telephones. Concerning the reality on the ground in Afghanistan, we might as well have been on the moon; we didn't have any more information on where UBL and his lieutenants were than we did back in 1998.

Guy-on-the-ground impostors aside, I believe that the most detrimental aspect of VTC is the opportunity cost it incurs to individuals and the overall team. Every minute we sat in a VTC was a minute we could have been using to better understand the environment by reading everything available on Afghanistan, studying maps, identifying and making contact with guy(s) on the ground, or using that same time to brainstorm the art of the possible. Four VTCs a day was robbing the key leaders of the much-needed time to saturate, incubate, and illuminate.

Within a few days my fellow Unit members and I began breaking away from the nonstop didactic planning sessions and VTCs, and started convening our own brainstorming sessions in the Delta tent. We weren't the only ones frustrated with our higher headquarters' lockstep approach and the all-or-nothing obsession with the two empty targets.

Men from every unit and every service (army, navy, and air force) joined us. I knew most of these guys from other real-world missions, or joint training exercises; none of them surprised me with their attendance. Why did they come? These guys came because they cared. None of us joined the military to conduct empty-target raids; we joined to make a contribution. These were the mavericks, banding together to find a way; there is always a way.

Our goal was straightforward: if we were to have any hope of finding these guys, we first had to figure out what was really happening on the ground in Afghanistan. Using all of our finely tuned lessons from the recent past, these sessions were marked by a raucous anything-goes mentality. Anyone and everyone who had an idea was welcome to throw it on the table. Much like our gorilla warfare sessions in Bosnia, humor was never in short supply. As frustrating as it was for all of us, the command's obsession and obstinacy around the empty targets provided ample ammunition for sarcastic witticisms.

Before we did anything operational, we had to wrap our collective heads around how to define the enemy. According to the conventional wisdom at the time, Afghanistan was a hostile environment, and almost everyone on the ground was in cahoots with UBL and Al Qaeda. This didn't seem right, especially to those of us who had read about and researched the history of Afghanistan and the Afghan people. Not a single hijacker or 9/11 planner was an Afghan. UBL himself, for that matter, is not an Afghan. But we knew the Taliban were Afghans. So should we consider the Taliban and UBL's Al Qaeda terrorists one homogeneous enemy force?

In the first few days following 9/11, I spent two nights from dusk to dawn searching, reading, and downloading papers and articles by authors from all over the globe concerning UBL, Afghanistan, Afghans, and Al Qaeda. I used LexisNexis, a popular searchable online subscription database containing content from newspapers, magazines, legal documents, and all other printed sources. Its primary customers are graduate students, journalists, academics, and lawyers; its slogan is "It's how you know." I brought copies of the papers I down-loaded with me.

One of the papers came from a Pakistani journalist named Ahmed Rashid, who wrote what is still to this day one of the best books for understanding the chronology of events that led up to the pre-9/11 situation in Afghanistan. The book is titled *Taliban*. The most insight-ful part of the work I read was the author's revelation that the Afghan people had a deep disdain for UBL's Al Qaeda occupiers. The reason was simple: UBL and his Al Qaeda charges had committed the cardi-nal sin of Maoist guerrilla warfare doctrine. Instead of making an ef-fort to win the hearts and minds of the people in Afghanistan, UBL and Al Qaeda had treated the Afghan populace as second-class citi-zens in their own country. The result was a growing disdain for the occupying Al Qaeda Arabs by the majority of the Afghan populace. This seemingly mundane tidbit of information changed everything about the way we thought about operating in Afghanistan. It was in direct contradiction to the conventional wisdom promulgated by most Western governments and by much of the international media at the time. Most everyone associated Al Qaeda with Afghanistan, and then jumped to the conclusion that all Afghans were the enemy—connecting the dots before collecting all the dots. The Pakistani author's on-the-ground insight provided the first chink in the urban legend of Afghan-istan impenetrability. If we could win the hearts and minds of the Afghan people, we realized, we could successfully conduct ongoing operations inside Afghanistan. A few months later, this information would turn out to be an indispensable insight for my men and me while interacting with the Afghan people during the mission-critical first few weeks after the Taliban and Al Qaeda fled to the frontier ar-eas of the country.

We had lots of other questions we needed answered before we could come up with something of substance that might convince our higher headquarters to drop the empty-target-raid concept. Where were the Al Qaeda and Taliban leaders? Where were the Al Qaeda fighters setting up their defenses? What was the condition of the dry lakebeds we wanted to land on? What kind of trucks and SUVs were most ubiquitous in the area around Kandahar? How navigable was the desert around Kandahar? How extensive was the ring of fire (anti-aircraft weapons) around Kandahar? What would a goatherd do if he ran into one of our teams outside of Kandahar? There was no doubt in my mind that we needed on-the-ground input from Afghans, and to understand the enemy, we desperately needed on-the-ground input from someone who understood Al Qaeda. We had neither. After our meeting adjourned, I realized I wasn't going to find the type of knowledge we needed by sitting around my tent inside our lunar planning compound; *I had to take action to make action.*

Sequestered on a desert island with no way to get off, communication technology was the only vehicle available to access sources of on-the-ground knowledge. An edict was issued a few days earlier that restricted the use of phones and the Internet to make contact with anyone except our own organizational headquarters back in the States. The purpose of the restriction was to prevent someone from contacting a friend or loved one and inadvertently leaking information about our location or mission to the public. In the context of personal phone calls and e-mails, the edict made sense. But I believed that the mission took priority here. I needed to use the satellite phone and our secure Internet connection to begin boundary-spanning with other government agencies, tapping into online search engines, and making contact with whomever I could find to provide us with guy-on-the-ground knowledge.

You may have heard the expression "In large organizations it's easier to ask for forgiveness than permission." Years earlier, while briefing Colin Powell on the missions we conducted in Colombia, I mentioned to him that we were successful because we were nimble. We didn't ask anyone to approve our concepts; we moved first, and figured things out as we went along. Listening intently to the story, he smiled and reflected to me that good leaders don't wait for official blessings to try things out. They use common sense to guide them because they understand a simple fact of life in most organizations: if you ask enough people for permission, you'll inevitably find someone who believes that they should tell you no.

So while the staff obsessed over the details of the weather, and whether they had enough fuel to get the helicopters to the empty targets inside Afghanistan, I started boundary-spanning with other government agencies (the state department, the FBI, the CIA) back in the States. There was a palpable "anything goes" spirit pervasive in our government during the months following 9/11. To me it was a prime example of how things should work all the time. During those weeks and months, the red tape that usually impeded nimbleness in government all but dissolved. No one ever told you they couldn't help you unless you went through the "proper channels," or until they "checked with their boss." No one was thinking, I'm military, or I'm FBI, or I'm Department of State. Instead, we were all part of the same organization—the United States of America. Everyone seemed willing to share whatever information and ideas they had for the greater good of the mission.

The phone I was using allowed me to talk to anyone anywhere in the world; it used specially developed technology to bounce the signal all over the world and make the call untraceable. One of the first calls I made was to an old friend who was once a high-ranking leader in the Department of State. He had recently retired and was now living in the idyllic Washington, D.C., suburb of McLean, Virginia. I explained what I was looking for, and he told me he had some Afghan-American friends he met with weekly at an Afghan restaurant just outside of D.C. He specifically mentioned an ex–Afghan general who had fought against the Soviets in the mid-'80s. The fact that he met with these guys weekly reassured me that he knew them well and more important, that he trusted them.

When we talked the next night, my friend handed his phone to the Afghan general. *I wondered what he told the guy about me.* My friend had obviously prepped him for the call, because the general spoke in a very deliberate and thoughtful whisper the entire conversation. His English was perfect. By the tone of his voice I imagined a large man with a thick salt-and-pepper beard. "I am an Afghan general who has fought in many battles. I left Afghanistan in the early '90s after the Soviets left." Although we were six thousand miles apart I could detect the emotion in his voice. "I love Afghanistan and am willing to do anything to help my people return Afghanistan to the Afghans. I had family members killed by the Taliban when they tried to join me in the United States." He continued, "I still have relatives living in terror of the Taliban, and I am prepared to offer my services to you in any capacity." He paused for a moment and continued, "I am prepared to fight with you on the front lines for as long as it takes. I can pack and be prepared to join you by tomorrow morning." *Another example of what makes America such a great country. Great men and women from all over the world come to the United States, and realize how lucky they are to live in a country that allows them to experience all the freedoms that the rest of us sometimes take for granted. They understand that freedom isn't free.* "I still have my uniform," he told me.

Now it was my turn, "Sir, I want to thank you for volunteering your services. We are going to need men like you. Your knowledge is very helpful."

The main thing I focus on when assessing someone's credibility is his or her motivation. Family, patriotism, revenge, and self-preservation are the motivations that are most often correlated with credibility. If, on the other hand, someone immediately begins discussing an extrinsic motivator, such as money or personal advancement, I maintain a healthy degree of skepticism of everything he or she tells me. Based on what I'd heard, I assessed the Afghan general to be credible.

The Afghan general told me that he stayed in constant contact with his relatives in Kabul and Kandahar. The general mentioned that he had talked with his cousin in Kandahar that very morning.

"Can you tell me what your cousin said?" I asked.

"Of course," the general replied. He went on to tell me a story of a city that was just beginning to realize what the implications of 9/11 might be to them. The land that time forgot was once again returning to its starring role on the world stage. "The people are confused; they fear the cruise missiles," he told me.

I thought I'd take a chance and ask him if his cousin knew anything about the enemy situation. "How hard is it to get around with all the military activity going on?"

"What military activity?" he responded.

"All the tanks and antiaircraft guns that encircle the city," I replied.

The Afghan general scoffed, and then explained to me that there were indeed tanks and antiaircraft guns all around the city, but that very few, if any, of them actually worked. Apparently when the Taliban took over, they disbanded the last of the Afghan military units that were trained to operate and maintain the equipment. Most of the tanks sat today where they broke down for the final time in the mid-'90s.

He paused, and I was speechless. When you talk to the person on the ground, you almost always experience an onslaught of insights on the problem or opportunity. It's like a skyscraper rising up out of the ground: suddenly you can see the entire girdered structure, and better understand how it is constructed to make optimal, reality-based decisions.

The general had just provided another prime example of why guy-on-the-ground input is so important to understanding the reality of the situation. Technology such as satellite photos and communication intercepts give us a one-dimensional view of the world. Although these can offer value as a baseline, they do so without one key factor: context. The satellite photos that the intelligence community was using to brief everyone, including the president of the United States, on the enemy situation in Afghanistan, portrayed what they referred to as "the ring of fire" surrounding Kandahar. A massive bombing campaign was planned to neutralize those defenses, and once again, massive amounts of time and effort that should have been focused on finding the living, breathing enemy was dedicated to neutralizing the bogus ring of fire. But in a single phone conversation with someone who was connected to on-the-ground knowledge, I had learned that perhaps all we thought we knew from our panoply of advanced technologies was a canard. Regarding the Al Qaeda fighters inside Kandahar, the Afghan general told me that Al Qaeda wasn't preparing defenses around the city as our intelligence officers had told us. Rather, they didn't seem to believe that the United States was actually going to attack them. They were just sitting around their tents and houses, with a business-as-usual mentality.

Next I asked the Afghan general about the weather. He compared it to Denver, Colorado, cold and snowy in the mountains but very temperate on the flatlands. More than any other aspect of the Afghan urban legend; it was the weather that seemed to put the biggest zap on the thinking of our military and political leaders.[9] The myth of the arctic Afghan winter was driving the thinking of our key military and civilian decision-makers in Washington, D.C. Bob Woodward describes Vice President Cheney's guidance to the presidential advisers: "I'm worried that we won't have anything concrete to point to by way of accomplishment. When the snow and bitter cold come next month . . . What is our objective for accomplishment before the snow?"

The reality, also available with the double click of a mouse button, is that the mean monthly temperature in the capital city of Kabul between December and February is in the mid-thirties, borderline balmy. Our lack of on-the-ground knowledge concerning the weather was forcing our leaders to believe that we were running out of time and that we had to do something, and do it quickly.

Slowly but surely, a different picture was beginning to form for me and my comrades as we accrued more and more on-the-ground information. We began to challenge everything we thought we knew about the reality of the situation on the ground in Afghanistan. There was no "ring of fire" around Kandahar; the Afghan *people* were not the enemy, the weather was temperate not terrible, and the enemy was far from being a formidable foe—they were actually low-hanging fruit ripe for the picking.

Back in D.C. both the secretary of defense and the president were expressing well-earned frustration with the dearth of intelligence being fed to them from a trillion dollars worth of space-age intelligence technology. Ironically just a few miles away from the White House, across the Potomac River in Virginia, there were men sitting around a table in an Afghan restaurant who had better, and more accurate, intelligence. The cost for anyone in D.C. to access and consume that intelligence—a hearty handshake, a few minutes of time, and maybe three bucks for a kabob and a Coke.

I passed the information on the Kandahar defenses ("the ring of fire"), the weather in Afghanistan, and the Afghan disdain toward Al Qaeda to one of the staff officers in our higher headquarters. I was only mildly surprised when he dismissed it outright. He was incredulous that I would even consider prioritizing what an ex–Afghan general who lived in the United States, told me over what hundreds of intelligence analysts were telling us about the reality on the ground. I didn't really expect that our higher headquarters would go all in and stop the presses on the current plan. After all, the Afghan general was a single source of information, and I had never even met him in person. But I did expect others to respect the primacy of the information he gave us as being equal to or more relevant than any other knowledge source we were currently using. In fairness to the staff officer, his job was to do what the commanding general told him to do, and he didn't have much leeway to do anything else.

Despite the frustrations with our higher headquarters, we realized we still had plenty of time. Although I felt good about the Afghan on-the-ground knowledge we were accumulating, the Afghans weren't the main enemy—UBL and the Al Qaeda foreigners were. We needed to get inside the heads of UBL and Al Qaeda. *There's always a way!*

11

IMAGINE HOW TO
SEEK OUT THE
GUY ON THE GROUND

The next night I went back to work on the phones. One of my first calls was to an old military intelligence operative who worked out of Washington, D.C. Frosty was a fiftysomething spook who was one of those guys who never told anyone anything about who he actually worked for or what his actual job was. To this day, I still don't know. He was an enigma, operating on the fringes of all of the three-letter spook clubs, but not part of the social fabric of any of them. I figured that he and his vastly networked web of contacts might be able to connect me or at least point me in the right direction in my search. I told him I was trying to better understand the on-the-ground perspective of the Al Qaeda fighters inside Afghanistan. He warned me that none of the three-letter clubs knew much about Al Qaeda. Then anecdotally he added that he had bumped into a friend of his from one of those clubs at breakfast that morning, and the friend mentioned an imprisoned Al Qaeda operative who had offered to cooperate in whatever way needed.[1]

"What's he in prison for?" I asked.

"For the Kenyan and Tanzanian embassy bombings. UBL sent

him there to oversee the planning. Supposedly he also trained UBL's security detail," he added dismissively.[2.]

"Has anyone taken him up on his offer?" I asked incredulously.

"No," he answered. "He's been in prison since 1998 so you have to understand that he has only limited value as a real-time intelligence source."

"You gotta be shittin' me," I replied. "If he trained UBL's bodyguards, he might be able to tell us how they operate. This guy could know things like how often they move UBL, or where they prefer to hide UBL, or how they communicate with other members of the terror network. If we understand how UBL's bodyguards think and make decisions, we can adapt to them, and anticipate what they'll do next."

"Okay, okay," he responded, "I get it." Frosty agreed to follow up with his friend and get back to me as soon as he had something.

Two days later Frosty called me and told me he had a document written by the "Al Qaeda guy" with some of what he termed "his ramblings" on the current situation in Afghanistan.

"Great" I said. "What kind of file is it?"

"It's a handwritten document on eleven-by-fourteen legal paper," he replied.

I asked him to scan it as a PDF file and send it to me ASAP. A few hours later, I had the document in my hands. After stapling it together, I settled down on my cot to check it out. Two paragraphs in, I jumped back up to get my Hi-Liter and colored stick-on tabs. Within minutes, I wasn't just highlighting anymore, I was coloring it in. These weren't just idle musings of an imprisoned madman, this was a dissertation on how to find, infiltrate, and defeat Al Qaeda in Afghanistan. The more I read, the more it became apparent to me that the author had his Ph.D. in understanding the enemy. It was around thirty pages long and formatted by questions that would have made anyone's top ten list for most in need of answers at that time. His eloquently simple answers to each question were all profoundly insightful.

Q: "How do you infiltrate Afghanistan?"

A: "You walk in. You can cross the border almost anywhere, and you can hire Afghan guides for almost nothing. Once through the mountains, walk to a house that has been prepared. You stay there until the intelligence is ready, you set up your radios and equipment, you can even test your weapons. *[This guy must have some kind of military background; these are exactly the types of questions my guys would want to know.]* The homes are really mud forts with walls twenty to thirty feet high. No one will bother you in there, and they will never know you are in there. You can move out at night in vehicles and conduct reconnaissance of the local areas or launch assault force if the situation warrants it!"

Eureka!—this was perhaps the most intractable barrier to imagining how we could sustain ourselves on the barren Afghan frontier. In much the same way we used cell phones to provide our cover and hide in the open in front of buildings in urban areas, in Afghanistan we could be right next door, but behind the towering mud walls and closed doors of the Afghan house/fort. The Lewis and Clark concept will work!

Q: "How do you infiltrate cities such as Kandahar and Kabul?"

A: "You dress like women and wear burkhas.* In teams of two, no one will bother you because the Taliban forbids men from talking to women in public. Just walk away if someone tries to talk to you. You can conceal your weapons under your burkha very easily, and when you get to your target you will have achieved complete surprise. You only need to do this once, and you will have terrorized the enemy. They will envision commandos under every burkha. They will be

---

*A burkha is the concealing overgarment worn by Muslim women for cloaking the entire body. Under the Taliban rule, all women were required to wear burkhas at all times.

forced to take drastic measures to check every woman in the city. They will never allow women to go without burkhas, so you will paralyze their security infrastructure."

This guy had obviously spent some time incubating on this one. From gorilla costumes to burkhas—this is right up our alley. I'll have our logistics guy find us some extra-large burkhas so we can begin tailoring them and getting used to the fit. We (the United States) need to conduct a few "burkha raids" just for the psychological effects it will have on the enemy. Once word gets around that the Americans are dressing up in burkhas, half the population will make the enemy jittery. The Taliban and Al Qaeda fighters will be forced to wonder if every woman walking toward them is about to pull a gun, which will cause them to devote precious amounts of manpower and time to set up and man checkpoints all across the city. Imagine a Taliban version of the Transportation Security Administration!

Q: "How can we find UBL?"

A: "Look for his security detail. He trusts only a handful of men, and they are the only ones who know where he is or where he will be. Don't waste your time trying to find him; he is too careful. You will increase your odds tenfold if you focus on his ten closest security guards. You must do 'police work' here, learn where the guards' families are and then focus your communication devices and surveillance on key members of those families. Then just wait for them to lead you back to bin Laden."

Common sense is knowledge of patterns!

Q: "Where will UBL hide?"

A: "Look for UBL where he has trusted friends. Always look in places he has been before. Like many who are on the run, he is a creature of habit because he can only go where he trusts the people around him. Look in Gardez, Khowst, Shahi Koht, Ghazni, Jalalabad, and Tora Bora."

We aren't looking at any of these places. This is the first I've heard of some of these cities. Shouldn't we drop the empty targets and start looking at these locations?

He ended the document with a message to the reader:

"I am willing to assist the effort in any way required. I don't believe in what Al Qaeda is doing, they are ruining the image of all Arabs and are doing great damage to the Arab cause throughout the world. I can find bin Laden for you. I am only asking for a chance."

Always listen to the guy on the ground! What a treasure trove of information. After tabbing every one of the thirtysomething pages, I read it again. As I did, I realized that there was more to this document than just sound tactical advice. Woven within every answer, every idea, and every explanation, the author was telling the reader all about himself. Indirectly, and at times directly pleading to help the cause in any way possible. In the opening paragraphs he fully admitted his complicity in the African embassy bombings, but he wanted to make amends for it. He made numerous references to how deeply he cared about his wife in California and how much he wanted to get back to her. The entire document was written with intense passion. To me, the validity of his writings was confirmed by the operational relevance of everything he wrote. And for this reason, even though I had never met him, I believed him. These weren't the idle musing of a deranged prisoner, or an attempt to deceive or distract; there was just too much context and connective logic. This was someone who knew a lot and wanted to use what he knew. But I wondered what his motivation was.

I was pumped; my mind was racing a million miles an hour. We needed to stop the planning for the empty targets and jump all over this information. When aggregated with what the Afghan general told us, and the Lewis and Clark concept, we definitely had some options. I couldn't wait to share it.

I hurried over to the JOC. Although there was no classification on the document, I handwrote "need to share" on the top so that every leader would understand how important it was for them to read, understand, and share with everyone else in their organization. I told the lieutenant colonel in charge of the JOC that I had something that every leader needed to read right away. He asked me what it was, so I explained how I got the document, who wrote it, and a summary of what the document said.

"How long's this guy been in prison?" he asked.

"Since 1998," I explained, but the nanosecond the eight came out of my mouth his eyes rolled topside with a dismissive smirk close behind. I hurriedly attempted to explain how the date really didn't matter, but the more I explained about the timelessness of key nuggets such as UBL being a creature of habit, the more I could see that I had lost him as soon as he heard 1998. His response would be the first in a long line of offhand dismissals of the credibility of Ali Mohamed's advice based on the 1998 date of incarceration. It was like they believed there was a shelf life on knowledge. Although it's true that it takes time to build context, it's also true that some context is timeless. Maybe the inability to understand this fact is why so many fail to heed the lessons of history. "That was then, this is now"; "things have changed"; and "that's old news" are all common reactions of those who dismiss the value of historical context.

"Pete, how can a guy who has been in prison for three years have better information than the satellite photos and signal intercepts we have from the here and now?" he asked as he held up a couple of pieces of paper that probably showed the latest satellite images of the "ring of fire," but I didn't look at them. "Would you dismiss a stock tip from Warren Buffet three years after he retired?" I asked him, but I could see in his eyes that it was already too late. He had already made up his mind; I was spitting in the wind. I'd have to find another way.

In October 2001, the military's institutional faith in the supremacy of technology was unimpeachable. We still hadn't conducted a single combat mission as part of the war against terrorists, so there were no empirical examples of guy-on-the-ground knowledge trumping the accuracy and collective value of satellites, listening devices, and database searches. We would have to learn that lesson the hard way—over and over and over.

I recommended that the commanding general read a copy, but I was told he was in the middle of a VTC, and was booked solid with VTCs for the rest of the night. So I dropped a copy off for him with a note that explained how important I believed the information to be. The lieutenant colonel told me he would personally try to read the document when he got a chance, but he had a planning meeting he was busy preparing for. My suggestion to make it mandatory reading for all leaders went over like a lead balloon.

"No one has time to read a thirty-page document. We're about to launch the longest helicopter raid in the history of warfare and we still have a lot of planning left to do," he lectured.

As frustrated as I was about not being able to share Ali Mohamed's operational insights with my own headquarters, there were other pieces of his document that I believed were equally important to share with the high-level decision-makers in Washington, D.C., as quickly as possible. Specifically, what Ali Mohamed said about sleeper cells:

"There are no sleeper cells left in the United States. Think like you are part of Al Qaeda. Would you want to try to hide in the United States right now? Al Qaeda leaders do not want anyone left who could be interrogated and lead the United States to find them. There is no threat from sleeper cells. You must understand that this operation was a huge undertaking for Al Qaeda. They don't have a lot of money and it took everything they could muster to pull this operation off. There is no threat from sleeper cells. It cost Al Qaeda a lot of money, and despite what some think, UBL and Al Qaeda don't have deep pockets, they watch their money very carefully. The way they operate is to always clean the table after an operation. There is absolutely no way they would leave anyone in the United States who could be captured and expose their leaders."

Even though we now had firsthand information from an individual who knew more about Al Qaeda than anyone in our government, there was no way to get this foundational information back to the key decision-makers in Washington, D.C. If I had the president's cell phone number I would have called him myself. But the mechanistic and hierarchical organizational structures of large organizations such as the military create layers upon layers of human barriers, each providing incremental friction to the flow of the information, which invariably ends up diluting or contaminating it so it never makes it to key decision-makers in a timely and accurate fashion.

If President Bush and Congress had been able to read what Ali Mohamed was saying, I have no doubt that they would have been able to make better, more well-informed decisions about homeland security and the establishment of new agencies such as the Transportation Security Administration (TSA) during those first few critical months.

As I walked out of the JOC into the dusty desert darkness with the Ali Mohamed document in my hand, I realized that once again, the tyranny of the plan was trumping updated situational awareness and common sense. There was no way to turn the planning machine off, and there was no way to alter its course. Even though we had updated information, the staff had put so much work into putting the plan together that the mission itself no longer had anything to do with the reality on the ground. The mission was to execute the plan.

Just a few days later, we conducted the opening raids of the war and confirmed that, indeed, both targets were empty. Both raids were filmed by military cameramen, distributed to all the major news organizations, and shown to the world the next day.

New Yorker writer Seymour M. Hersh published an article on November 5, 2001, which described the empty target raids. In the critical passage, he described the raids in detail—who, what, where, and when—and ended with a devastating quote attributed to an anonymous senior military official:

U.S. Special Forces conduct their first two significant raids in the Afghanistan war on this day. In the first, more than a hundred Army Rangers parachute into a supposedly Taliban-controlled airbase near Kandahar. But in fact, the airbase had already been cleared by other forces, and the raid apparently is staged for propaganda purposes. Footage of the raid is shown that evening on U.S. television. In the other raid, a combination of Rangers and Delta Force attack a house outside Kandahar occasionally used by Taliban leader Mullah Omar. This raid is publicly pronounced a success, but privately the military deems it a near-disaster. Twelve U.S. soldiers are wounded in an ambush as they leave the compound, and neither Mullah Omar nor any significant intelligence is found at the house.

One senior U.S. military officer criticized the planning for the October 20 attacks as "Special Ops 101." "I don't know where the adult supervision for these operations is," the officer added.

The article from the *New Yorker* was widely distributed and read by most everyone in our desert compound, as well as by the military and civilian leadership back in D.C. and Tampa. Our highest-level civilian and military leaders in D.C. reacted by questioning our commanding general as to what he was actually thinking by attacking the empty targets.[3] I have no idea what his response was, but that series of events taught me firsthand how valuable the press can be in wartime. The *New Yorker* article may not have been 100 percent accurate (none of our men were wounded in the raid) but it exposed the operational futility of the empty target raids, as well as the senseless risk incurred by sending all those men and machines on such a perilous operation with no potential upside to the overall mission.

Make no mistake about the heroic role of the commandos and pilots who participated in these raids. They risked their lives and showed uncommon valor in the execution of an incredibly complex and high-risk mission. Those men were doing what they were told to do, based in large part on their faith in their chain of command to always make the type of decisions that prioritize the mission and the men. As we would learn in the coming months, the real tragedy of the empty target raids was the opportunity cost.

Enemy accounts of life inside Kandahar revealed that the Taliban and Al Qaeda fighters made no discernible effort to prepare defenses or to vacate their camps in the weeks between 9/11 and the early November raids. The Al Qaeda leadership clearly believed they were invincible in Kandahar, often directly quoting media comments about their impregnable geographic defenses and their undefeatable tactical acumen, as exemplified by their victory against the Soviets. They had a "come and get me, I dare you" mentality that made them ripe for the picking during those early weeks and months. So the reality was that the majority of Al Qaeda and Taliban leaders were sitting in their tents in Kandahar, while we were sitting in our tents a thousand miles away planning to attack a couple of empty targets. Instead of focusing our efforts on finding the enemy and attacking them before they fled to Pakistan, we focused all of our time and resources trying to psych them out.

In the days following the empty target raids, the sitting-duck Al Qaeda and Taliban leaders fled from Kandahar for the border region near Pakistan. The list of terrorist leaders sitting around Kandahar at the time included Mullah Omar, Abu Zubeida, and Abu Zarqawi, two of whom would form the foundation of our Worldwide Most Wanted List for many years to come.[4] Zarqawi went on to lead the Al Qaeda resistance movement in Iraq, which was responsible for thousands of American and Iraqi deaths during the six years that followed.

With the 5th Special Forces Group and CIA making quantum progress in northern Afghanistan, the pressure was now on our commanding general and our higher headquarters to actually provide some sort of contributory return on the hope and expectation our country had invested in us to make a positive difference in Afghanistan.

The day after the Seymour Hersh article came out, our higher headquarters called a meeting with leaders of the subordinate special operations units. Once everyone was seated, a high-ranking officer stood up, cleared his throat, and announced unabashedly, "Our work here is done; we'll start planning for the redeployment immediately."

We're throwing in the towel? I couldn't contain my shock.

"Sir, why would we go home now? We have—"

He interrupted me before I could continue. "Because we need to be in a position to react to other contingencies around the world," he responded. Sometimes when someone says something that is so bizarrely illogical, it momentarily stuns the listener into a state of incoherent speechlessness. *The mission was to destroy UBL and Al Qaeda. They were here and we were here. What in the world could possibly be more important than hunting this guy down?*

"But, sir—"

That was all I was able to get out of my mouth before he turned around and rushed out of the tent, slamming the tentflap behind him. I had just spoken what history confirms are the two most notorious last words by a subordinate to his commander.

Then a funny thing happened in that tent. What everyone was actually thinking I'll never know. But it appeared to me that all eyes in that tent zeroed in on me with that familiar eyebrow-raised, pursed-lips look that asks, "What the hell should we do now?" No one uttered a word when I got up from my ass-aching metal folding chair, walked up to the front of the tent, and plugged my thumb drive into the USB port of the laptop computer that was projecting on the screen. *Here goes:*

"Gentlemen, I think going home would be a huge mistake. We need to present the commanding general with some options. As most of you know, we've been conducting brainstorming sessions over the past couple of weeks, and I've got a few options that I'd like to share with all of you for your intellectual refreshment."

I opened the file up and the first slide on the screen was a quote from Thomas Friedman that I downloaded from LexisNexis on September 14. Much as Thomas Paine's treatise *Common Sense* captured the essence of the argument for America's rights to independence and freedom of choice in 1776, I believed that more than any other written word after 9/11, Thomas Friedman's treatise captured the common sense essence of what the global war against terrorism was all about.

> *The people who planned the 9/11 attacks combined world-class evil with world-class genius to devastating effect. And unless we are ready to* **combine our best minds and our best organizations** *to combat them (the World War III Manhattan Project) in an equally* **daring, unconventional and unremitting** *fashion, we're in trouble. Because while 9/11 may have been the first major battle of World War III, it may also be the last one that involves only conventional, non-nuclear weapons.* (Emphasis added.)

By stripping away the emotion and bombast of the event, he put both the enemy and the complexity of the challenge in bare-bones context for all to understand. He also illuminated the key ingredients for future mission success—combining our best minds, daring, unconventional, and unremitting—into sharp focus for all to recognize.

"Consider this as our foundational logic for everything we do from this day forward," I commented. I could tell Friedman's common sense inspired the group. I could see it in their eyes.

Next, I toggled through the Lewis and Clark slide deck.

"But what's the mission?" someone asked. "Yeah, and what's the target?" said someone else with a slight hint of skepticism.

"The mission is to develop the situation—we're going to get on the ground, build our situational awareness, and then let the teams develop options based on what is actually happening around them. Think of it as taking action to make action."

The response was a collective "hmmmmm."

I finished with a couple of slides that summarized Ali Mohamed's advice. The title of the slides was "The Art of the Possible." I used bullet points and amplified each with an explanation of his key insights: wearing burkhas, hiring Afghans, the people are on our side. When the men and woman in that room heard his advice and insights, I detected a collective hint of reflective frustration regarding how cautious and constrained we had been up to that point. I closed by advising everyone to read the entire Ali Mohamed document.

Whether it was Thomas Friedman's quote or Ali Mohamed's audacious insights into the art of the possible, or the seed planting that our entrepreneurial comrades had done leading up to the meeting, it was blatantly obvious that there was no need for any more convincing. It was as if someone slapped all of us in the face and shouted "Snap out of it! Where are the gorilla costumes?" It was time to get innovative; it was time to adapt; it was time to get audacious!

The colonel in charge of our higher headquarters staff jumped up from his chair and began barking out new guidance and timelines. Within five minutes everyone in the tent was up and heading out the flap to start working on the new concept. The staff went back to work, this time directing their energy toward the coordination and execution of the Lewis and Clark concept. *We're in business,* I thought.

Our higher headquarters still had to go through the military decision-making process to plan the Lewis and Clark concept, so it would be ninety-six hours—or four days—until the first teams would get on the ground. Although the empty-target raids hadn't accomplished anything of operational significance, they had definitely alerted the enemy that the United States had the capability and resolve to put forces on the ground in Afghanistan. The enemy would be waiting for the next attack. So we wanted to ensure that we maintained the advantage of surprise, but to do this we needed to minimize the enemy's ability to detect our landings. *How can we reduce the enemy's situational awareness?*

That night we got back together in the Unit tent and began brainstorming ideas. If situational awareness is knowing what's going on

around you, then our objective was to confuse and confound the enemy so they had no idea what was going on around them. This is the
essence of effects-based warfare: taking actions to influence the way
the enemy thinks and makes decisions.

When you unleash the creative floodgates of a bunch of special
ops warriors, you better be ready for some of the wildest, most diabolical ideas imaginable. The wake-up call from Ali Mohamed for
thinking creatively and using our imaginations was heeded; the operational handcuffs were now off. I think it was Rob who came up with
an official name for our group: the Ministry of Dirty Tricks, a name
supposedly used by an obscure British team that developed the deception activities to fake out the Germans before the D-Day invasion.

The first concept we came up with was to fly over Kandahar in
C-130s and drop parachutes attached to giant ice blocks in the hills
around the town. The goal of the phantom parachute drops was to
strike terror in the hearts of the enemy by making them believe that
the hills were alive with commandos. Once the ice blocks hit the
ground they would melt away into the desert, and each parachute would
blow free across the hills until it was captured and reported by whoever
came across it. Where are the commandos? they would wonder.

We would follow the phantom parachute operations by dropping
resupply bundles around the same locations a few days later. Boxes
stuffed with fake letters from home, along with appropriate amounts
of food, batteries, and water, were all part of the phantom resupply.
We also would send false radio and cell phone signals that simulated
the chatter between nonexistent teams in the hills around the city. At
this point, the staff of our higher headquarters was ready to approve
just about anything we brought to them—and they did.

Twenty-four hours later, phantom parachutes dropped from the
sky around Kandahar. *We were getting nimble!*

As the Ministry of Dirty Tricks continued to piggyback ideas and
stretch the limits of outrageousness, the ideas grew bigger and bolder.
The pièce de résistance, in my opinion, was the concept of creating a

false helicopter crash on the outskirts of the city. We'd first drop an unflyable helicopter full of fuel and explosives on the edge of town. As enemy soldiers rushed to the fiery crash site like bugs to a light, in hopes of capturing or killing the defenseless American pilots, we would identify and engage them using an aerial gunship circling out of sight and sound high overhead.

That concept was overtaken by events, but it definitely would have made any enemy throughout the world think twice before approaching the next downed U.S. helicopter. We later learned that the phantom parachute drops not only confused the enemy, they also terrorized the enemy. Once they discovered the infiltration evidence, every bump in the night, and every seemingly out-of-the-ordinary occurrence around the town of Kandahar was attributed to the phantom "American Commandos." As their diaries would later expose, the enemy wasn't sleeping very well during that period. *In paranoid times, people see connections where there aren't any.*

Four days later, phase one of the Lewis and Clark concept was launched and we were landing on the same dry lakebeds we pinpointed in 1998 (and the same dry lakebeds we briefed the defense contractors on in August). We had teams and vehicles all over the southern deserts of Afghanistan. For the enemy, there was one unsettling difference; these teams were firing projectiles at them before melting away into the surrounding desert.

The remaining enemy reacted as most fighting forces do when completely confounded by the chaos of unconventional tactics: they panicked and fled for the mountains. The Taliban government of Afghanistan collapsed within days, while the Northern Alliance, accompanied by the heroic men and teams of the 5th Special Forces Group and the CIA, rushed in from the north to fill the power vacuum and occupy the capital city of Kabul.[5]

But the fall of the Taliban regime only marked the end of the beginning; we now had to get on the ground and find UBL and his Al

Qaeda army. The footprint moved forward onto Afghan soil to occupy an abandoned Soviet airbase called Bagram.[6]

The men who had conducted the empty-target raids and the initial
reconnaissance missions into Afghanistan were all sent back to the
States as part of an administratively driven rotation plan. I also returned to the States, and I knew exactly what I needed to do when I
got there.

12

IMAGINE HOW:

THE COUNTERFEIT DOUBLE AGENT

December 2001

Reading the Ali Mohamed document was illuminating, but I wanted more; I wanted to look him in the eye, listen to his words, and understand what made him tick.[1] There was no doubt in my mind that if we as a nation were going to take full advantage of his unique insights and perspectives, someone needed to talk to him face-to-face. The reality on the ground in Afghanistan had changed significantly since he wrote the original document, so I figured he'd have lots of new insights and ideas, given the amazing turn of events.

I had only limited time at home before I'd be heading back to Afghanistan, so as soon as I got there I began coordinating to visit Ali Mohamed in prison. It wasn't difficult, because no one considered him to be any kind of big deal—after all, he had been in prison since 1998. Additionally, the anything-goes spirit was still alive and well throughout the government, so coordinating with the various government agencies that were involved in his case was a simple matter of a few phone calls and a few lunches.

While I waited for confirmation of my request, I prepared myself by learning as much as possible about Ali Mohamed the person: What

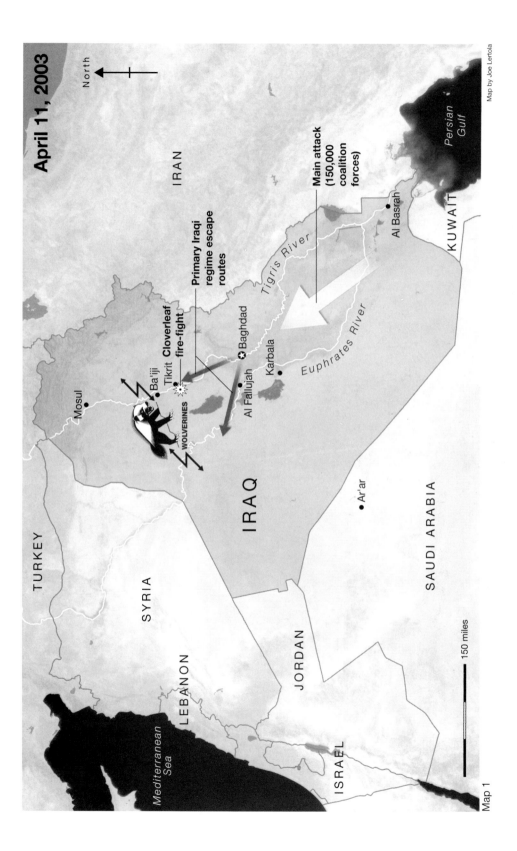

April 11, 2003

North

Map by Joe Lertola

Persian Gulf

Main attack (150,000 coalition forces)

Al Basrah

KUWAIT

IRAN

Tigris River

Primary Iraqi regime escape routes

Baghdad

Euphrates River

Karbala

Tikrit Cloverleaf fire-fight

Ba'iji

Mosul

WOLVERINES

Al Fallujah

IRAQ

Ar'ar

TURKEY

SYRIA

LEBANON

Mediterranean Sea

JORDAN

ISRAEL

SAUDI ARABIA

150 miles

Map 1

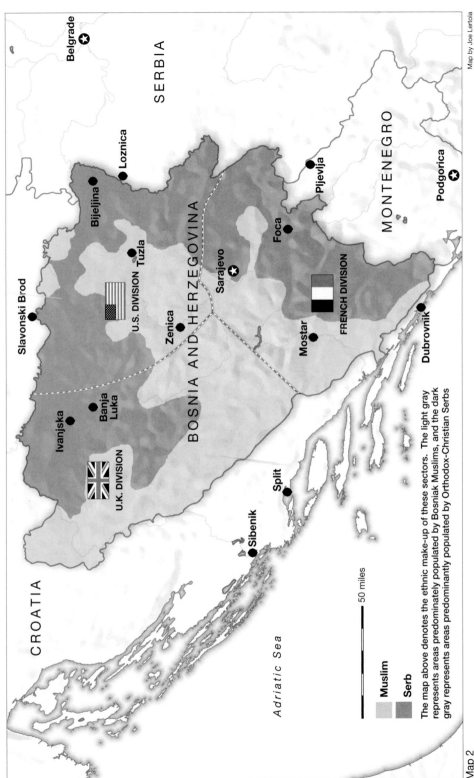

The map above denotes the ethnic make-up of these sectors. The light gray represents areas predominately populated by Bosniak Muslims, and the dark gray represents areas predominantly populated by Orthodox-Christian Serbs

Muslim

Serb

50 miles

CROATIA

Adriatic Sea

Split

Sibenik

Dubrovnik

Slavonski Brod

Ivanjska

Banja Luka

U.K. DIVISION

Zenica

U.S. DIVISION

Tuzla

Bijeljina

Loznica

BOSNIA AND HERZEGOVINA

Sarajevo

Mostar

FRENCH DIVISION

Foca

Pjevlja

SERBIA

Belgrade

MONTENEGRO

Podgorica

Map by Joe Lertola

Map 2

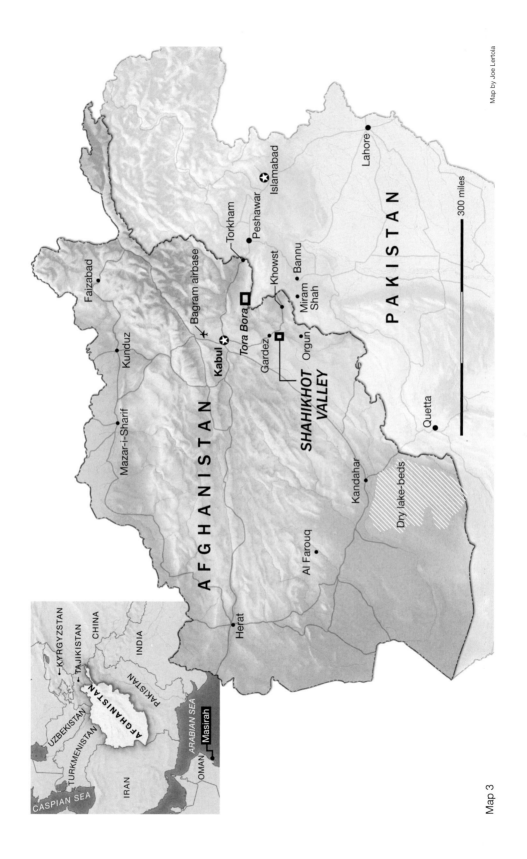

Map by Joe Lertola

Map 3

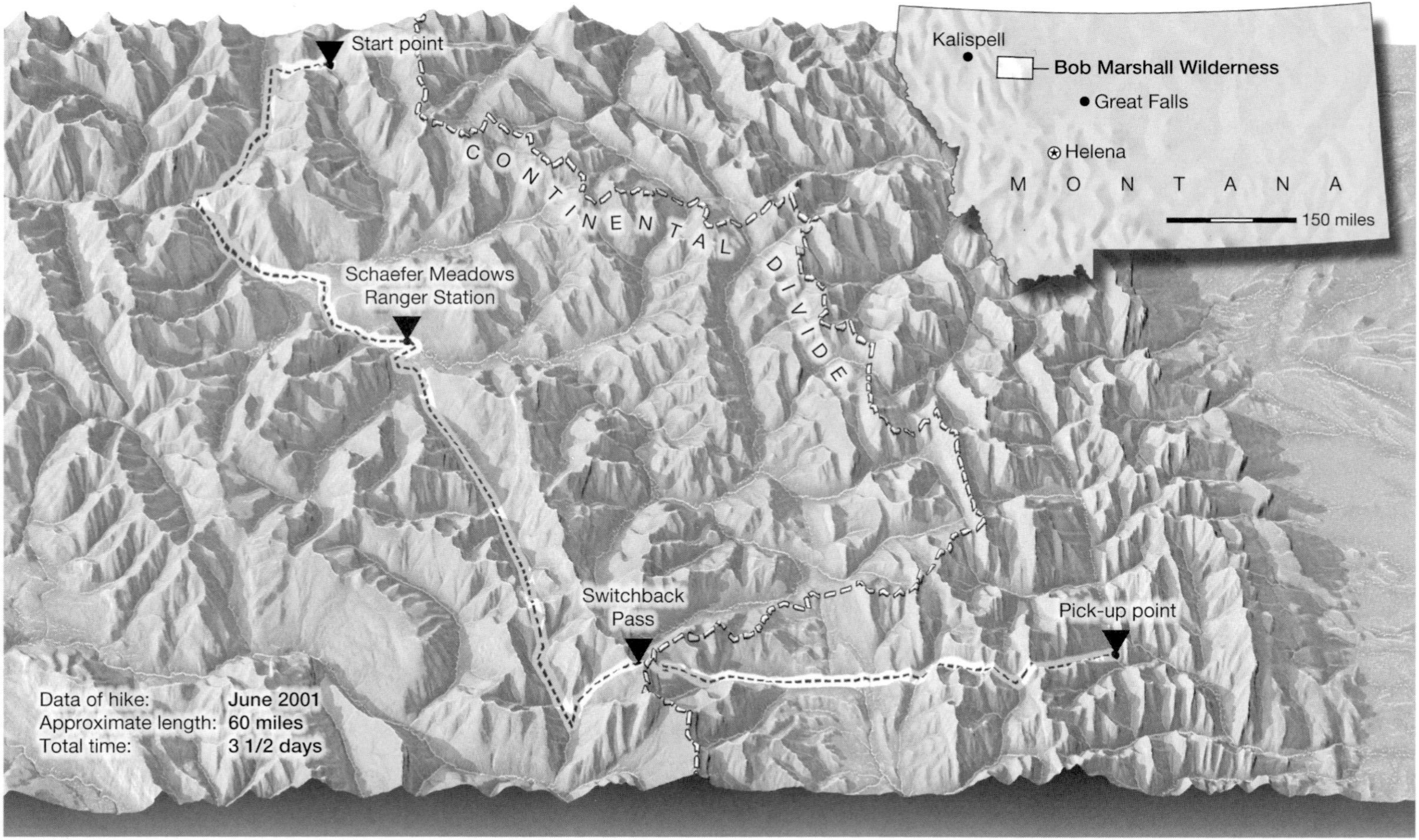

Start point

Schaefer Meadows
Ranger Station

Switchback
Pass

Pick-up point

C O N T I N E N T A L

D I V I D E

Kalispell

Bob Marshall Wilderness

Great Falls

M O N T A N A

⊛ Helena

150 miles

Data of hike: June 2001
Approximate length: 60 miles
Total time: 3 1/2 days

Map 4

Map by Joe Lertola

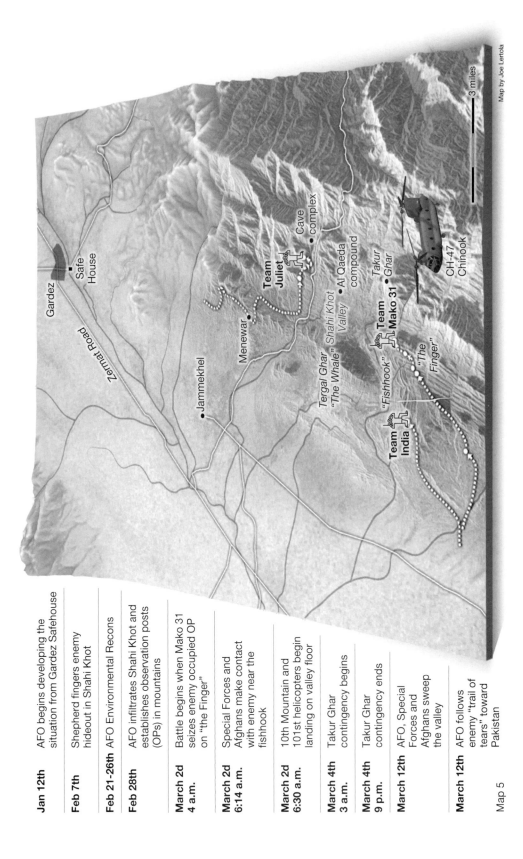

Jan 12th	AFO begins developing the situation from Gardez Safehouse
Feb 7th	Shepherd fingers enemy hideout in Shahi Khot
Feb 21-26th	AFO Environmental Recons
Feb 28th	AFO infiltrates Shahi Khot and establishes observation posts (OPs) in mountains
March 2d 4 a.m.	Battle begins when Mako 31 seizes enemy occupied OP on "the Finger"
March 2d 6:14 a.m.	Special Forces and Afghans make contact with enemy near the fishhook
March 2d 6:30 a.m.	10th Mountain and 101st helicopters begin landing on valley floor
March 4th 3 a.m.	Takur Ghar contingency begins
March 4th 9 p.m.	Takur Ghar contingency ends
March 12th	AFO, Special Forces and Afghans sweep the valley
March 12th	AFO follows enemy "trail of tears" toward Pakistan

Map 5

Map by Joe Lertola

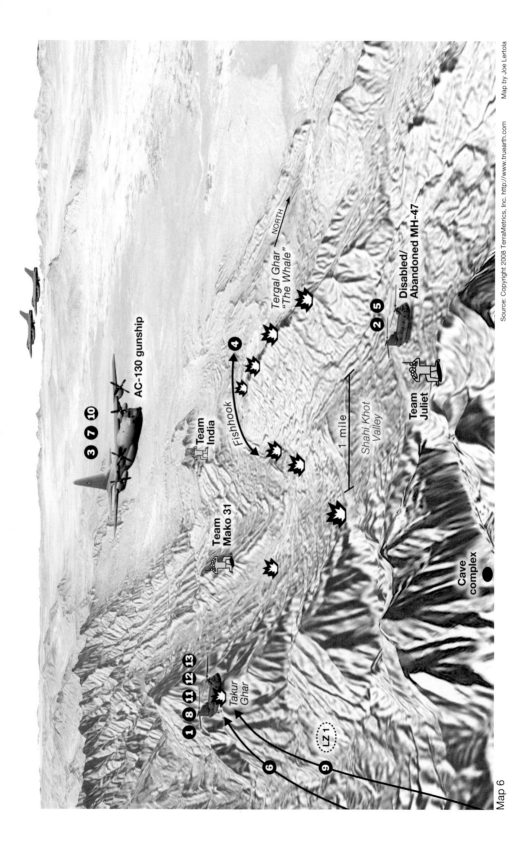

Map 6

NORTH

Tergal Ghar
"The Whale"

AC-130 gunship

3 7 10

Team India

Fishhook

4

1 mile

Shahi Khot Valley

Team Mako 31

Team Juliet

2 5

Disabled/
Abandoned MH-47

Takur Ghar

1 8 11 12 13

LZ 1

6

9

Cave complex

Source: Copyright 2008 TerraMetrics, Inc. http://www.truearth.com

Map by Joe Lertola

March 4th Takur Ghar Chronology

1 Mar 4th, 3 a.m. MH-47 carrying Mako 30 attempts to touch down on Takur Ghar peak. RPGs and machine-gun fire pound the aircraft. One member of Mako 30 (Neil Roberts) is thrown out the back of the badly damaged helicopter.

2 Unable to regain control of the crippled aircraft, the pilots set it down on the valley floor. Slab requests permission to return to peak and rescue Roberts.

3 An AC-130 gunship and a Predator arrive in the sky above Takur Ghar. Status of Roberts is unknown.

4 Slab calls Pete at fishhook and they agree to use AC-130 to suppress and destroy the bunched up enemy on peak before Mako 30's helicopter lands to rescue Roberts.

5 4:34 a.m. Another Chinook in the area picks up Mako 30 and the crew of the disabled Chinook and flies them back to Gardez safehouse to drop off crew.

6 4:45 a.m. Slab and Mako 30 reload the aircraft and fly back toward peak to rescue Roberts.

7 Unable to understand what is actually happening on the battlefield and believing Roberts fell out on the valley floor, Headquarters TOCs at Masirah (1,100 miles away) and Bagram (100 miles away) change the satellite radio frequency and cancel the AC-130 mission seconds before Mako 30 lands on the peak.

8 4:55 a.m. MH-47 carrying Mako 30 attempts to touch down and is shredded by enemy machine-gun fire. Slab leads Mako 30 off the helicopter and charges the enemy positions in attempt to locate and rescue Roberts. MH-47 flies away. Air Force communications specialist John Chapman is killed while assaulting an enemy bunker. Mako 30 takes cover on side of mountain.

9 5 a.m. Ranger Quick Reaction Force (QRF) is launched from Bagram on 2 MH-47's, without being told what has happened to Mako 30, and without working satellite radios to communicate.

10 6 a.m. AC-130 departs protective perch in sky above the peak.

11 6:10 a.m. Ranger QRF helicopter #1 attempts to land on Takur Ghar and is knocked out of the air 20 feet above the peak. 3 Rangers and 1 crew member are killed before they can get off the aircraft by reinforced enemy.

12 7-10 a.m Enemy attempts to outflank Rangers but are (exposed) by Juliet team who can see them move, and reports their position to attack aircraft overhead, which neutralize the last of the enemy fighters.

13 9 p.m. All American forces off of Takur Ghar.

Something other than what it seems: Tanks
in the Iraqi desert.

Humor your imagination: Man, beast, or metaphor?

Ali Mohamed
Department of Defense

John Walker Lindh
Department of Defense

Always listen to the guy on the ground: (L to R) Andy, Pete, and Predator, back together again on top of the Continental Divide in September of 2005, four years after the original trek. In June ten to twenty feet of snow covers this same spot.

Developing the situation: Jimmy and I paying our respects to the great Afghan leader, Ahmed Shah Massoud, near his grave in the Panjshir Valley.

View from hill where Shepherd fingered the Shahi Khot.

Don't plan, prepare: Afghans in formation before loading "Jingha" trucks for transport to Shahi Khot valley. Within a few hours, three of the Jingha trucks would overturn, killing and injuring more than twenty Afghans. The view is from the Gardez safe house watchtower on the evening of March 1, 2002.

It's not reality unless it's shared: March 4, 6:20 A.M., at the "fishhook," minutes after we discovered the Ranger QRF helicopter had been shot down on top of Takur Ghar. The view is looking eastward toward the Shahi Khot.

Reality check: What's your recommendation? Clearing the Shahi Khot with our Afghan comrades. Even without maps, they always seemed to know exactly where to go to find the enemy, the best way to get there, and what to do when we arrived. All we had to do was ask. March 12, 2002. Note the physical diversity of the Afghans.

Once you recognize the patterns that inform the behavior of your enemy, you can adapt to them, and your enemy's toast: Enemy artillery positions found in the dry creek-beds of the Shahi Khot, exactly where history books revealed the Mujahideen always put them, and exactly where the Russian combat reports said they would be.

Recognizing patterns: Levitating above the divisive influence of emotion and politics allows us to operate at an altitude where we can recognize and adapt to life's underlying patterns.

was his background? What shaped his values and beliefs? What motivated him to do what he had done? There wasn't anything available on him in the military intelligence database, so I figured I'd do what everyone does when they need background information on someone; I sat down at my computer at home and Googled the name Ali Mohamed.[2]

Although I felt like we missed some opportunities to take advantage of his insights during the initial invasion, once I started researching his past, I learned that those missed opportunities in October and November 2001 paled in comparison to the missed opportunities in the prior ten years. There was lots of information about him online. The most difficult part of culling through it was separating the facts from the fiction around the man and his complex life journey. I would soon discover that much of what the media and the government thought they knew about Ali Mohamed was based on misinformation, and dot connecting without adequate dot collecting.

Today there are TV documentaries, books, and numerous official reports that promulgate what has become the accepted version of the Ali Mohamed story: that of a terrorist double agent, most commonly referred to as bin Laden's military mole, who infiltrated and duped multiple U.S. government agencies to pilfer their most sensitive secrets.[3] But as I was about to discover, the reality behind the story of Ali Mohamed was quite different.

Ali Mohamed was incarcerated in a federal penitentiary for masterminding the surveillance and planning of the U.S. embassy bombings in Nairobi and Tanzania. In late 1993, Al Qaeda leadership ordered Mohamed to scour Nairobi for targets that would avenge the U.S. involvement in Somalia. While in Nairobi, Ali Mohamed was responsible for training at least two of the members of the East Africa cells directly involved in the attacks, Abu Jihad and Fazul Abdullah Mohammed.[4] He taught them how to conduct surveillance and how to preserve operational secrecy by moving around Nairobi undercover. His favorite disguise tip to his trainees was always to wear a pair of sunglasses and a baseball cap. During his guilty plea Mohamed told prosecutors, "We used various code names to conceal our identities; I used the name Jeff."[5]

Mohamed drew maps and diagrams of the U.S. embassy in Nairobi and rigged a darkroom in a colleague's apartment. When Mohamed showed the embassy surveillance drawings and photos to UBL, UBL pointed to the rear parking garage as the optimal place for detonation of the truck bomb by the suicide bombers.

The tactics, techniques, and procedures Mohamed taught the suicide bombers, such as how to case targets, how to photograph them, and how to write detailed attack plans, came right out of U.S. military manuals. But he didn't steal the manuals, nor did he have to purchase them on the black market; the manuals were issued to him while he was serving as a member of the U.S. Army Special Forces.

Born in 1952 in Egypt, he joined the Egyptian army where he rose to the rank of major. In 1980 he was chosen by the Egyptian military to take part in the highly coveted U.S. military exchange program. He was sent to Fort Bragg, North Carolina, to spend four months learning about the U.S. military. He trained alongside U.S. Special Forces (Green Berets), learning firsthand how to plan and coordinate Special Forces missions such as deep reconnaissance, unconventional warfare, and counterinsurgency operations. After four months, he received a diploma with a Green Beret on it, and then returned to Egypt where he spent three more years in the Egyptian military before leaving to work as a security adviser for Egypt Air.[6] But Ali Mohamed wasn't satisfied. Like many foreign exchange officers before him, he had acquired a taste for the freedoms and liberties he experienced while living in America, and now found himself hungering for more.

At this point, what we know about Ali Mohamed's journey gets a bit tangled. We know that he approached the U.S. embassy in Cairo and volunteered for service with the FBI and the CIA.[7] We also know that the CIA sent out a worldwide cable to all its stations asking if anyone needed someone with Mohamed's skills. The CIA station in

West Germany was interested, and subsequently hired him to infiltrate a mosque in West Germany. He didn't last long. According to the unclassified reports available at the time, Mohamed was terminated for "talking to known terrorists," which resulted in the CIA determining him to be untrustworthy.[8] *Isn't that what we hired him for?*

In 1985 Ali Mohamed returned to the United States. On the plane ride over, he met and fell in love with an American woman who would eventually become his wife. They moved into a tidy two-bedroom duplex in the central California town of Santa Clara. Santa Clara residents who met him described him as cordial, well spoken, and physically fit. Mohamed often introduced himself as a former Egyptian army officer who hoped to someday do intelligence work for the United States.[9] *Is that how an undercover terrorist introduces himself to strangers, or does that sound like someone who is trying to network for a job?*

In 1986 Ali Mohamed approached a U.S. army recruiter in Oakland and volunteered his services. The army liked what they saw and signed him up as an enlisted soldier. He was thirty-four. Although unusually old for a new recruit in the mid-'80s, he was in excellent physical condition and possessed a trait found in all prized recruits: he was highly motivated. He told his recruiter he was joining because he wanted to "serve the United States." After graduating from basic training, he was assigned to the army Special Forces at Fort Bragg.

Every article and interview written about Ali Mohamed in the hyper-paranoid fall of 2001 concluded that he was a double agent who specifically chose the Special Forces so he could siphon and export the skills he learned to train future terrorists. But the more I read and learned about his life, and the more I thought about his actions in the context of my own (I joined the military in 1985), the less the double-agent theory began to make sense to me. The dots were not snapping together.

As the name implies, the Special Forces is a refuge for those who are special—as in a bit different from everyone else. The Special

Forces soldier is a unique breed of cat, a breed that doesn't lend itself to any specific psychological profile. But there is a pattern of common individual traits such as mavericks, adventurers, and patriots; one or more of which are almost always present in the pedigree.

Like a lot of men who joined the Special Forces during the peace years of the 1980s, Ali Mohamed seems to have possessed varying levels of all three. The dictionary definition of maverick is an un-branded range animal that belongs to the first person who puts a brand on it. Remember that definition. When Mohamed left Egypt; he packed his worldly possessions in a suitcase and used every dollar he had to buy a ticket to the United States. At the age of thirty-four, his search for adventure still not satiated, the former Egyptian Army officer decided to enlist in the U.S. army as a private. Like many fellow adventurers, both inside the military and out, he dreamed of someday upping his game and joining the CIA or FBI to become a covert operative similar to the James Bond–like image propagated in books and movies all around the globe. Ali Mohamed also was keenly aware that honorable service in the U.S. military portends fast-track status to U.S. citizenship.[10] Thus, it was with high hopes and great expectations that he reported for duty on his first day with the U.S. Army Special Forces at Fort Bragg, North Carolina.

Although Mohamed was administratively slotted as a supply sergeant, the Special Forces have always put a premium on difficult-to-learn language skills, and word spread quickly of Ali Mohamed's fluency in Arabic, Hebrew, French, and English. He was soon spending most of his time as a language instructor, and also teaching classes to soldiers about the culture of the Middle East. Although his contributions were appreciated, he didn't join the Special Forces to be a language instructor; he was, at his core, a warrior, and he yearned to be an elite combat soldier like those he was teaching. Within a few months, he filed the paperwork to go through Special Forces qualification training, which was a prerequisite for anyone who wanted to become a member of one of the small, closely knit Special Forces teams that had the mission of going behind enemy lines and conducting unconventional warfare. His request went nowhere.

In 1988, Mohamed approached his commander (a lieutenant colonel) and told him he wanted to use his upcoming thirty days' leave to go to Afghanistan and fight alongside the Afghanistan resistance fighters (the mujahideen) against the Soviets. At the time, the United States was secretly supporting the mujahideen by supplying them with hundreds of millions of dollars' worth of weapons and equipment.[11] Much like today, the agents working the situation in Pakistan in the '80s were in dire need of Arab Americans who could speak the language and move into and out of the border area between Afghanistan and Pakistan with impunity. Instead of seeing Mohamed for the unbounded potential he so blatantly represented for both current and future Middle East operations, his commanding officer saw him as a problem, and openly labeled him as a fanatic.[12]

In post-9/11 newspaper and television interviews, Ali Mohamed's commander described his rationale: "Ali Mohamed was hellbent on fighting against the Soviets," which he described as being "contrary to all army regulations." The commander added that when he asked Mohamed about the Anwar Sadat assassination, Mohamed told him that "Sadat was a traitor," and then "showed no remorse for Sadat's death."[13] His commander also claimed he "wrote reports to get Mohamed investigated, court-martialed, and deported." This struck me as odd.

I was a Ranger lieutenant in 1988, and what Mohamed was proposing to his commander was very similar to what most if not all special operations soldiers I hung around with were thinking and hypothesizing about during that period. Like most Americans, we fervently believed in the mujahideen cause of liberating their country from an invading army and freeing the Afghan people from the oppressive shackles of a Communist political system. There was an additional and more palpable motivator for those of us in the military. Many a young American soldier was killed or wounded in Vietnam due to Soviet-supplied advice and ammunition; helping the mujahideen seemed like a prime opportunity to conduct some payback. If the option to go to Afghanistan and help out the mujahideen during leave had availed itself to me or any of the cats I hung with from the Ranger pedigree, I'm certain every last one of us would have pounced on it.

As far as Ali Mohamed's supposedly fanatical opinions on Anwar Sadat, I thought about the U.S. presidential election in 2000. If a person is to be labeled a fanatic for stating his dislike for the president of his country, then judging by some of the hate-filled bumper stickers, radio talk-shows, and demonstrations seen and heard around the United States at the time, this country had a large fanatic problem.

Despite his commander's retrospective reaction, there is no record of him ordering Mohamed not to go to Afghanistan. Therefore, and perhaps because of, Mohamed followed his heart and headed off in search of adventure in Afghanistan. We only have Mohamed's version of what transpired while he was gone, but thirty days after he departed, he returned to Fort Bragg. Bedraggled and twenty pounds lighter, he walked into his commander's office and presented him with a souvenir from his trip, a Russian belt buckle that he claimed to have taken off a dead Russian officer.

What was he trying to do? If he was a double agent, why would he tell his Special Forces commander what he had just done instead of laying low and keeping his Afghanistan war stories to himself? It didn't make sense. Was the belt buckle a token of his fanaticism, as his commander described it, or was this an act of desperation to prove his worth as a warrior in hopes it might finally earn him the rite of passage into the elite brotherhood of the Special Forces operational teams? The image of a cat or dog trying to please its master by dropping a mangled bird carcass at their feet came to mind.

Whatever his intent, it didn't fly; there was no rite of passage for Ali Mohamed. His commander was incensed, and once again Mohamed was harshly rebuked for his actions. As a U.S Army soldier, he technically was not allowed to fight in an armed conflict unless it was with his army unit. But ignoring and admonishing him after he returned didn't seem to make much sense. As hard as it may be to remember now, in 1988, U.S. military doctrine was 100 percent focused on defeating the Soviet Union in an armed conflict. All of our tactics, techniques, and procedures were based on this doctrine. It seems like it might have been a good idea to at least listen to the insights and perspectives of someone who was resourceful enough to travel from North Carolina to Afghanistan and engage in real combat on the ground against real Soviet forces.

Ali Mohamed's commander, like the FBI and CIA before him, just could not see it. Perhaps it was because Ali Mohamed was Egyptian, or perhaps because he was older (then thirty-six years old), or perhaps it was the combination of the two that made Ali Mohamed the human equivalent of the four-inch knife blade.

With the harsh rebuke and cold shoulder he received from his commander, along with the lack of progress concerning his repeated requests to transfer to an operational team, Ali Mohamed began to grow frustrated. Like water flowing through rocks, Ali Mohamed's thirst for action and adventure—preferably as a U.S. operative—was going to be quenched. It was only a matter of time before he found the path of least resistance to get there.

In the fall of 1989 Ali Mohamed received an honorable discharge from the U.S. military and was subsequently granted his U.S. citizenship. He returned to Santa Clara, California, where he continued to serve in the U.S. Army Reserve while trying, and ultimately failing, to get a job as an FBI interpreter.

At this point in his life, Ali Mohamed had a résumé of one-of-a-kind skills and knowledge: fluent in four languages, Special Forces training, Afghanistan combat experience, U.S. citizen, Arab, physically fit, good-looking, and intelligent. When viewed in aggregate, his curriculum vitae would put him in the "highly coveted employee" category with almost any organization operating on the world stage at the time, whether for business, diplomacy, espionage, military, or terror. It didn't take long for one of those potential employers to take notice. The group that recognized his unique buffet of skills found him in much the same way they found John Walker Lindh and all the other American jihadists—through the mosque network in the United States. In 1989 Ali Mohamed wandered into, and was welcomed with open arms by, the Al Farooq mosque in New Jersey. Al Farooq was home to some of the charter members of what would eventually become Al Qaeda, and they were looking for someone to provide weapons and tactics training to their members. Ali Mohamed was just what they were looking for, and in short order, he would exceed all of their expectations. *The terrorists, on the other hand, thought of that same four-inch knife blade as a powerful instrument for terror and coercion.*

Ali Mohamed had found his path of least resistance. Here's what I learned about his journey from that day forward:[14]

• **1990:** Ali Mohamed makes another attempt to join the FBI in San Francisco, but is only put on retainer as a translator.

• **November 5, 1990:** One of the men Ali Mohamed trained to shoot on the firing ranges of New Jersey, Al Said Nosair, is arrested after the murder of a radical Jewish rabbi Meier Kahane. When authorities searched the home of Nosair, they found U.S. Army training manuals, secret documents, and videotaped talks that Mohamed delivered at the Kennedy Special Warfare Center at Fort Bragg.

• **1992:** Ali Mohamed travels to Khowst, Afghanistan, trains Al Qaeda soldiers in basic military training, and establishes a reputation as a hard-core trainer who is very strict but also very proficient.

• **1993:** At the request of Al Qaeda leaders, Ali Mohamed conducts visual and photographic surveillance on the U.S. embassy in Nairobi, Kenya.

• **1994–1996:** UBL's second-in-command, Mohamed Atef, refuses to let Ali Mohamed know what name and passport he is traveling under. Captured U.S. embassy bomber L'Houssaine Kherchtou would testify in his U.S. trial in February 2001 that Atef "doesn't want Abu Mohamed al Amriki [Ali Mohamed the American] to see his name, because he [is] afraid that maybe he is working with United States or other governments."[15] Other captured terrorists will later report that Ali Mohamed had numerous falling-outs with Al Qaeda leaders after 1994, over a wide range of issues, from his handling of money to his suspected relationships with the FBI.[16] He also is labeled by many of his fellow terrorists as a bad Muslim who isn't fanatical enough.

• **1996:** He helps supervise the security for UBL and his family's move from Sudan to Afghanistan.

• **1998:** The U.S. embassies in Kenya and Tanzania are bombed. Within two weeks, FBI agents use a key supplied by Mohamed's apartment manager to search his apartment in Sacramento, California. According to testimony at his trial, his computer hard drive contained files and photographs from the cell he set up in Nairobi and numerous how-to documents for terrorist training. He was arrested on September 10, 1998.[17]

The FBI has acknowledged in court filings that its agents interviewed Mohamed at least three times between 1990 and 1998. So how could a man be a key participant in Al Qaeda's most diabolical terrorist activities in the 1990s, while simultaneously volunteering to work with and for the FBI, without being killed or imprisoned by either side? Was this the behavior of a highly accomplished and fanatical double agent, as is the conventional wisdom today? Or was there some other explanation?

There was only one way to find out: a face-to-face meeting with the guy on the ground.

To help me separate the facts from the fiction, before I talked to him, I boned up on my counter-elicitation skills. I had gone through a commercial counter-elicitation course a few years earlier. Taught by retired CIA case officers, the course has since become popular with police departments all over the U.S.[18] Counter-elicitation uses neuro-linguistic techniques to build rapport and detect deception. The main premise of counter-elicitation is that the best way to tell if someone is lying or being deceptive is by recognizing the patterns of his or her body movements. Forget about eye movements: some people habitually roll their eyes, and some people just like to check out your shoes; neither are accurate indicators of truth or deception. But body movements, in conjunction with responses and reactions are. When people tell the truth they are smooth, natural, and still. But when they engage in deception or lack confidence in what they are telling you, their bodies betray them and they make subtle, abrupt body movements—the instructors call it "coming off one's base." All the techniques apply cross-culturally and cross-gender, and therefore are effective in all parts of the world. The training video used in the course I attended showed a clip of O. J. Simpson answering questions from a couple of Chicago Police Department detectives the day after the murder of his ex-wife and her friend. It was routine questioning. O.J. wasn't a real suspect yet—after all, why would O.J. kill someone?—he was rich, famous, and had it all. During the initial stages of questioning O.J. was very still, he was on his base. But when questioned about his whereabouts during the killing, and how he cut his hand, he rocked and rolled off his base as he explained that he was nowhere near the scene of the murder, and that he had cut his hand when he broke a glass in his hotel sink. O.J. was lying.

But that was the classroom; I had to test it out in the real world. So I added counter-elicitation techniques to my repertoire for dealing with intelligence sources and paid informants while operating around the world. It proved its worth many times over.

Armed with a witches' brew of facts, fiction, assumptions, and suppositions about Ali Mohamed and his complex life journey, I was ready to meet with him at the maximum-security prison where he had taken up residence. There was no fanfare, nor any bureaucratic red tape to pass through; in retrospect, I don't think anyone really gave a hoot about the guy, or, for that matter, who was visiting him. The prison was located smack in the middle of a sprawling urban metropolis. Ten feet from a newspaper stand bustling with businesspersons, I walked through a thick tinted-glass entrance door and found myself standing directly in front of a bulletproof glass–cocooned guard booth. Dressed in a sport coat and tie, with long hair and a goatee, I slid my military ID card through the slot. The guards seemed a bit incredulous at first, then pushed a clipboard back to me and told me I had to sign a safety waiver acknowledging that if I were taken captive during a prison uprising, the prison would not be held liable for whatever happened to me. It was a bizarre way of reinforcing that it was time to switch out of my "I'm walking through a safe U.S. city" mind-set into a "I'm about to walk through a building full of desperate criminals" mode. *Situational awareness is knowing what's going on around you.*

I had never been inside a maximum-security prison before, so I didn't know what to expect. What I remember most about the place was how completely antiseptic it was. Everything was either made of stainless steel or painted white, and everything was either rounded or completely flat. No doorknobs, no handles, no chair legs—there were no protuberances of any type that could potentially be broken off or re-formed for use as a weapon.

The guard escorted me into the visiting room where I sat in a white plastic chair, its legs molded into the floor. The room was bathed in sunlight, but the thick walls and shatter-resistant windows completely soundproofed the room from the bustling city just a few feet away. After a couple of minutes of waiting, a large steel door off to my left slid open and in walked Ali Mohamed. Wearing an orange jumpsuit and leg chains, he shuffled purposefully to his seat and sat across the table from me. He didn't look anything like his picture, but I learned long ago that not many people do. His hands were unencumbered. *Do you shake a terrorist's hand when you first meet him?* I was told ahead of time that Ali Mohamed wouldn't be told anything about my background or my purpose. He would only know that I was a government employee who wanted to ask him some questions.

He extended his hand across the table. "Hello. What do you do to stay in such great shape?" he asked in perfect, unaccented English.

"Nothing," I replied as I clasped my hands together on the table then pulled them back and rested them on my thighs. *He's trying to figure out what government agency I'm from,* I thought. If I had truthfully told him about my intensive workout routine, he would have pegged me as a special ops guy right off the bat. *Next time, stay on your base,* I scolded myself.

I explained to him that I had read his paper, which seemed to put him at ease; authors like to know that someone has actually read their work. From my briefcase, I pulled a manila folder that contained some maps and photos and placed it on the table. He had an eight-by-fourteen legal pad in front of him with what looked like a hundred dog-eared pages of handwritten notes that he was adding to as we talked. *Maybe he's writing a book,* I thought.

Without prompting, he jumped right into his thoughts on the current situation in Afghanistan. The prison must have allowed the prisoners unlimited television access, because he had up-to-the-hour information on what was going on on the ground. I pulled out my map of Afghanistan and Pakistan, and he immediately put his hands on a section of the map around the border region between the two countries.

"How can we find Al Qaeda in Afghanistan?" I asked.

He looked at me and smiled, as if to say, I thought you'd never ask. He oriented the map and ran his finger along a five-hundred-mile contiguous series of mountains above and below the cities of Gardez and Khowst (see Map 3).

"This is where you must go," he said. "You want to find Al Qaeda and UBL—yes?" I nodded my head nonchalantly. "Okay, then this is where you need to go."

He paused for a minute then continued, "Go out into the Afghan frontier and ask the shepherds, because the Arabs must have lamb meat to survive. Ask the shopkeepers, because Arabs consume special spices that Afghans rarely use. Ask the money exchangers, because the

Arabs get money delivered to them from home by couriers and must always convert the money to dollars. Ask the taxi drivers, because very few Arabs drive and none bring cars into Afghanistan!"[19]

I was writing as fast as I could. Having been through a couple hundred man-hunting missions, I recognized his counsel for what it was: simple genius. *The wisest guy on the ground will always defer to other guys on the ground.*

As he elaborated, I wished I could have put him on a speakerphone so that every soldier, every agent, and every leader in Washington, D.C., who was involved in the Afghanistan mission could have heard firsthand the pearls of tacit knowledge that were coming out of this guy's mouth. *Tacit knowledge is contextualized knowledge of people, places, ideas, and experiences.* This was tacit knowledge on steroids. He was telling me where to go, what to do when I got there, and how to accomplish my mission. This was why I came here—to get to the real nuggets that are available only through face-to-face conversation. You have to let the person tell his story.

For the next three hours I asked him questions, challenged his answers, and listened to Ali Mohamed while he told me about UBL, Al Qaeda, his life, his motivations, and his dreams. He never rocked off his base. He watched my responses with great introspection. Whenever I appeared to ponder or doubt one of his responses, he would quickly challenge, "If you don't believe me, let me take you there myself." He'd then add, "You can kill me if you find out I'm lying.

"Take me with you to the Northwest Frontier Province, I can find him."

"How?" I asked.

"You have to ask the right questions and follow leads," he told me. *He was rock solid—no movement.*

U.S government psychologists developed a simple mnemonic to describe the primary motivators of individuals who are willing to betray their country or parent organization. The concept of "MICE" is based on historical examples of hundreds of cases (including Aldrich Ames, the most notorious "mole" ever to penetrate the CIA) over the past fifty years. MICE stands for money, ideology, coercion, and excitement. Intrigue is sometimes substituted for ideology. We know from the testimony of Ali Mohamed's captured Al Qaeda comrades that he wasn't motivated by religion or by money. We also learned that there was no coercive pressure on him from either the United States or Al Qaeda. So what motivated him to work both sides of such a combustible counterfeit coin?

As I sat across from him and listened, I began to recognize that his life experiences had instilled in him a completely different set of values and beliefs than I had. He spoke nonchalantly about teaching Al Qaeda fighters how to commit acts of terror, while seamlessly transitioning to explain his willingness to work undercover to infiltrate and capture those same terrorists. I began to realize that he had what is sometimes referred to as "moral flexibility." Commonly found in master criminals, hitmen, and white-collar criminals, Mohamed was the type of guy who could rationalize just about any behavior based on his own belief that it was the circumstance of the moment that mattered most, not the conventional distinctions between good and evil or truth and lies. In other ways, though, he wasn't so different from me or many of the guys I worked with. He was an adventurer, genetically addicted to both the thrill of the hunt and the thrill of the chase, and a maverick, someone who exhibits great independence in thought and action.

Patterns were beginning to coalesce. He spoke with devout reverence as he continually referenced secret organizations and secret missions. He rarely missed an opportunity to pay homage to, and convey his admiration and respect for secret operatives, especially those in what he described as "the almighty" CIA and FBI. That's when it hit me: this was the missing piece of the Ali Mohamed puzzle.

The more I listened to what he told me, and the more I thought about it in the context of his life journey, the more I began to understand that the real or perceived intrigue, excitement, and adventure of becoming a U.S. secret agent was the common thread that wove through his pattern of seemingly inexplicable life behaviors. His moral flexibility was what allowed him to do it so effectively.

He was not a fanatic, as his Al Qaeda brethren correctly surmised. Nor was he a double or triple agent, as most books, documentaries, and conventional wisdom still promote. Instead, Ali Mohamed was an adventurer and maverick, with a certain moral flexibility who believed that by keeping his options open as a terrorist, he would increase his value as, and correspondingly his potential to become, a U.S. secret agent. Interviewed by the FBI one day, ignored the next. Entrusted to conduct surveillance on the Nairobi embassy one day, distrusted with key information concerning Al Qaeda leaders the next. He was hedging his bets and developing the situation on both fronts, hoping to discover the options that would allow him to find his path. An advanced version of the same belt buckle behavior he exhibited at Fort Bragg, hoping that maybe, just maybe, his credentials as a terrorist insider would earn him affirmation from his American handlers and the rite of passage to become a U.S. secret agent.

In the end, the option to become a U.S. secret agent never availed itself to Ali Mohamed, and without the option to become a U.S. secret agent, he had no other choice—he went with the only option available to him, the option to work for Al Qaeda. *The unbranded range animal belongs to the first person who puts a brand on it.*

I left my first face-to-face meeting with Ali Mohamed with confidence. As events continued to unfold on the ground in Afghanistan, I became even more confident that the knowledge he had shared was credible. On December 12, 2001, an intercepted radio transmission by UBL confirmed that he was indeed hiding in Tora Bora.[20] Ali Mohamed's seminal document had advised looking for UBL in Tora Bora in early October, and two months before the first U.S. forces arrived there. He was right about how to infiltrate Afghanistan, he was right about sleeper cells, and he was right about Tora Bora—a pattern of

accurate advice and prognostications. Deductive reasoning told me
that the rest of the information he provided was likely accurate too.

I felt that I was uniquely qualified for the toughest and most complex challenges our country was facing at that time. All I needed was
a mission. And for all my efforts, I was about to get one.

Imagine the Possibilities of the Guy on the Ground

The stories of the defense contractors, the Afghan general, and Ali
Mohamed are all stories of the amazing synergy between imagination
and guy-on-the-ground knowledge. Imagine everyone's potential as
the guy on the ground. Imagine how to seek out the guy on the ground.
Imagine how.

An object lesson for the utility of this guiding principle was an
intangible tipping point in the mid-'90s. At that time Al Qaeda and
the U.S. government were conjoined by their common interest in Ali
Mohamed. Both sides recognized that Ali Mohamed had one-of-a-kind
skills and experiences to support each side's uniquely self-serving interests. Both sides had independently come to the same conclusion: Ali
Mohamed was not the type of individual they could trust to become a
card-carrying member of their respective organizations. The tipping
point was how the two sides reacted. Al Qaeda leaders were able to
overlook Ali Mohamed's lack of Muslim fanaticism and his erratic
connections to the U.S. government because they couldn't imagine
how they could achieve their ultimate terror objectives without the
mission-essential knowledge and skills that only he possessed. Ali
Mohamed's U.S. government handlers, on the other hand, just plain
could not imagine. The result of the tipping point was 9/11. Ali Mohamed wasn't directly responsible for the execution of 9/11, but it's
easy to imagine how he could have been directly responsible for preventing it.

The only ways we can ever hope to see these types of events unfolding before they occur, is to look at the world around us through the minds and eyes of others. It's the person who has walked the specific ground, lived the specific lifestyle, and possesses a specific psychosocial mind-set whom you need. They are very rarely cut from the same cloth as you and I.

PART 4

1 3

ON THE GROUND
IN AFGHANISTAN

RIDING THE EDGE OF CHAOS

November 2001

Perhaps one of the least recognized and most misunderstood aspects of combat is that the true moments of battlefield genius almost always occur during periods of complete chaos. In the Unit, we had a name for these moments: we called them operational sweet spots. They usually occur during the early phases of a battle or mission, or during unanticipated contingencies such as surprise attacks, or accidents. It's during these operational sweet spots that entrepreneurial warriors recognize the chaos of the moment as opportunity, and break free from the prison of the plan and the shackles of the hierarchy, to achieve effects way out of proportion to the effort expended.

American military history is replete with such examples. The men who parachuted into Normandy prior to D-Day weren't successful because someone was directing their every move, or because they were following a highly scripted plan. Instead, they were successful because they were dropped in the wrong locations, were separated from their chains of command, and collectively decided to throw away the plan. In the chaos of the moment, they innovated, they adapted, and they were audacious. As a result, the Nazi enemy were completely confused, confounded, and quickly collapsed.

In the final months of 2002, this same pattern of battlefield chaos and genius was repeating itself in Afghanistan. In late November, one of the most potent entrepreneurial combinations ever to self-organize on any battlefield took advantage of the chaos of the moment to achieve one of the most astonishing battlefield successes in the history of warfare.

As phantom parachutists dropped from the sky and melted into the desert in the south, derring-do CIA officers made something out of nothing by organizing and supplying superempowered Northern Alliance militias, while small, highly adaptive Special Forces teams, sometimes riding into combat on horseback, guided both the militias and their laser-guided arsenal from the sky against the enemy.[1] Confused and confounded, the hapless enemy quickly collapsed.

These astonishing battlefield successes weren't the offspring of some master strategist standing on a hilltop and spouting orders. Nor did they come from a master plan; none existed. Instead they were spawned during an operational sweet spot, when fewer than five hundred American special operations and CIA warriors were unleashed to do what American warriors throughout history have always done best: they developed the situation.[2]

14

IT'S NOT REALITY
UNLESS IT'S SHARED

December 2001

By late December, the situation in the main Afghan cities of Kandahar, Kabul, and Mazer-e-Sharif was settling into normalcy, if normalcy were possible where none had existed for over twenty years. As for the rest of the country, no one had a clue. No Westerner had been out in the frontier areas of Afghanistan where the enemy was now hiding since the late '70s. To find the enemy and figure things out, the United States needed to get people on the ground in the unexplored frontier areas; that's where the concept of AFO entered the picture.[1]

AFO stood for advanced force operations. More a verb than a noun, prior to Afghanistan, advanced force operations described what small special operations teams were supposed to do in a hostile country in preparation for potential future missions.[2] If necessity is the mother of invention, then in the case of AFO in Afghanistan, serendipity was the father, because AFO, the organization that was about to make the biggest impact on the Afghan battlefield, wasn't planned; it just happened.[3] There was no charter; no organizational structure; no budget; and best of all for me, no real constraints or limitations on creating any of the above. The operational sweetspot was still open.

"Get some men out into the frontier to figure out what's going on," General Tommy Franks told us.[4] As commander in chief of U.S. Central Command, General Franks commanded all American military forces in Afghanistan. "Find the enemy, then kill or capture 'em," he added. That was more than sufficient guidance for me; it was a blank canvas on which I could paint whatever was required to accomplish the mission. Whether I created a masterpiece or piece of crap would depend on my ability to apply all the guiding principle lessons I had learned over the years as an artisan of the art of war.

My plane landed at Bagram Air Base (see Map 3), thirty miles north of Kabul, and taxied to a parking spot between two rusting Soviet MIGs that had long since seen better days. With the engines still screaming at ear-splitting decibel levels, the hydraulic ramp on the back of the aircraft lowered slowly, revealing the bone-chilling blackness of the Afghan winter night. The only thing I could see was a blinking red light twirling in circles from a few hundred meters away. *That would be Jimmy.*

Jimmy didn't have a formal title; no one in AFO did. I guess you could say he was my deputy. Jimmy was one of those guys everyone remembers. With a billboard-handsome face, now carpeted with a thick black beard, Jimmy was well liked by just about everyone who met him. "*Salaam alaikum*, Panther!" he bellowed, "*Salaam alaikum*, Jimmy. You look like a real mountain man," I told him as we shook each other's hand while executing the patented no-touch warrior hug. His eyes lit up and he pointed at me while saying, "Blend in anywhere."

I was genuinely ecstatic that Jimmy was going to be working with me; he was a rare breed of warrior: superfit, commonsense smart, and a superb organizer. Unlike a lot of us, Jimmy was as lethal with a keyboard and pen as he was with a knife and a gun. Best of all, Jimmy was what Malcolm Gladwell calls a "connector," someone who is extraordinarily gifted at making friends and acquaintances and then linking them all together to create a productive network.[5] With the ever-increasing cornucopia of organizations and units that AFO would be interacting with, Jimmy's skills as a connector would prove to be as important to our success as any weapon, radio, or tactic. After forty-eight hours of mostly sitting on my ass on planes, I badly needed to stretch my legs, but I also needed to get an update from Jimmy, so he and I did what we would do all across Afghanistan over the next hundred days; we went for a long walk, and we talked.

So it was when I arrived in Afghanistan in early December 2001. There was a lot of uncertainty on the ground, with a country in need of rebuilding and a terror network in need of being found and destroyed. I realized I had to do two things: I had to develop the situation to find and destroy the enemy, and I had to create and lead an organization to do it. This was my mission!

The next day we headed out to the frontier to get the lay of the land and to meet with and listen to our men on the ground. At this stage in the war the other key players on the ground in Afghanistan were the army's 5th Special Forces Group and the CIA. Both had already begun following the enemy's trail, and both were pushing out into the frontier to recruit and train Afghan militias while trolling the waters for any and all useful information about the enemy.[6]

AFO had about forty-five men in country, spread out in six teams across the 647,000 square kilometers of Afghanistan. Most of AFO came from Delta, but because AFO was a top priority of General Franks, we were able to tap into the best of the best from the navy and air force special operations forces.[7] All of these men were seasoned veterans of numerous other battlefields, and only a few were below age thirty. This was no insignificant factoid. As warriors throughout history can attest, there are few shortcuts to combat wisdom; acquiring it requires travel on the long, winding, and hazard-laden road of real-world experience. Combat experience provides context, and context provides common sense. There were two other virtues that all of these men had: the first was a skill: they all possessed highly advanced strategic reconnaissance skills; and the second was a mind-set: they were all highly adaptable.

At that time, most AFO teams were either operating by themselves or within close proximity to the Special Forces and the CIA, who were now working together in what was referred to as "pilot teams."[8] The AFO team in Orgun (see Map 3) was different. They had already integrated with the Special Forces and the CIA as part of the pilot team working the area. No one told them to do this; they did it because it made sense.

Living together in a sprawling, mud-walled safe house, the pilot team in Orgun was busy developing the situation when I arrived. Tall, thickly muscled men with long hair, spontaneously barbaric beards, and dark sunglasses scurried around the compound like ants. No one appeared wanting of a task. These men formed the initial impression by which most Afghan frontiersmen thought of Americans.

Orgun was one of the closest outposts we had to the Pakistan border. Perhaps because of its proximity to the border, enemy activity in the area was constant, which made the Orgun safe house not so safe. The area around Orgun was distinctive because it had something you rarely saw in other areas of Afghanistan: trees. There were no forests, but thousands of copses dotted the green, rolling hills that defined the area. Somehow this area of the country had escaped the insatiable axes of the starving and freezing populace during the Soviet War.

On the third day of my stay at the Orgun safe house, Rex, the AFO team leader, woke me at sunrise and told me that the Afghan warlord I had met two days earlier was at the front gate asking for a personal meeting with "the American commander."[9] Establishing relationships and building alliances with the local warlords was a top priority at that time, and the team was anxious to bring this particular warlord into the fold. Two decades of nonstop civil war had disintegrated all established central government institutions in Afghanistan. Filling the power vacuum were ethnically aligned leaders of war bands, called warlords, who ruled the frontier areas. They built their power bases on a combination of benevolence, bravery, brutality, and a heavy dose of swashbuckling theatrical flair thrown in for good measure. They provided the only line of defense and security for the people of their specific tribal ethnicity, which earned most of them the genuine loyalty and support of the majority of their constituents. With names such as Dostom, Kahn, Najibullah, and Noorzai, these guys were essentially land pirates.

I threw on my shirt, tucked my pistol inside my belt holster, and told Rex to bring the warlord into the courtyard where I'd be waiting to meet with him.

The warlord strode through the center opening gates into the dusty courtyard flanked by two heavily armed bodyguards, who shadowed him cockily from a pace or two behind. The guard on the right immediately gave me pause. A black charcoal substance coated his eyelids, and his unnaturally pursed lips were coated with some kind of pink, gooey substance. *An Afghan drag queen; I never thought I'd see that.* But it was his finger, planted firmly on the trigger of his AK-47 that really concerned me. Psychological instability and finger on the trigger do not a healthy combination make in a combat zone. Rex had zeroed in on the same thing. In a polite yet stern tone, Rex used pantomime to communicate with the bodyguard. "Take your finger off your trigger," he commanded while wagging his bent index finger. Unbeknownst to the bodyguard, he was about a pound of trigger pressure away from having his head explode like a watermelon. Danno, one of the other AFO members in Orgun, was, at that moment, on sight security detail in one of the four corner watchtowers that surrounded the safe house. The protocol we used for meetings such as this was situationally driven. If the U.S. participant ever put his hands up or scratched the top of his head, the sniper was cleared to use his best judgment and mitigate the situation.

Likely believing his original purpose for meeting with me now in jeopardy, the warlord harshly rebuked the bodyguard, who turned around and stormed out of the courtyard, stomping his feet in what could only be described as an Afghan version of an effeminate tantrum.

Wrapped in a claret robe, with a jet-black beard that flowed from his cheekbones to his chest, and well over six feet tall (without turban), the warlord presented an imposing figure. Judging by the depth of the wrinkles etched into the few visible inches of his fully bearded face, he was likely fifty to sixty years old. His furled brow and frenetic eyes gave him the look of a man who had fought his way to the top of the heap and now spent all his time worrying about defending his roost.

After greeting him in Pashto and shaking his hand, I allowed him to initiate the conversation. He began in a slow baritone rustle, but within a few seconds he worked himself into a saliva-spitting frenzy. He explained to me (through a translator) that the evening before, his cousin—a truck driver—had been murdered, his gut-shot body left in a bloody heap on the side of the road just a few miles from our safe house. "Please accept the condolences of me and my men," I replied. "What can we do to help?" With the look of a man who is about to ask a really big favor, he replied, "I was wondering if you could use your computer to find out who killed my cousin."

I was puzzled, so I paused and feigned indecision to buy time. As I did, I happened to glance over the warlord's left shoulder toward the entrance to our living area. Set up close to the door for fresh air and generator power access were our laptop computers, clearly visible from where he and I were standing in the courtyard. During his prior visits to our safe house, the warlord likely noticed the computers' mystical glow radiating from the darkened interior; it must have seemed like space-age magic to this Afghan frontiersman, who almost assuredly had had no prior contact with the technocentric outside world. I put my hand on his shoulder and replied with open-minded sincerity, "I'll take a look, but I'll need a few hours." His eyes widened as he shook my hand with grateful vigor, bowed slightly, then yelled something unintelligible to his drag queen security guard and headed for the gate.

I walked back into the communication room where Rex and five to ten of our Special Forces and CIA comrades were anxiously await-ing my return. "What'd he want, boss?" Rex asked while everyone else stopped what they were doing and listened. I explained what he told me and then asked the group what they thought. The senior Special Forces sergeant was the first to respond. "Well, if we can do something for the guy that motivates him to cooperate with us, I'm up for just about anything. Without the support and cooperation of his tribe against the enemy in this area, we're just spitting in the wind." He paused for a second and then continued, "Why don't I go and check out the spot where he said his cousin was killed." "I'll go with him," Rex added. As both men walked out the door, they simultaneously checked the chambers of their M-4 rifles. This was a reflexive habit that served the dual purpose of confirming a round was ready to fire if needed, and to cue each man's psychological transition from the semi-relaxed, inside the compound mind-set, to the fully alert, all-senses-scanning mind-set required any time any of us headed out into the frontier.

Without looking up from his computer, a guy who I assumed was an intelligence analyst chimed in next: "I'll send a request back to my headquarters to probe last night's satellite imagery and see if we had coverage of that area; maybe it will reveal something. I can also run the warlord's name through our relationship database and see who his cousin actually was." He didn't need me or anyone else to give him permission, or to tell him it was good idea. Of all the organizations on the battlefield in Afghanistan, the CIA was by far the most nimble. They allowed their people to make decisions as far forward as possible, and seemed to live by the philosophy "When it's the right thing to do, just do it."

A few hours later, the analyst called me over. "Bingo!" he announced while an "I-told-you-so" smile crept onto his face. I walked over to see what he had on his computer, which was surrounded by a thick nest of candy bar wrappers, cracker crumbs, Kleenex, and half-eaten MRE cookies. A grainy black-and-white aerial picture of the truck appeared on his laptop's dusty screen. He zoomed in and then hit the return button a couple of times to get the next time-phased pictures to sequence in. "There it is." The picture showed two trucks parked back end to back end. The image was clear, but too grainy to read a license plate—not that they had any in that part of the world anyway. "Find the driver of the other truck and you'll find the murderer," the analyst declared with great conviction. Just then, Rex walked in. "How'd it go?" I asked. "We found the truck," he reported while looking over my shoulder at the satellite photo on the computer. "We found wood chips all over the bed of his truck, and all around on the ground. At first we figured the warlord's cousin was carrying wood and was killed when someone else tried to steal it—"

The intelligence analyst interrupted. "Hey, man, I could have saved you guys the time and the risk you took by driving all the way out to a murder scene in the middle of bad-guy country—the satellite photos prove that whoever took his load of wood is the killer."

Rex didn't respond; he just smiled and continued talking. "While we were snooping around we noticed a couple of kids playing in the rocks nearby. They looked hungry, so we gave 'em some MRE crackers. While they were munching away we asked 'em if they knew what happened to the guy who got killed. One of the kids told us he saw the whole thing while he was drawing water from the well behind his home just before sunrise. He told us that he saw the cousin's truck driving slowly down the road with its lights off. The kid showed us how the cousin backed his truck up to the other guy's truck, then jumped out and started transloading the wood as fast as he could. He was halfway done when the other guy came walking out of his house and caught him in the act. The warlord's cousin pulled his pistol first and started blasting away, but the kid said the other guy was a better aim, and shot him dead with one shot."

The warlord returned that evening. This time he didn't have his bodyguards with him. Instead he brought his daughter. Perhaps five or six years old and too young to wear a burkha, she had dark brown hair and strikingly catlike eyes, in stark contrast to the jet-black hair and dark eyes that most of us think of when we think about Afghans.

Whether for trade or to conquer, people had been passing through Afghanistan for thousands of years, creating one of the world's most diverse melting pots. While the majority of Afghans are of Persian or Turkish descent, there are also many other ethnic roots still visible across the frontier. The girl's dark brown hair and greenish eyes were likely genetic markers of those thought to be descendants of Alexander the Great and his invading army in 330 B.C.

I didn't attribute the little girl's presence to happenstance—he had a specific reason for bringing her. *But what was it?* While the little girl waited submissively near the gate, her father and I walked circles around the courtyard. Through my Afghan-American interpreter, I shared what we discovered, specifically, that it looked like his cousin was shot because he was attempting to steal wood from another man. For obvious reasons I didn't mention the kids.

I could see something connect behind the warlord's eyes as his facial expression cycled from receptiveness, to enlightenment, to anger, and finally to resignation. I got the feeling that his cousin was a known troublemaker, and our explanation confirmed what the warlord already suspected. He sighed, shook his head, then looked me in the eye and whispered, "You must find Al Qaeda and kill them all." I wasn't sure what to say back; it seemed kind of random, considering what we had just discussed, but I was more than willing to hyperlink. I figured he knew a heck of a lot more about how to find Al Qaeda than I did—this was his backyard. "How do you recommend we find them?" I asked through my interpreter. He seemed bewildered for a moment, maybe because I was deferring to him instead of going into the house and typing the question into my all-knowing computer. Then he smiled and whispered, "The mountains around Gardez, you must look for them in the mountains." Interested in his motivation for helping us and not the enemy, I asked him why he disliked Al Qaeda so much. He looked back at his daughter for a few seconds, and then whispered just loud enough for me and my interpreter to hear, "Because I want my daughter to go to school, I want her to be a person."

As he walked away with his daughter in tow, I suddenly understood why he brought her with him that day. It was so we could see her with our own eyes and put a face on the future of Afghanistan. It worked. From that day forward, I never needed anyone to tell me why we were in Afghanistan, and I'll never forget that little girl.

The experience with the warlord was an example of the kind of situation that our guys on the ground in Afghanistan dealt with almost every day. Since nothing dramatic occurred, such as a firefight or a captured enemy combatant, episodes such as the warlord encounter rarely got passed on, or for that matter, remembered by most of the participants.

As we drove away from the Orgun safe house, staring at the copses of trees dotting the hills, I was reminded of how important it is to see the world around us through the minds and eyes of others. To understand the way others interpret reality, we have to interact with them, and we have to share information. Sharing information creates a shared reality. Not only does it make the whole wiser than the individual parts; it also serves as an effective system of checks and balances to correct misinterpretations by individuals who don't have all the pieces of the puzzle.

The satellite photo portrayed two trucks parked together at a specific point in time; this information was useful, but only as a one-dimensional portrayal of reality. As our intelligence analyst exemplified, the reality the satellite photos portrayed were highly susceptible to the perspective and corresponding misinterpretation of whoever was looking at them. Only when Rex and the Special Forces sergeant drove out to the scene of the crime were we able to understand the reality of what had actually occurred. As is so often the case, the key piece of the puzzle came from the guys on the ground, and in this case, the kids on the ground. Technology was still valuable; it both confirmed and corroborated the kids' account of what happened. Each piece was important alone—the wood chips, the kids on the ground, and the satellite imagery of the two trucks—but only when shared did they portray the context-rich reality of what actually occurred.

As we passed the last of the Orgun tree copses and entered the barren, brown beauty of the "other" Afghanistan, I recognized that to successfully develop the situation and accomplish our mission on the complex and unforgiving Afghan frontier, AFO would need to create and maintain a shared reality. As I was about to learn, it would be more than just mission-essential. The lives of my men would depend on it.

15

ORGANIZING FOR COMBAT:

DEALING WITH A NATURAL DISASTER

January 16, 2002

The final stop on my journey across the frontier was the capital city of Kabul, where I was scheduled to meet with my counterparts from the Special Forces and the CIA.[1] One of the common denominators of every successful mission I had taken part in over the years was unity of effort among the government agencies involved, such as the CIA, the Defense Department, the State Department, and the FBI. Whenever we achieved interagency unity of effort, we were successful. When we didn't, we weren't. The CIA was the key government agency on the ground at that time. Not only did they have the best understanding of Afghanistan and the enemy, they also were best equipped to translate that knowledge into action. For AFO to succeed, I had to ensure we had a shared reality with the CIA.

Once the premier luxury hotel of Kabul, the war-scarred building we would be meeting at was in the center of the city, just a stone's throw from the presidential palace.[2] Surrounded by twelve-foot-high walls topped with concertina wire, the building was guarded by hardscrabble Northern Alliance soldiers who had to earn the "right" to perform this lucrative duty with battlefield bravery and conquests.[3]

After giving my name and a password to the guard at the gate, Jimmy and I drove into the compound and headed up the once-grand, cracked and crumbled curving marble stairs to our meeting room on the second floor. The stench of piss and Pine-Sol hung thick in the air. Waiting for me inside the room were my Special Forces and CIA counterparts. John was a thin, scholarly looking fellow, who sported the Jesus hairdo and beard.[4] Chris H. was the battalion commander of all the Special Forces teams arrayed around the eastern part of Afghanistan. His men were some of the first in, and the first to ride horses in combat since who knows when. Built like an offensive lineman, he had an unexpectedly high-pitched voice and an always jovial disposition. For the first hour or so we sipped green tea and engaged in a free-flowing conversation that spanned a wide variety of topics, all centered on the topic du jour: how to find the enemy![5]

There was still plenty left to do. The Taliban were gone and Al Qaeda's foreign fighters were on the run. It was up to our three organizations to band together and hunt them down. Within a few minutes we all agreed on one central organizing principle: the power of combinations. Both Chris and John had already heard from their people about the incident with the warlord in Orgun.

"If we can create that kind of synergy everywhere in country, we'll be in really good shape," Chris reflected out loud.

"We can, but we all need to agree to work together, we gotta be boundaryless, and we gotta share everything," I emphasized.

"I'm all for it," John chimed in

"Me, too," Chris added.

With our unofficial union, we had mixed together the key ingredients for man-hunting success. The CIA would provide the ability to produce and process intelligence, the Special Forces teams would train and equip the Afghans, and we—the AFO—would operationalize the entire effort by conducting on-the-ground reconnaissance to find and destroy the enemy.

"Building out the AFO concept across the country is the right first step, but we need to focus our efforts where the enemy is," I commented. "So where do you guys want to focus next?" Chris asked. John was pensive. Chris looked at his watch and announced that he had to get back to his compound, just down the street. "Let's meet again tomorrow at Bagram," he said, hurrying out of the room.

John stood up and stared out the window. The currency of spies is information, and the highest-value currency is information that no one else knows about. Once a spy acquires it, he's trained to lock it up, guard it, and only give it to others for something in return. As a result, spies tend to overcompartmentalize their most credible information, even in an atmosphere of complete cooperation, such as existed in Afghanistan at the time. I could tell John had something on his mind, some juicy morsel of context locked inside his head, available for release only if I could come up with the right password. "John, we have to keep the pressure on these guys—the enemy's on the run, they're desperate, and desperate men make desperate moves. They're vulnerable right now, but the longer we allow them to re-arm, refit, and reorganize, the harder it will be for us to find 'em and accomplish our mission." He walked over to the window, and closed the thick curtains. Darkness now cloaked the room. *Bingo.*

"We're getting a lot of reports that Al Qaeda forces are regrouping in an area in the mountains between Gardez and Khowst," he whispered. "What's it called?" I whispered back as I yanked my Day-Timer out of my cargo pocket. "Shahi Khot," he whispered. I thought I'd heard the name before, but it didn't immediately register. *Probably a phonetic thing,* so I asked him to spell it for me. "S-H-A-H-I-K-H-O-T."[6] He spoke each letter with the slow deliberateness of a man who is going to say something only once.

As Jimmy and I drove the thirty miles from Kabul back to Bagram, my head was awash with dots. After three weeks of living with and listening to Afghans and Americans all around the country, I felt confident that we now knew where to focus our search (in the mountains around Gardez, near this place called Shahi Khot). Thanks to the team in Orgun, I had a living, breathing example to use as a model for organizing AFO. It was time to reorganize.

One thing that always frustrated me about the military was the way we organized for combat missions. No matter what the mission, no matter who the enemy was or what country we were operating in, we always organized the same way. Platoons, battalions, army, navy, air force; no matter how complex the mission, we used the same administratively driven organizational approach every time. Over the past two hundred years, U.S. history has taught us that no two wars, engagements, or enemies are ever alike. Yet to this day, we continue shoving organizational marshmallows into operational piggybanks. In combat as in nature, if you don't adapt, you die. *How would large organizations such as the military organize if they didn't know how they were supposed to be organized?* I wondered.

Outside, a fierce blizzard was howling. Visibility dropped to front bumper. Jimmy violently jerked the wheel to the left in an attempt to avoid an elephant-sized pothole. Too late, and too big: the pothole swallowed the right front corner of the vehicle. The tire was flat and the rim destroyed. Jimmy pulled over to the side of the road. Without saying a word, each of us buttoned up our coats, slipped on our gloves, and jumped out into the blizzard. I grabbed the jack, and Jimmy grabbed the spare. While I pumped, Jimmy grabbed the nuts, and we started talking about what would happen if a natural or man-made disaster struck Afghanistan and isolated all the Americans currently inside the country, from all connectivity to the outside world. After a few days of no communications or guidance from their parent organizations, everyone would likely do exactly what Jimmy and I just did: they would come to the realization that they had to get on with the mission. AFO, Special Forces, CIA, 10th Mountain, Department of State, anyone and everyone on the ground would size up the situation, and self-organize in a way that was optimized for only one thing: to accomplish the mission—just like the teams and the teamwork we saw in Orgun.

With AFO, we had the opportunity to break out of the business-as-usual mode and organize according to the current mission and the environment. We didn't need a natural disaster; we knew what the right thing was to do right then. With the wheel repaired, Jimmy and I jumped back in our vehicle and continued our journey back to Bagram. Along the way we started the reorganization.

The first step was to flatten AFO headquarters by pulling all of our intelligence analysts and communications specialists out of Bagram and pushing them out to the pilot teams in the safe houses.[7] The communications specialists brought with them a suite of communications technologies that would enable each team to talk to anyone anywhere on the globe. They could also upload or download data (photos, articles, and maps) whenever they needed them. The intelligence analysts provided the team's face-to-face interaction with a single point of contact, who was completely dedicated to aggregating the teams' requests and feedback, and diving into research whenever required. There was no protocol for communications among teams. "Boundaryless" meant just that: if the teams needed to coordinate, they were encouraged to work freely with each other at any time. With the intelligence analyst and communications pipes, the teams would have the key enabling tools to collect, analyze, and act on intelligence in real time, without depending on a staff a hundred miles away. We were getting nimble.

Next we integrated all AFO teams with their CIA and Special Forces brethren as pilot teams. No two pilot teams would be organized the same way. Each mission-tailored team would operate in a decentralized fashion to develop the situation in a specific enemy-focused region of the country. The people, the geography, and the enemy required different approaches in each area. We were going for multiple actions at the fringes, with each team developing the situation in their own area, then sharing that information in all directions to ensure we created and maintained a shared reality. It was my responsibility to make sure we were boundaryless. No boundaries between teams, no boundaries between AFO and any other organization operating in Afghanistan, and no boundaries for what we could imagine and accomplish.

As for me, if I was going to effectively lead AFO, I needed to be up front where I could look a warlord in the eye, and where I could experience the effects of the cold, the altitude, the lack of supplies, and the same resulting frustrations that my men were experiencing. To understand the guy on the ground, there is no substitute for face-to-face interactions. There was another reason why I knew we had to move out of Bagram. The awesome transformative power of the U.S. military logistics system was changing Bagram from a South Bronx shithole into an Upper East Side condominium right in front of our eyes. Technology and comfort items such as the Internet, satellite television, and hot chow, are hugely net positive for men and women serving long tours in a combat zone. But they also combine to create subtle intrusions that slowly but surely rob a warrior of his most precious weapon: time to saturate, incubate, and illuminate. I turned to Jimmy, "What's up, boss?" he asked. "Let's pack it up, Jimmy," I answered. "We're heading for the frontier."

16

EXPLORING
THE FRONTIER:

RECOGNIZING ENEMY PATTERNS

January 12, 2002

The safe house in Gardez (see Map 5) was a typical Afghan rural home that consisted of four thirty-foot-high mud walls anchored by watchtowers in each of the four corners, which encased a large, barren courtyard the size of a football field in the middle. Calling it a home comes with an asterisk. In Afghanistan, most homes could architecturally qualify as what the rest of the world calls a fort. Thousands of years of invading armies cutting through their backyards and front yards, compounded by never-ending ethnic and tribal infighting, were the likely reasons for this uniquely Afghan interpretation of a home's functionality. To most Afghans the home isn't so much a place you stay in to live, as it is a place you live in to stay alive.

We were hunters, and hunters have to be where they can access their prey, but hunters also have to understand, respect, and interact with the locals whose lands the prey inhabit. We believed in Mao's axiom on guerrilla warfare: warm the waters and the fish will flourish, chill the waters and the fish will die! The people are the waters and at that moment, we were the fish. We spent a lot of time and effort building relationships and establishing rapport with the locals.

I stared out from my panoramic perch on the southeastern watchtower of the safe house and studied the terrain of the treeless, snow-blasted mountains that surrounded us. Spread out all around the safe house was a scene reminiscent of a Civil War bivouac site: more than a hundred white tents that housed more than four hundred of our Afghan allies. Each cluster of tents had a small campfire with five or six newly recruited Afghan warriors sipping green tea and likely reflecting on their new lot on top of the Afghan food chain.

There were about fifty Americans living in and operating out of the safe house. At 7,800 feet above sea level, the thin air provided the added bonus of allowing us to acclimate for future forays in the surrounding mountains. The courtyard was the hub of all combat preparation activity; vehicles were constantly being loaded, unloaded, or maintained. Men of all shapes, sizes, ages, and ethnicities were constantly milling around and mingling. The one common denominator among all of us was weapons: everyone had a weapon of various size, shape, caliber, and origin strapped to whatever part of the body individual preference and physiology allowed them to get to it the quickest.

Sleeping arrangements reflected the age-old war-zone law of first mover advantage. While the Special Forces and CIA teams slept inside the warm, protective bosom of the fort's spacious, hollow walls, AFO occupied a large tent in the courtyard. No one complained: I liked the fresh air and the chance to stare at the stars each night before I went to bed.

Air force C-130s air-dropped food and water once a week. There was no running water and no plumbing; we crapped in a gigantic hole that the medics covered with chemicals at the end of each day. The tactical operations center (TOC), where we prepared for and monitored our missions, was austere but incredibly functional. Probably designed as a living room it measured about twenty feet by thirty feet. Glenn (our intel analyst) transformed the room within minutes of his arrival. Maps were pinned to the mud walls, plastic sheets were used to cover the glassless windows, and radios and laptop computers were slaved to generators that hummed away in the courtyard 24/7.

In a few days, without any official document or directive to guide us, we had dramatically reorganized the U.S. force structure occupying outposts in the frontier areas all across Afghanistan. The whole, made up of AFO, Special Forces, and the CIA, was now much stronger, and much more lethal, than the sum of its parts.

The lack of distractions and the medieval ambience made it as good as it gets for a warrior. This was our hunting lodge, and I felt like we were ready to start the hunt. It was time to start developing the situation in the mountains around Gardez.

A few days after I settled in, Chris H. (the Special Forces commander) arrived, and we agreed to join his Special Forces TOC in the same room with our AFO TOC. A few days later, the best combat leader in the CIA showed up; we called him Spider. Physically unremarkable, he wore his six-foot, superwiry frame like his nickname. Spider and I had met while conducting gorilla warfare operations in Bosnia a few years earlier. Everyone has different opinions of the CIA, but like the military, their effectiveness in most situations depends in large part on the leaders they have working the mission. Spider was a living, breathing example of how good the CIA could be when they had their best leaders on the ground. His affable personality and deep, passionate dedication to the warriors working the mission on the ground earned him great respect among my military comrades wherever he showed up.*

As the pilot team in Gardez continued to gather intelligence and build situational awareness, we made sure we took time to think. We

---

*For security reasons I have chosen to leave out much of the detail around AFO interactions and coordinations with the CIA. What is important for the reader to understand is that for Operation Anaconda, we were one organization. Without the CIA, and especially Spider, Operation Anaconda and most of the early success in the war against terrorists would never have happened.

created a "required reading" table with a sign above it that read "Need to Share." Strewn across the table were the seminal documents, books, maps, and reports that were required reading for everyone on the team. Together they formed our foundational logic.

Before deploying to Afghanistan, the Unit gave each of us two books on the Soviet war in Afghanistan: The first, *The Other Side of the Mountain*, contained firsthand accounts of combat lessons from the perspective of mujahideen fighters. The second, *The Bear Went over the Mountain*, contained firsthand accounts of combat lessons from the Soviet perspective. Both books were cowritten by Lester Grau, a retired U.S. Army officer, and Ali Ahmad Jalali, a former Afghan mujahideen commander.

We learned a lot from these books; they were chock-full of insights, and over many nights of discussing and thinking about them, three key points stood out. The first was affirmation of what Ali Mohamed told us: the mujahideen were creatures of habit—they almost always returned to terrain they were familiar with and had fought from before. Both books contained detailed maps portraying the exact locations of the battles the mujahideen fought and the redoubts from which they based. We cross-referenced the locations with other intelligence we had, and then marked all of the locations on our own maps. The other two points were as much clues as they were key learnings. First, the mujahideen were not a self-sustaining fighting force. They didn't live off the land like the Viet Cong, who at times subsisted on wild plants and wild animals. Instead, the mujahideen were almost completely dependent on what we called an urban umbilical cord—close proximity to an urban area for food, water, and sustainment items. Last, both books continuously referenced a legendary mujahideen commander named Jalaluddin Haqqani.[1] Haqqani commanded more troops, and perhaps more respect than any other mujahideen commander. While reading the books, we discovered one of Haqqani's greatest battlefield victories occurred near a little-known place called Shahi Khot.

Clues are really just dots that lead you to other dots. To follow up the clues from the two books, we searched the greatest clue depository in the world: the World Wide Web. A couple hundred hyperlinks later, our efforts were rewarded. First we located a declassified Soviet report with lessons learned from the battle at Shahi Khot. The Soviet report described in detail how the mujahideen had used the mountainous terrain around Gardez to their advantage. They always fought from the high ground. "Look up," the Russian extolled, "you will find them up, always up." The report also described how the mujahideen fighters used the dry creekbeds to position their artillery and as lines of communication to bring in food and water from nearby towns.

Next we discovered that Jalaluddin Haqqani was now the senior military commander of the retreating Taliban army. In late October, after retreating to his sanctuary in Pakistan, he gave an interview to a mysterious Arab journalist who somehow talked his way into Haqqani's secret lair. The Internet enabled us to find the interview; our Arab-American adviser allowed us to translate it from Arabic to English. Here's what Haqqani had to say:

"We will retreat to the mountains and begin a long guerrilla war to reclaim our pure land from [American] infidels and free our country like we did against the Soviets. The Soviets were a brave enemy and their soldiers could withstand tough conditions. The Americans are creatures of comfort. They will not be able to sustain the harsh conditions that await them. . . . Afghanistan will prove to be the graveyard of the Americans."[2] (October 29, 2001.)

Haqqani was telling us that he and his fighters were going into hiding in the mountains in preparation for guerrilla warfare against U.S. forces. This creature of habit was sure that the "creatures of comfort" he was fighting wouldn't be willing or capable of coming up into the harsh Afghan mountains and finding him and his men. They would be safe in the mountains! Haqqani believed what he was saying; it was his reality.

All of us read the Haqqani reality.

Despite all the clues that continued to congeal into patterns that pointed us to this place called Shahi Khot, we still didn't know where it actually was, or, for that matter, whether the enemy was actually occupying it. There was no place called Shahi Khot on any map of Afghanistan. As it turned out, it was Ali Mohamed's "dated" tacit knowledge that allowed us to track it down.

"To find Al Qaeda, ask the shepherds, ask the shopkeepers, ask the taxi drivers," Ali Mohamed had told me. The Special Forces had already established ties with most of the local mayors and tribal chiefs. This was a critical component of what they called foreign internal defense. But Ali Mohamed didn't advise us to ask the mayor, and ask the tribal chiefs for good reason: to him they weren't the guys on the ground. So we decided to spread out across the frontier and double our efforts with the common folk. I was part of a team consisting of four Americans and two Afghans trolling the countryside east of our safe house. We had been at it all day and had learned a lot, but as we were driving back to the safe house we spotted a shepherd tending his flock a few hundred meters from the road. Up to this point, we hadn't come across any real shepherds; the shepherd was only a metaphor. But there was something about the way this guy stared at us. It wasn't the stare of cautious concern or contempt that we most often encountered in those early days; instead, it seemed beckoning, like he had something he wanted to say. Abdul, our Afghan driver, must have been thinking the same thing because he slammed on the brakes and without saying a word all six of us jumped out of the vehicle and headed across the muddy field to meet the metaphor.

An old man with gentle eyes, he greeted us with a placid smile. He seemed genuinely appreciative when we politely asked for permission to speak with him. After twenty or so minutes of small talk with our Afghan allies, Abdul asked him if he knew where the Al Qaeda Arabs were hiding. He didn't answer; he simply gestured for us to follow him as he turned and headed for a nearby hill. Most Afghans we encountered had never seen or used a map; they simply pointed or sketched terrain features in the dirt to describe directions. Although the shepherd looked to be at least seventy-five years old, he quickly shattered any preconceived notions we might have had about age and fitness when he put his hands behind his back and power-strode up the hill like a gold-medal speed skater. We followed him up the steep, thousand-foot grade like a bunch of backpackers following an attractive forest ranger. Arriving a few minutes behind him, our band of superfit but nonacclimated and out-of-breath athlete warriors put our hands on our knees and gasped for oxygen as we shook our heads in awe. We had a newfound appreciation for the disparity between us and the locals concerning acclimation to altitude. In a few weeks we'd close that disparity, but we never eliminated it.

Waiting patiently at the very top of the hill, the shepherd stood, pointing. My eyes tracked along his arm to the tip of his gnarled and weather-beaten finger. There, guarding the eastern horizon stood a daunting palisade of ten-thousand-foot cross-compartmented escarpments; most of which defied accepted topographic symbology. The shepherd mumbled something; I only understood two words: "Shahi Khot."

Abdul translated. He told us that Shahi Khot was actually the local name for the villages inside the valley, but most now referred to the entire valley as Shahi Khot. We stood spellbound for what seemed like a couple of minutes. From our hilltop perch it was easy to understand why the enemy believed the area to be all but inaccessible. A force that held the high ground around the valley enjoyed commanding views of all likely approaches and would have plenty of early warning to prepare for an attack.

For me, staring at those mountains was like staring at a gift horse. It reminded me of Montana. *In combat, once you recognize the patterns that inform the behavior of your enemy, you can adapt to them, and your enemy's toast.*

As we continued our long, slow drive back to the safe house, my mind raced ahead. To understand what was going on inside Shahi Khot we needed to put guys in the mountains. We had to get "eyes on the target." Our challenge was how to get close enough to confirm the enemy's presence without compromising the potential for a larger operation to destroy them.

Inside the dimly lit TOC that night, we brainstormed the dilemma. To "find 'em and destroy 'em" we would have to maintain the advantage of surprise. To the Unit guys who had worked with me on other battlefields, there was no surprise when I reiterated to everyone present that "there will be no direct helicopter infiltrations of AFO teams anywhere near the valley." There were plenty of helicopters flying around Afghanistan during that time; I just didn't want any going near Shahi Khot. If the AFO reconnaissance teams were going to get close enough to confirm the enemy's presence, they would have to do it without the enemy knowing they were there; they would have to do it the old-fashioned way, by walking through the mountains without being seen.

I had a personal "no heavy-lift helicopter" policy for any operation I was involved in. The historical pattern of failed missions and squandered opportunities in Vietnam, Iran, Somalia, and the "empty-target" raids, were deeply etched in my mind. Two common-denominator lessons linked all of them; first, the obvious: helicopters make it all but impossible to achieve surprise on an enemy-occupied target. The long-range *wap-wap* and *thumpity-thump* created by the turbo-powered heavy-lift rotors inevitably alert any and all enemy personnel occupying a target to the approaching heliborne assault force. After Somalia, every despot, drug kingpin, and dictator who had any reason to believe that the United States might be coming for him expected that when and if we actually came, we'd come in helicopters.[3] Imagine the hyperparanoid UBL sitting in the middle of nowhere in Afghanistan, hearing the distinctive Doppler-induced noise signature of multiple heavy-lift helicopters flying toward him. It wasn't likely that he was going to mistake or dismiss the sound as that of a wayward traffic helicopter that took a wrong turn in New York.

Second, I believed that operationally defaulting to the use of helicopters stymies any potential to discover the type of out-of-the-box creative options required for successfully accomplishing the most difficult missions. The art of war is the art of outthinking your enemy with strategies and tactics such as disguises, deception, diversions, and stealth. There are no shortcuts; you have to immerse yourself in the essence of the situation and imagine every possibility. At the opposite end of the spectrum is the medieval mindlessness of the head-on assault. Once it's decided that helicopters will be used to attack a target, there's no longer any perceived need to develop a high-resolution understanding of the enemy situation, and no need to develop out-of-the-box options to address them. Defaulting to helicopter-centric operations is an intellectual cop-out from a leader's responsibility as an artisan of the art of war. Planners spend all their time focusing on weather and fuel loads instead of whether the enemy posts a guard at night, or when the enemy gathers for their daily meals. Helicopters also usually end up becoming the end-all component of the mission; in other words, leaders end up making key decisions about the mission based solely on the capabilities and limitations of the helicopters instead of how to best take advantage of the enemy situation to accomplish the mission. A prime example is weather. Bad weather is the best time to attack a target; the enemy is usually buttoned up to stay warm or dry, and visibility is limited, which almost always favors our forces and our superior ability to operate in harsh conditions and limited visibility. But bad weather also means that the helicopters either can't fly or won't fly as well, so even if the enemy situation looks good, the decision is usually to postpone the operation until the weather improves. Helicopter-centric operations are the modern-day equivalent of the head-on assault, and history attests that head-on assaults usually result in mission failure. It's common sense to use your head instead.

Before we sent teams into the mountains to risk their lives for the actual mission, we needed to know how the environment affected their life-support equipment. We needed to conduct environmental recons. These were not practice runs. Years of recon training in the military, and years of long-range backpacking excursions while off-duty had taught me that every mountain environment is slightly different, and that it's the little things you have to overcome to master the mountains. We needed to see how far we could travel each night; what type of clothing we'd need to keep warm and dry; whether there were any water sources available; and in aggregate, whether it was even feasible to infiltrate through these barren inhospitable mountains without being detected.

To conduct the ultra-aggressive recons, I needed more men. Not just any men, mind you: there were only a handful of men on the planet who could attempt the kind of mission I had in mind and have any chance of succeeding. Luckily, I knew some of them personally; they were the same men I had commanded while walking through the mountains of Montana six months earlier. I figured that at least three teams of four or five men each would suffice. I called back to the Unit that night and gave the men a heads-up. "Start getting your stuff ready," I told one of them. "Do you have permission from the commanding general?" he asked with an air of heavy skepticism. "Not yet," I replied, "but I'm working on it."

In his seminal account of Operation Anaconda, *Not a Good Day to Die*, Sean Naylor describes AFO's higher headquarters during the early days of January:

> *It started the war as Task Force Sword, but by January had been renamed Task Force 11. Task Force 11 had only one goal: to kill or capture so-called "high-value targets" (HVTs), the phrase the U.S. military used to describe senior Al Qaeda and Taliban leaders. Reporting to TF 11 was a small organization that would soon have a major impact on the war. Called Advance Force Operations, or AFO, its mission was to conduct high-risk reconnaissance missions deep into enemy territory. AFO was not a standing organization back in*

the States, but rather a concept . . . that could draw personnel
from any special operations unit to meet a particular mis-
sion's requirements. . . . "The intent is to tailor the force for
the situation, so it's never quite the same, but it's always
small, it's always cross-functional, and it's always the best of
the best working in it," said an officer familiar with AFO.

As Naylor points out, AFO was only a tiny slice of TF 11. In early
January, the main body of TF 11, also known as the assault force,
consisted of the navy SEALs, Army Rangers, and a large armada of
special operations helicopters, all co-located at Bagram Air Base.

The commanding general of TF 11 had returned to the United
States immediately after the Tora Bora effort.[4] To act as his proxy in
country, he left his deputy commanding general (DCG), who was a
one-star air force general.[5] The DCG was a fervently religious officer,
who sported a tall gangly frame and a perfectly coiffed helmetlike
hairdo, which he constantly raked back with a purple plastic palm
comb he kept in his cargo pocket. With thousands of hours flying aircraft all over the globe, the DCG was an exceptionally experienced
special operations pilot. But with thousands of hours flying aircraft all
over the globe, he was also an exceptionally inexperienced special operations ground commander.[6] Without any firsthand experience in any
type of maneuver warfare, when it came to commanding a highly complex manhunt in an unforgiving environment such as Afghanistan, he
was the military equivalent of a caveman staring at a rocket ship.

But the DCG wasn't the architect of this quixotic command ar-
rangement; the Department of Defense assigned him to his position as
the second in command of our higher headquarters under the guise of
"jointness," and the commanding general appointed him to command
our task force in Afghanistan under the guise of dogma; the military's
rule of thumb in Afghanistan, was that no organization could operate
in country without a general officer commanding and controlling it.
With an open disposition and the right people around them, an ac-

complished leader can effectively lead just about any type of organiza-tion. Even without context-specific experience, a good leader can contribute by adding a perspective that looks at things through a fresh, untainted lens. But to do this effectively, a leader must possess some key traits, specifically openness, an adaptive approach to think-ing and making decisions, and constant deferral to the guy on the ground. By this point in the war on terror, I had gotten to know the DCG. He was a nice guy, but an accomplished leader he was not. As one of my comrades from the Unit had so sagely reflected, "My uncle's a construction worker—and a really nice guy—but I would never al-low him to command my men in a combat zone."

To assist the DCG in Afghanistan, he had a staff of more than a hundred men and women occupying a small operations center in Ba-gram, and a massive tactical operations center (TOC) a thousand miles away in the Persian Gulf.[7] These well-meaning and highly edu-cated military professionals worked long hours and with great passion to do whatever the DCG told them to do. With all the latest whiz-bang technology and massive databases and communications pipes at their disposal, there was a constant self-generated pressure to put all the technology to good use, to do something. Unfortunately, that some-thing was the unending creation of timelines, policies, and plans—the embalming fluid of organizational nimbleness. The unfortunate object of their bureaucratic embalming fluid was the TF 11 main-body—the SEALs and the Rangers.

Despite the obvious benefits of going where the enemy is located in order to hunt him down, and organizing special operations forces based on the mission and the environment, the commanding general had left strict orders to his staff on how the SEALs and the Rangers were supposed to conduct operations to accomplish their mission. As Naylor describes it:

Some in TF 11 were also unhappy with commanding general and DCG's concept for how the task force was to operate, which was to keep the direct action force . . . based intact at Bagram, waiting for intelligence . . . . to pinpoint a high-value target, at which point the door-kickers would launch on a raid to kill or capture the target. The hours required to fly from Bagram to the eastern provinces where bin Laden and the other senior enemy figures were probably hiding made some think it would have been better to divide the direct action force into smaller elements and push them out to safe houses in those provinces. "It became an unwieldy process," an operator said. "Most of the guys knew it wasn't the best way of operating. . . . You cannot fly in a helicopter in real time to a target from Bagram and have a high likelihood of killing or capturing someone. You have to be deployed forward."

Despite having two of our operational hands tied behind our backs, there was no wall-kicking frustration among my comrades and me. By this point in the War on Terror we were accustomed to the obstinacy and illogic of our organizational reality. *Don't attack the machine-gun nest, go around it.* We would have to adapt!

Although there were plenty of recon specialists in country, the most important task I had as the leader of AFO was to make sure I got the best people "on the bus" for this mission. To get approval, I flew back to Bagram for a video teleconference (VTC) with the DCG, who was in his tent in Masirah, and the commanding general, sitting in his office in North Carolina.[8] I was genuinely proud of what we'd accomplished thus far. I was confident that we had very likely found the general location of the enemy; now all we needed was a few good men so we could pinpoint their location for destruction.

The VTC was contentious; the commanding general openly scoffed at AFO's presumption that there was a large "pocket" of Al Qaeda fighters hiding out in the Shahi Khot Valley. From his office in North

Carolina, it just didn't make sense to him. But in the end, he begrudgingly approved two-thirds of my request for additional men. I would learn later that his skepticism of AFO's ability to find a "large pocket" of enemy was more than just operational; it was also personal. This quote in Sean Naylor's book from one of the general's most trusted confidants describes his perspective on our relationship:

> *"Their personalities are oil and water—they don't mix," said a JSOC officer who knew both men. "There's not a lot of love there."* . . . *[The commanding general] thought Blaber and his AFO troops in Gardez were exceeding their authority with their ambitious plans for the Shahikot and their close coordination with the CIA and, when they arrived, the conventional forces. The JSOC commander found this frustrating. . . . [T]he perception is that Pete Blaber is running the show and running amok," the JSOC officer said.*[9]

I was aware of the commanding general's personal animosity toward me. I was also aware that the independent role we had carved out by reorganizing and operating from our frontier outposts had some high-ranking staff officers at TF 11's Masirah headquarters referring to me as "Peter the Great" and "Colonel Kurtz" from the movie *Apocalypse Now*.[10] None of this gave me the least pause. I could understand why many of them were skeptical of what we were doing. This wasn't how they were trained to conduct military operations; to them it was surreal.

But I saw the skepticism and sarcasm as net positives, because it bought us time. I was convinced that it was far better to be doubted, mocked, and ignored than to be micromanaged. The technological and proximal isolation of the Gardez safe house greatly inhibited the generals in Masirah and North Carolina from interfering with our ability to be innovative, to be adaptive, and to be audacious.

February 14, 2002

Our recon specialists arrived via C-17 only forty-eight hours after I had requested them. All were from the same squadron I had commanded a year earlier. Coincidence? Perhaps! No strangers to Afghanistan, all had been in Afghanistan during the empty-target raid and had taken part in the first reconnaissance missions in and around Kandahar. I gathered all of them in our TOC in Gardez to explain our mission. Spider and some of the Special Forces guys also attended.

"Our mission is to develop the situation to find the enemy; to do this, we need to recon the routes around, and eventually into the interior of the Shahi Khot Valley. We're operating in the enemy's backyard, so we have to ensure we understand how he thinks. I want every man to read everything available about this area, talk to our Afghan allies about the enemy, and constantly ask yourselves, 'If I were the enemy, how would I defend this valley?'" Finally, I summed up my guidance to them by reiterating Patton's three principles of war: audacity, audacity, and audacity. I wasn't trying to give a Knute Rockne speech. That stuff doesn't really hold water with the type of mature warrior who made up AFO. Instead I was trying to underscore something I was just coming to grips with myself—that to be successful at developing the situation, you have to be audacious. Anyone can recognize a pattern; it's having the courage of your convictions to act on it that matters. Audacity isn't taking senseless risks, or being rash; it's a natural by-product of confidence and knowledge, and I was supremely confident in my people and in how much we knew about what was going on around us.

We divided our initial recon missions into two phases. The first phase consisted of vehicle recons. We considered the roads and trails around the valley as our enablers. These were the access corridors that would allow us to infiltrate, exfiltrate, and resupply our reconnaissance teams. Opening the roads would turn out to be the decisive point for us to execute our mission in Shahi Khot, in much the same way as slowing the vehicle down was the decisive point for us to execute our gorilla warfare mission in Bosnia.

The second phase was what we called our environmental recons, with two teams, one from the north and one from the south, probing the perimeter of, but not entering, the Shahi Khot Valley. Each team would establish an observation post in the mountains, and then return to Gardez to share lessons and prepare for the actual mission into the valley.

The newly arrived operators from the Unit organized themselves into two teams: India team and Juliet team. Juliet team was the larger of the two. Master Sergeant Kris K. led a team that totaled five men. Kris was from West Virginia, in his mid-thirties, and about five feet ten with a very athletic build. He was quiet and reserved, and his work reflected his demeanor: always precise and always thorough. Accompanying Kris were three other Unit members and an air force combat controller (CCT).

India team had only three men. Not the optimal number for a mission such as this one, but what they lacked in numbers, they more than made up for in skill and experience. The team leader was a thirty-six-year-old Kentuckian we called Speedy. He did everything—run, shoot, and talk—fast. Born and raised in rural western Kentucky, Speedy grew up in the woods. Legend had it he once shot an acorn out of a squirrel's paws—with a BB gun. Speedy's partner was a man I considered to be the poster child of a Delta operator. Bob was born, raised, and still longed to return to Austin, Texas.* He was as all-around fit as anyone in the Unit, and like Speedy, a world-class hunter who never came home from a hunt empty-handed.

---

*Bob was killed in action in Iraq on June 17, 2005. "Every man dies, but not every man truly lives." Bob truly lived, for family, for nation, and for the guys around him.

As I told Sean Naylor, "If you needed two men to track a chipmunk in a hundred-thousand-acre forest and kill it with one bullet, these were the two. Although two operators were less than I would have said were needed for a mission such as this, these two were living proof of why you never say never with regard to rules governing tactics. Having Speedy and Bob on a team together was like having Daniel Boone and Simon Kenton together in the frontier days—as hunters and athletes, they had no peer, anywhere."

The teams approached both phases of the recons with true entrepreneurial spirit—always pushing the envelope with a "whatever it takes" approach and a "nothing ventured, nothing gained" perspective on risk. To find their way, they did what successful explorers and entrepreneurs have always done: they experimented. They experimented with every conceivable method of movement—trucks, cars, horses, donkeys, and of course feet. You name it—they tried it. They tried different routes to get into and around the mountains. They tested different camouflage patterns, different night vision devices, and different weapons. Little by little the guys were developing the situation, and in the process figuring out exactly what they needed to accomplish their mission.

Most everything they came up with they came up with on their own. My job as the leader wasn't to try to tell them how to do their jobs; rather, it was to provide an environment that fostered experimentation, followed by thoughtful and honest reflection on what we learned and how we could apply it. As the leader of AFO, my most important task during this phase was to ensure that my men and I had time to develop the situation. *You have to make time to saturate, incubate, and illuminate.*

While the teams experimented, they read all the same books and papers that the rest of AFO had already read. The TOC was busy twenty hours a day. Most of us slept about four hours a night during that period—not because we were on any type of time schedule but because we couldn't lie down without a new idea popping into our heads. The saturate, incubate, illuminate cycle never ends. The teams never stopped preparing. They pored over maps and satellite photos to study the terrain and search for evidence of enemy activity. Our Afghan allies proved invaluable during this phase. The teams continuously bounced ideas off the Afghans, and tapped into their on-the-ground knowledge of the terrain, weather, and local populace.

During the environmental recons, both teams probed deep into the mountains under the worst possible conditions—driving snowstorms and ice storms combined with uncharted and unforgiving mountainous terrain. Harsh landscape and weather aside, the fact that we still didn't know how many enemy were out there, or where they actually were, never wandered far from any of our thoughts.

Within a week, we felt we had a high degree of familiarity with the lay of the land around the Shahi Khot. We had solid time/distance estimates for all the roads, and felt confident traveling on them as long as we stayed small, fast, and unobtrusive. With regard to the terrain, much like in Montana, we learned we could move up, over, and through the toughest of Afghan mountain terrain in one twenty-four-hour period. Also like Montana, we discovered that the hard-packed snow, which blanketed the mountains made it easier for us to move. The frostbite-inducing temperatures made it unlikely that our ill-equipped and ill-prepared adversaries would be out and about to bump into us. We had the finest cold-weather clothes, boots, and equipment that science and money could produce. The harsh weather and inhospitable conditions were definite advantages for us. But the more we learned about the vastness of the Shahi Khot Valley and surrounding mountains, the more we became convinced we needed another team.

While Jimmy was running things for AFO back at Bagram, my sidekick while I traveled the Afghan frontier and operated around Gardez was a wizened SEAL sniper, appropriately named Homer. A large lumbering man in his late thirties, Homer had long wavy black hair and a mad, triumphant smile. I rarely went anywhere without Homer. It's hard to describe how valuable a top-notch sidekick is for a leader in a combat zone. Homer's advice and counsel were nested in just about everything I did. "You're on the right track, you're smoking crack, let me and the guys handle that," all those little things that in aggregate, allowed me to maintain a cruising altitude where I could filter out the white noise of pride, prejudice, and politics and hone in on the key patterns that were essential for understanding what was going on around us. While Homer and I were checking on our Afghan guards late one night, he mentioned to me that some of his SEAL reconnaissance brethren were growing restless waiting for actionable intelligence back at Bagram. "They're chomping at the bit to get out of their barracks and into the hunt," Homer implored. The next day I contacted the SEAL commander at Bagram, and asked him for "however many reconnaissance men he could spare." Within hours he quietly sent us a five-man team. The team's call sign was Mako 31. Mako 31 was led by a lanky, good-natured SEAL named Mike, but known to most everyone simply by his diminutive Goody.

I continued to report everything our teams discovered from our recons and from our day-to-day interactions with the people on the frontier in a document we called the AFO commander's sit-rep.[11] It was our way of sharing everything we discovered each day, along with how each new discovery fit into the overall pattern of enemy activity in and around the Shahi Khot. Unbeknownst to me, these reports were also the first thing General Tommy Franks read each day back at his headquarters in Tampa. He would turn out to be a huge supporter of our entrepreneurial efforts, constantly lecturing subordinate generals that AFO was the most efficient and effective force he had on the ground in Afghanistan. Even though our own chain of command didn't believe our efforts would amount to anything, General Franks did. So he assigned the mission of destroying the enemy that he was now sure AFO was within days of pinpointing to the only conventional infantry unit in country, and they were more than willing to get in on the hunt.

On February 14, Major General Buster Hagenbeck and his 10th

Mountain Division staff assumed control of planning for what his staff would soon name: Operation Anaconda. Under General Hagenbeck were three battalions of U.S. conventional infantry, consisting of two battalions from the 3rd Brigade ("Rakkasans") of the 101st Airborne Division and one battalion—the 1st Battalion, 87th Regiment (1–87)—of the 10th Mountain Division.

General Hagenbeck assumed operational command of all American forces in Afghanistan, with just one exception: TF 11 and, by proxy, AFO. Despite the fact that we had no official command and control link to either General Hagenbeck or the 10th Mountain, I immediately moved Jimmy into the 10th Mountain TOC at Bagram, so we would be hardwired into his people and organization. Both Jimmy and I agreed that there was no sense in building this wealth of situational awareness without sharing it with the staff and commanders whose troops would be with us on the ground, fighting the enemy. So while I commanded AFO from Gardez, Jimmy ensured that everything we discovered was shared with General Hagenbeck and his staff. Jimmy also attended every important briefing and rehearsal that the 10th Mountain held. Critically, Jimmy occupied a table within arm's length and whisper range of General Hagenbeck. With a wall of tech gear in front of him, Jimmy was able to share everything AFO learned in real time by simply leaning back on his chair, putting his lips together, and you know the deal.

To officially kick off preparations for Operation Anaconda, a meeting was set up for all participating units' key leaders. The meeting took place at the Special Forces safe house in Kabul.[12] The goal for the meeting in Kabul was to get everyone on the same sheet of music. My personal intent was to share everything AFO had learned to this point, and to build a good enough shared vision of what was actually happening on the ground. I wanted to create a shared reality, not a plan.

To kick off the meeting, Glenn shared everything we knew about the enemy. All source intelligence led us to believe that there were between two hundred to a thousand enemy fighters in the valley. The terrain and weather were harsh, and the people in the area were precariously ambivalent.

Glenn was followed by a major who was serving as the operations officer for the infantry units from the 101st Airborne Division. The 101st is the army's only all-helicopter, all-the-time division. They were one of the first units to adopt the air-assault concept in the mid-'60s, which at the time was considered a revolution in military tactics and techniques. The air assault was first used in combat during the opening battle of the Vietnam War, the Battle of LZ X-ray, which was later made famous by the book *We Were Soldiers Once . . . and Young.*

The major didn't waste any words; he unabashedly announced to everyone in attendance that "the key to success here is the air assault [helicopter assault]. Throughout history the helicopter has struck fear in the enemy's heart. The psychological impact of helicopters full of troops descending suddenly out of the sky will unhinge the enemy fighters." With jaws agape, most of the special ops guys in the room just stared, waiting, hoping that maybe, just maybe, there was a punch line, but there was none. I knew the major from many years back when I was a Ranger. He was a fine infantry officer. I also understood that this was how he was trained: he believed what he was saying, it was his reality. The meeting ended like most meetings do, with a decision to meet again the next day.

The meeting took place at Bagram inside a tent that bizarrely was located inside a warehouse. Many of the same "players" were present for this meeting, but in the twenty or so hours that had passed since the "psychological impact of the helicopter" comments were made by the major, his recommendation to go helicopter-centric had calcified into "the plan." AFO's approach to preparing by developing the situation was colliding head-on with the Military Decision Making Process.

Standing in the back of the overcrowded tent, I listened to the same major brief, but this time he wasn't talking about a concept, he was talking about a plan. The 101st was advocating a daylight air assault into the valley. As he talked, a couple of leaders from the CIA and Special Forces who were standing next to me near the back of the tent leaned in close and implored me to share my perspectives on the enemy, the terrain, and the use of helicopters. "Maybe you can convince them of the error of their ways," they whispered. At the end of the briefing, the staff officer who was facilitating the meeting asked if there were any more questions. I strode up to the front of the tent, introduced myself, and began sharing everything I knew about the enemy, the terrain, and the environment in and around the Shahi Khot.

"What do you think of our plan?" the major interrupted.

I chose my words carefully. "Understand that because of the terrain and altitude, there are only two air corridors the helicopters can use to fly into the valley, and you should assume both will be covered by heavy weapons. Remember that every enemy on the planet expects the U.S. military to attack using helicopters; this enemy will be no different. The time it will take the large, lumbering Chinooks to brake, flare, hover, and then land will make you highly vulnerable to the enemy's antiaircraft weapons." As I finished up my eyes were drawn to one of the leaders in the front row whose head spastically rocked backward with narcoleptic indifference. *Like many leaders, he likely was burning the candle at both ends, and having a hard time adjusting to the vampire cycle of combat operations. The reality was that he didn't hear a thing I said; in actuality I hadn't shared anything with him. The planning continued.*

REALITY CHECK:

WHAT'S YOUR RECOMMENDATION?

THE ENEMY: *Our early presence in it gave us sufficient experience and much knowledge of it inside and out, its dangerous parts and the ways out of them, and allowed us to master their use—by the bounty of Allah the Most High—for our operations with the Americans when Allah caused us to encounter them in that area. Maulawi Jawad was Saif-ur-Rahman Mansoor's military commander for the duration of the previous phase of battles. He had been involved in preparing the bases and occupied with arranging and fixing ambushes. We planted land mines accurately in the main roads, which led to the village, and we set up heavy artillery on the surrounding mountain peaks.*

In the early days, we spent all our time preparing the area. Our numbers totaled 440 mujahideen in all, comprising 175 Afghan mujahideen from Saif-ur-Rahman Mansoor's group, 190 mujahideen from the Islamic Movement of Uzbekistan under the command of Qari Muhammad Tahir Jan (this was the largest group), and about 75 Arab mujahideen, the majority of whom had previous military knowledge and training."[1]

To ensure we stayed in sync with the 10th Mountain Division, Spider and I traveled from the Gardez safe house to Bagram once or twice each week to meet face-to-face with General Hagenbeck. Dressed in the half-Afghan, half-commando motif of scarves, chitrali hats, hip holsters, and long, unkempt hair and beards, we blended in well with the Afghans, but stood out like sore thumbs back at Bagram, where the desert utility uniform was all the rage.

By this point we had developed a solid relationship with General Hagenbeck. Based mostly on mutual respect, Spider and I admired the guy as both a general officer and as a person. He was a great listener and seemed to have a mission-first, people-first approach to every decision. He didn't always agree with what we had to say, but he was always willing to discuss and dive deeper in an attempt to come to a mutual understanding.

Although he technically had no formal authority over either of us, I didn't need a memo or an organizational line and block chart to tell me that I worked for him. He was the commanding general of all forces that were going to fight the battle, and I was the commander of the interagency reconnaissance effort—my information was his information.

I believed our boundary spanning to be nonnegotiable at this stage of preparation for the operation. I was going to send my men into the valley ahead of his troops, and both of our forces were going to be fighting the same enemy on the same chaotic battlefield. Lack of communication and coordination between our organizations would be a surefire recipe for fratricide and squandered opportunities. Unfortunately, my belief in the import of boundarylessness was not shared by my administrative higher headquarters.

Somehow, word of AFO's collaborative relationship with the CIA and General Hagenbeck got back to the TF 11 commanding general in North Carolina, and word on the street was that he was furious.[2]

Later that night, after returning to Gardez, I was talking with Speedy in the TOC when the satellite phone rang. It was a colonel from the TF 11 headquarters back in North Carolina.[3]

"Pete, the CG [commanding general] is really pissed at you. He thinks you're pushing the envelope by sending your guys into that valley, and it's infuriating him that you're working so closely with the 10th Mountain and CIA. He's talking about relieving you and bringing you home unless you stop."[4] I didn't respond; I couldn't respond; I was floored. *How much more bizarre could this get—up until this point I had been dealing with three major obstacles: the terrain, the weather, and the enemy. Now there were four.* I thanked the colonel for the heads-up (he was taking a huge career risk by calling me and sharing that information) and told him I needed time to think about what he said.

I hung up the receiver and walked outside. The road in front of the safe house was closed to vehicular traffic. We had two checkpoints manned by our Afghan allies; each checkpoint was positioned one and a half miles down the road in opposite directions from the safe house front door. With the ever-present howl of wild Afghan dogs in the distance, I buttoned up my collar, pulled my chitrali hat down over my ears, leaned westward into the wind, and started walking.

Even though it was freezing cold outside, I was smoking-hot pissed-off on the inside. As I walked, my emotions began to run rampant over my common sense. *What the hell does this guy got against me? What the hell did I do to piss him off? Screw him, screw me, screw this, screw that* was pretty much the upshot of my irrational and short-lived brooding. Time spent walking through the Afghan night was the best prescription to counteract and stabilize my emotionally plagued mind. The common sense of the 3Ms provided the cure.

What was my mission? I asked myself. Go out there and find 'em, then kill or capture 'em, was what General Franks told me. It also was what I was sure the American people and the president expected me and my men were risking our lives for. That was my mission, and we were doing the right things to accomplish it.

What was my responsibility to my men? Under my command in Gordez were three operational teams totaling thirteen men, seemingly paltry numbers by classical dismounted warfare standards, but they were thirteen of the finest warriors to have ever stepped foot on any battlefield. They had prepared their entire lives for a mission like this one. Over the past few weeks they had repeatedly risked their lives to develop the situation and the opportunities that now lay before us. We weren't in competition with the 10th Mountain or the CIA, and I never thought of them as separate organizations; I considered them as fellow Americans. To accomplish our common mission, we had to work with a common purpose, not at cross purposes. Those were the men, and I was sure I was doing the right thing by all of them.

As for me, I wondered what the opportunity cost would be if we didn't take advantage of this situation. We estimated that there were three hundred to a thousand enemy fighters occupying the same valley stronghold where the mujahideen had fought and defeated the Soviets just fifteen years earlier. The enemy was concentrated in one large—albeit difficult-to-access—location. How many of them were directly or indirectly involved in 9/11? How many future suicide bombers could we kill or capture now, while they were clustered together in the Afghan mountains, before they had an opportunity to disperse across the globe and kill innocent civilians in the future?

By refocusing on the mission and the men, and leaving the *me* out of the equation, I was able to view the overall situation from an altitude that allowed me to understand the key underlying patterns through the unemotional lens of common sense.

I vowed I wouldn't waste another precious second worrying about why the commanding general disliked me, or whether he would relieve me from my command and destroy my career. Operationally pushing the envelope and closely coordinating with General Hagenbeck and the CIA were the right things for the mission, the right things for my men, and (as an American citizen) the right thing for me. I had a mission to accomplish, and the men were waiting.

February 26

In the small windowless rooms below the towers, the three AFO teams conducted final preparations for their infiltrations. The teams pored over maps and imagery of their routes and objectives in an

attempt to collaboratively update what they already knew, and cor-
roboratively refine what they still needed to know. Not a single Power-
Point slide was ever shown, there were no VTCs, and there was no
traditional plan.

Later that day, a thin, unkempt Afghan male, with dust on his
face, an AK-47 on his back, and a chip on his shoulder, walked up to
one of our checkpoints and requested to "talk with the Americans."[5]
The individual professed to be a Taliban squad leader with thirteen
soldiers in his squad. He estimated there were somewhere between
580 and 700 enemy in the Shahi Khot Valley, occupying fighting positions in the mountains. He explained that the fighters came down
only to get food, which was delivered daily by couriers from a nearby
town. When asked about his motivation for telling us the information,
he explained that it was because he was fed up with the way the foreign Al Qaeda fighters treated the Afghans. "Like we are dogs," he
explained. The enemy segregated itself into three tiers, with Al Qaeda
(foreign Arabs) on top, Uzbeks and Chechens in the middle, and Afghan Taliban on the bottom. A caste system of sorts, where the Arab
fighters actually forbade the Taliban from speaking directly to them.[6]
*A rigid hierarchy, no communication, no shared reality, we're in busi-
ness,* I thought.

Sunrise, February 27
The teams were now ready. All of AFO gathered in the Gardez TOC.
A vicious blizzard howled outside, the wind pounding the loose plastic on the windows with every blow. It was really cold, so everyone
migrated toward the potbellied stove in the center of the room. Spider
and many of the Special Forces leaders along with the overall Afghan
commander also were present. Each team shared the details of their
mission—their routes, their observation post (OP) locations, the equipment they would carry, their communications information, and anything else they could think of.

Everyone in the room had the opportunity to ask questions and provide advice. The Afghan commander opined that avoiding contact with civilians was likely our toughest challenge for remaining undetected during infiltration. "Whenever possible, avoid contact. If they get only a brief look at you, they will be unsure of themselves, and it may be days before they come in contact with anyone to tell. But if they see you face-to-face, they will likely feel they have to report you for fear of Taliban retribution," he explained in broken English. We took his commonsense advice to heart. All the teams added clothing accessories that helped disguise their non-Afghan profiles when viewed from afar, or from cursory glances closer up. The teams never stopped adjusting and refining their concepts; for AFO, the window for good ideas never closed.

Juliet team (five men) would infiltrate from the north and occupy the high ground on the east side of the valley (see Map 5). They would not be walking. After hundreds of hours of experimenting and studying the northern approaches to the Shahi Khot, Kris K. and his team came up with a novel idea for their infiltration—the use of all-terrain vehicles (ATVs), to penetrate the valley and climb up the eastern ridge.[7] But these were not your run-of-the-mill ATVs; they were specially modified by the Unit mechanics. Engines and suspensions were beefed up, and superquiet mufflers were the standard. Juliet team would be riding into battle on four-wheeled chariots.

India team (three men) would walk into the valley from the west and occupy the high ground in the southwestern portion of the valley. They would overwatch the main enemy (and friendly) avenue of approach into the valley, which was shaped like and appropriately named the fishhook.

Mako 31 (five men) would move along the route that India team reconnoitered during their environmental recon, to a spot that all of us believed to be the key piece of terrain in the valley. Called the finger, it was on the southern edge of the valley, and jutted northward like a dagger at the heart of the valley. If you controlled the finger, you could control the entire valley (see Map 5).

When occupied, we believed these three positions would provide us with an eagle-eye view of the entire valley; and collectively allow us to see the entire battlefield.

After all three teams had shared their concepts, I gave them a quick recap of my expectations. We had three primary tasks: to confirm or deny the presence of the enemy; to check that the helicopter landing zones were clear for the 10th Mountain troops; and to destroy or capture the enemy. While I talked, I looked into the eyes of each man and sensed that this might have been the first time that some of them grasped the collective audacity of what they were about to carry out. Sneaking up and over ten-thousand-foot snow-covered mountains into a valley occupied by three hundred to a thousand hard-core enemy fighters without being detected hadn't been attempted too many times before in the history of modern-day combat, so they definitely had reason to be reflective. Most of the guys were also still a bit skeptical that we were actually going to get final approval for the mission. Like me, they had all been through a lot of mission preparations that went right up to the threshold of execution before someone lost his nerve and called the whole thing off. "Guys," I told them, "at this point we're not waiting for permission; we're going in tomorrow night. The mission's a go."

Afterward, I walked outside with Speedy. As so often happened in Gardez, the weather changed 180 degrees in minutes. The sky was now clear, the moon was full, and its reflective glow off the surrounding snow-covered mountains made it seem like daylight in a black-and-white movie. With one of his signature sarcastic smiles creeping onto his face, Speedy spoke first. "Sir, now I know for sure you don't really care whether I live or die." I smiled back and replied, "Speedy, your dying is none of my concern. It's not that I don't care, it's just that I know how good you are, so I don't have to worry about you dying. You're uniquely qualified to execute this mission. This is your destiny." We shook hands in the moonlight; then Speedy turned and headed back to his tent. "Thanks, sir!" he yelled over his shoulder. "For what?" I yelled back. "For letting me fulfill my destiny." I couldn't tell if he was being sincere, sarcastic, or both.

Next I headed over to see if Goody had any final issues or questions. I wanted to make sure I reinforced to him how important I believed his mission was. Since Goody and his SEALs were late arrivals, they hadn't had time to participate in the environmental recons with the other two teams. But Goody had done a great job of tapping into the other teams' knowledge and lessons, and he had read all the context-rich information that the rest of us had. He and his team were in the courtyard conducting final precombat checks: test-firing weapons, conducting radio checks, and ripping apart their backpacks one last time to see if they could find any weight savings.

"So what do you think?" I asked him. "Sir, this is one hell of a mission. I really appreciate you bringing us out here to be a part of it." "Hey, I'm really glad you're here," I told him. Then I nudged his shoulder to ensure that he was looking at me. "Goody, the success or failure of your mission will predicate the success or failure of the entire operation; you have to make it to that OP [observation post] before H-hour." Goody didn't flinch; it seemed like he had already internalized how critical his OP was to the overall mission. He responded with the courage and candor of a true warrior. "Sir, I'll make it to my OP come hell or high water, if we're hurting on time, we'll drop our rucks. If we're still having problems, we'll keep dropping gear until five naked guys with guns are standing on the OP at H-hour." *Where do we get such men?* I thought as Goody went back to his precombat checks. As I walked away, Goody yelled to me, "Hey, sir, do you think I should take a camera with me?" "What's your recommendation?" I responded. "Well, if we find some critical intelligence that's important to the rest of the force, I always figure a picture is worth a thousand words, so I think we should take it." He didn't need me to affirm his rationale; he was already stuffing the camera back into his backpack. "Hey, Panther," he added, "just make sure those 10th Mountain guys know we're up there." Like the rest of us, Goody was worried about the high potential for fratricide.

The 10th Mountain plan was based on the classic military "hammer and anvil" maneuver. The Special Forces in Gardez (the hammer) would lead a truck convoy of Afghans from our safe house to the fishhook (see Map 5) and enter the Shahi Khot Valley from the west to clear the western portion of the valley. Planners believed this maneuver would cause the enemy to flee east—into the anvil. The responsibility for the anvil went to the soldiers from the 101st and 10th Mountain, who would fly into the valley on CH-47s, and land on eastern sections of the valley floor.*

The plan didn't make much sense to a lot of the participants, especially the Special Forces. With well over four hundred Afghans they had the biggest force on the battlefield, and had the most to lose if any of the complex intricacies of the plan, such as the timing or the location of the CH-47 landings didn't occur exactly when and where they were supposed to. An anvil is by nature supposed to be solid, yet the plan for the positioning of the anvil seemed quite porous. There was a lot of derision back at Bagram between leaders of the Special Forces and the 101st over the plan, but I couldn't worry too much about what was out of AFO's control. I figured that as long as the three AFO teams got into position to dominate the valley from the key terrain, we could buy time for the troops on the ground until they got it right.

---

*The CH-47 is a twin-engine, tandem-rotor helicopter designed for transportation of cargo, troops, and weapons during day or night. The aircraft fuselage is approximately fifty feet long. With a sixty-foot rotor span on each rotor system, the effective length of a CH-47 (with blades turning) is approximately one hundred feet from the most forward point of the forward rotor to the most rearward point on the aft rotor. Maximum airspeed is 196 miles per hour.

Sundown, February 27, 2002

On the road in front of the safe house, the three teams prepared to move out. Two Toyota 4x4 trucks, driven by five AFO members would carry India and Mako 31 teams to their drop-off points south of the valley. Lined up behind the Toyotas were the four ATVs, on which the five members of Juliet team would ride into battle (one ATV would carry two men). Up in the air, prowling the teams' routes ahead of them was an armada of pilotless surveillance aircraft that beamed their images back to our TOC and many others around the globe.

Seconds after darkness won its nightly duel with light, I watched through my night-vision goggles as the convoy slowly rolled away from the safe house and headed southeast toward the mountains surrounding Shahi Khot. Within seconds Juliet team split off from the convoy and headed overland to proceed with their infiltration.

With night-vision goggles on their heads and ATVs beneath their hinds, they used GPS navigation devices strapped to the gas tank between their legs, to pick their way through the hardscrabble and deeply rutted terrain along their route. The radio headset each man wore allowed him the option of talking to his teammates, talking directly with the surveillance aircraft flying overhead, or talking with me and Glenn back in Gardez. Even though their original route had them circumnavigating all human-occupied areas, the canalized terrain left them with no choice but to drive smack through the middle of the tiny enemy-occupied town of Menewar (see Map 5). The superquiet mufflers and their 20/20 night vision capability allowed them to surgically pick their way through the town with only a few dogs detecting their presence. Outside the town they broke into the gently ascending slopes of the Shahi Khot Mountains. The team passed through an enemy minefield, underneath an enemy-occupied heavy machine-gun position, and up the side of the eastern wall of the valley. Their first-choice observation post (OP) didn't have sufficient cover and concealment, despite what the map and satellite photo had portrayed, so they continued moving south along the ridge toward their alternate OP, which they found to their mission-oriented liking.

At 4:45 A.M., Kris called me: "Juliet team is in position."

South of the valley, two 4x4 pickup trucks approached India and Mako 31's drop-off position with lights off, night-vision goggles on, and guns up. As soon as the vehicles stopped, members of India and Mako 31 unloaded in slow motion, taking great care to prevent any hard object from clanging against the metal cab of the vehicle. Once unloaded, the men silently slung their backpacks over their shoulders, tightened their straps down as tight as their biceps allowed, and began their stealthy treks upward into the mountains.

After a kilometer of moving together, the teams split toward their individual OPs. India team's route was short and steep; a seven-kilometer movement seemed like park strolling compared to the "into thin air" movement they made during their environmental recon, just three days earlier. At 10,500 feet, India's team of three stopped just short of the edge of the cliff. All three India team members laid down flat to avoid being silhouetted from below. After unshouldering his ruck, Bob H. scootched forward on his belly. He stopped behind a small pile of rubble. Canting his head slowly, he spied the valley below. His eyes and ears strained to detect any unnatural noise or movement; Bob was focused, like a man whose finely tuned autonomic nervous system is programmed to maintain perfect equilibrium between the thrill of the hunt and the thrill of the chase. Bob understood his status as both the hunter and the hunted. He liked it that way. If you could have peered back through his thermal scope, you would have seen an unmistakable gleam in his eyes—it was the gleam of pure, unadulterated courage. Courage has been called a contradiction in terms, meaning a strong desire to live manifest as a readiness to die. It described Bob and his mates to a tee.

From their perch, India team could directly overwatch the fishhook as well as the southern end of Tergal Ghar. They were in position to cover the route that the Special Forces and Afghans planned to use to enter the valley. As was so often the case, India team confirmed to their toughest critics—themselves—that they had chosen their position well.

At 5:22 A.M., Speedy radioed me with a simple message: "India Team is in."[8]

After breaking away from India, Goody and his team of five plodded upward. Snow, rain, and fierce winds swept the ridgeline in waves. Sometimes misery comes with an asterisk. It's much easier for men to tolerate the unrelenting hell of wet-cold, when they understand it also provides them with a hell of an advantage over the enemy. Although the weather treats both sides with equal disdain, in this case, the weather definitely favored the attackers. The enemy guards standing watch around the valley were confined to the abridged time-distance umbilical cord of their shelters or warming fires, which meant they wouldn't be out checking the perimeter for potential Goodys or Bobs.

Goody coaxed his men onward. Despite their best efforts, as light began to peek over the mountains, Goody realized he would not have sufficient cover of darkness to reach his OP before daylight. The final portion of his route required tortoiselike movements and surgical care to avoid detection by the enemy. Goody stopped the team a thousand meters from the OP. At 5:15 A.M. Goody called me and passed both his location and his intention of staying still until the next night. It would turn out to be a sagacious decision.

Sunrise, February 28

Throughout the night Juliet team methodically trolled the surrounding valley with their thermal night sights, catching numerous enemy while they moved around their well-concealed fighting positions. They immediately went to work pinpointing and plotting the locations. As the sun rose, Kris and team carefully studied the Tergal Ghar ridgeline with their high-power spotting scopes. Their assessment: Tergal Ghar was infested with enemy fighting positions. After five or six separate reports, he called me on the satellite radio and summarized, "The enemy is everywhere."

At about midday, Juliet team alerted to the sound of snow-crunching footsteps approaching their OP from behind. With cheeks melded to their M-4 stock-welds, the entire team watched as four fast-talking enemy fighters, carrying their RPGs and AK-47s like luggage, walked directly in front of their position and stopped. The enemy stared at the ATV tracks in the snow. While Kris watched the drama unfold from his well-concealed nook on the boulder-strewn cliff, he steadied his team. Then, using the slow, deliberate whisper of a man within spitting distance of the enemy, he contacted me on the radio and asked, "What do you want me to do?"

"What's your recommendation?" I whispered back.

"Well, if we kill 'em now, the whole valley will know we're up here, and we'll lose the element of surprise. Let me see what they do next. I'll call you back."

While literally scratching their turbans in complete befuddlement, they appeared to be discussing the same question. Mother Nature made up their minds for them with gale-force winds and thick, eye-poking snowflakes. The four fighters ducked their snow-caked beards into their coats and continued on their fast-talking way down toward the valley.

Kris called me and described the situation. "They didn't seem that interested, almost like they were too busy, or had to be somewhere."

Then he added, "We've plotted the grid for the cave entrance they walked out of and will coordinate a bombing mission on it at H-hour." For the four enemy fighters, it was not a good day to die.

I sent a summary of Juliet team's reports to all other units involved in the operation. I ended the message with three words: *We're in business.*

THE ENEMY: *The snowfall upon the area intensified until it was entirely covered, which delayed the time of battle we had scheduled. We took* *advantage of the fact that it was Eid* and we spent the day in renewing our resolves, preaching to one another, and praying for victory or martyr-dom. The Uzbek mujahideen also held a big party, which was attended by most of the mujahideen in the area.*

Sundown, February 28

When night returned, Goody and his team began methodically sloth-ing their way through the rocks toward their OP. Once again, the treacherous weather befriended them. Thick snowflakes mixed with fog erased their image from sight of any eyes more than a few feet distant. Six hours hence, Goody called and reported he had stopped a few hundred meters short of the OP.

A few moments later I received word from Jimmy that H-hour (the scheduled start time for the 10th Mountain attack) was delayed twenty-four hours. "Why?" I asked. "The bad weather made it too risky for the helicopters to fly," Jimmy replied. Once again, the capability and limitations of helicopters, instead of the enemy situation on the ground, were driving the operational decision-making. H-hour was now set for March 2, at 6:30 A.M. Although less than thirty hours away, it was thirty additional hours that the three AFO teams would need to re-main undetected from the enemy while expending another day's worth of life-sustaining battery power and water in the process.

Dawn, March 1

Despite the reassurances that "every available satellite and sensor" was focused on the valley the week prior, none of the satellites or spy planes that scoped the area had detected or revealed any enemy activ-ity or weapons in the mountains around the Shahi Khot.[9] The techno-logical all-clear further convinced some leaders back in the States that

---

*Eid ul-Fitr or Id-Ul-Fitr, often abbreviated to Eid, is a Muslim holiday that marks the end of Ramadan, the Islamic holy month of fasting.

it made no sense to risk men's lives conducting long-range infiltrations through the mountains in inclement weather. After all, the most technologically advanced surveillance sensors had produced pictures that proved there were no enemy and no weapons to be found. The sit-reps from Juliet team already told us they were wrong, Goody and his team were about to prove it.

Much like in Vietnam, the enemy's use of low-tech guile in the form of camouflage tarps and face-to-face communication was proving to be an able match for the highest of our high technology. The military and civilian technocrats back home didn't understand that you can't enforce Moore's Law* on a jurisdiction such as Afghanistan: Hajji don't play that game.

Worming their way forward, the SEAL snipers spotted movement. There, just fifty meters in front of them, casually strolling around the rock cliff at the end of the finger, was a clean-shaven enemy fighter with reddish-brown hair, camouflage pants, and a Gore-Tex jacket. Off to his right was a large tent, too large for a single man. A small pipe protruded from the tent top venting smoke from what was likely a heating and cooking stove. The snipers scanned back to the left; there, on the tip of the finger, the exact spot we had designated as key terrain in the valley, stood a tripod-mounted DShK antiaircraft weapon. With ammunition loaded and stacked to the side for immediate reload, the heavy machine gun was perfectly oriented toward the main helicopter infiltration corridor through which the lumbering helicopters planned to fly at sunrise.

The SEAL snipers steadied their handheld digital camera to capture clear pictures of both the DShK and the enemy fighter. They then wormed backward to their hidden cove in the rocks.

Goody worked with the sense of urgency driven by the under-

---

*Generally refers to the unrelenting advancement of technology and computing power and the resultant ability to do more with less.

standing that he had life-or-death information that needed sharing. Blowing on his exposed fingers to make them nimble, he pulled out his Libretto mini-laptop computer, and connected it via a USB port to his satellite radio. He then downloaded and labeled the photos "AFO commander eyes only." He sent the photos to me a minute later. The label Goody chose was meant to connote the "stop the presses" importance of the pictures. He knew these three or four pictures captured a reality that up until that moment had only existed in the heads of the men in the Gardez safe house.

I forwarded the photos to Jimmy so he could share them with General Hagenbeck and his staff. I also attached a note underscoring that the fighters seen by Mako 31, India, and Juliet were well armed, on the high ground, and ready to fight. Then I added, "The three AFO teams are now occupying dominant terrain and are a few hours away from being in position to control the entire valley."

Because Goody was within whisper range of the enemy, he used secure text messaging to discuss the situation with me:

Goody: What do you want me to do about the enemy?

Me: What's your recommendation?

Goody (long pause): I want to make sure we maintain the element of surprise as close to H-hour as possible. I will wait until H minus two [hours]. At H minus two I will start moving; that will allow me to take my time getting in position. I'll engage at H minus one, and then follow up with AC-130.

He then sent a follow-up message: I understand that you have to make the decision on this and I'll support any decision you make.

I sent him a two-word reply: "Good hunting."

Goody would later tell me how relieved he was to get my response. He was worried that someone higher in the TF 11 chain of command would disapprove of his recommendation to take out the enemy OP because Mako 31 was a reconnaissance team, not an assault team.[10] As it turned out, he was right. The message I sent with the pictures attached caused quite a bit of anxiety at Masirah. E-mails bounced back and forth advising that AFO should not jump to conclusions that this was the enemy, and that Mako 31 did not have the sufficient amount of men to attack the position, or the doctrinal authority to conduct a direct action mission. None of those staff officers fully understood AFO's mission, AFO's men, or me!

A few minutes later I sent Goody his mission statement.

"Terminate with extreme prejudice."

"Aye aye," Goody responded, using his Navy vernacular.*

With each new report of enemy activity and each interactive communication among the teams, I was learning that commanding a mission such as this one required a delicate balance between asking and telling, and between working with and working for my men. As the central gatekeeper of information to and from the teams, I may have had the best-aggregated understanding of what was going on all around the valley, but my understanding of what was going on in front of each team was dated by the time the descriptive words left their mouths. I could never understand the reality on the ground in front of each of the teams as well as they could. That's reality, and coming to grips with it was empowering. The success or failure of our mission depended on their ability to execute; my job as the commander was to make sure they had everything they needed to make it happen.

Both Goody and Kris had asked me for guidance concerning the life-and-death situations confronting their teams. My response in both situations was the question "What's your recommendation?" While listening to their responses, I discovered that once the man on the ground begins describing the situation in front of him, he almost always ends up revealing the solution nested within his description. For AFO, the primary purpose of the radio wasn't command and control; it was to network ideas and insights and create a shared reality.

---

*In the navy, *Aye aye* means, "I understand the order and I will carry out the order." The army uses the term *Roger* to convey the same thing.

While Goody and his men laid in wait a few feet from the DShK position, India and Juliet continued scrolling their prying eyes across the valley. As the day wore on, their reports of enemy activity continued to pile up. They grew concerned.

"I would highly recommend against landing on the valley floor," India team said.

"If they land as planned, they'll be pinned down, and there's no way we'll be able to prevent them [the enemy] from escaping," Juliet advised.

The plan was based on the supposition that the Afghans and Special Forces would flush the enemy from the villages, directly into the air assault–enabled blocking positions. But the reality in the valley was that the enemy was dug in on the high ground, not the low, and they appeared ready to fight, not to flee. If the infantry landed on the valley floor, the only thing they would end up flushing was the plan.

Jimmy passed everything the teams reported, along with AFO's recommendations concerning the plan, to the mountain staff. Nothing changed. So Jimmy gathered up all the pictures and reports and laid them out for General Hagenbeck's chief of staff (a full colonel). "Sir, do not land those helicopters [there]," Jimmy pleaded while pointing at the valley floor. "The current plan is not going to work out for you." The chief of staff replied apologetically, "I know, Jim, but it's too late to do anything about it."

Authors of the plan at Bagram would later explain that it was unreasonable to expect wholesale changes because writing the plan had been such a painful process of compromise and negotiation that nobody could face the prospect of tearing it up—or even significantly modifying it at the eleventh hour simply because the enemy might not be where they were supposed to be.

Jimmy called me back with the sobering news. "They say it's too late to change it; they're still planning to land on the valley floor."

I stepped outside into the courtyard and realized that once again the tyranny of the plan was trumping updated information from the man on the ground and its by-product, common sense. There was no way to turn the planning machine off, and there was no way to alter its course. Even though we had updated information, the plan was the plan, and the staff had put so much work into putting it together that the mission itself no longer had anything to do with the reality on the ground; the mission was to execute the plan on time.

To me that moment perfectly summed up the futility of traditional planning versus the utility of developing the situation. By pledging their allegiance to the plan, the 10th Mountain had inadvertently surrendered their freedom of choice. As a result, the entire force was operationally incarcerated in the prison of the plan, and this plan appeared to be escape proof.

THE ENEMY: *"The traitors and their American allies are going to attack soon, we need to bring reinforcements to the village."*

"There is no need," Maulawi Saif-ur-Rahman Nasrullah Mansoor responded. *"We were in Shahi Koht during the first Afghan jihad [against the Soviets]. There were six mujahideen in total and we were surrounded by ten tanks. Over five air attacks were staged on us in a single day and there were about one hundred Soviet soldiers who attacked us from the land. But all Praise belongs to Allah alone—they were not able to set foot on a single hand-span of the village, and we remained in this same state for about one week."* (These were the words by which Maulawi Saif-ur-Rahman Nasrullah Mansoor responded, when asked about the possibility of increasing the reinforcements for the village, to prepare for the anticipated American attack.)

Ignoring the advice from his foot soldiers on the ground, the enemy commander was adamant that there was no need for reinforcements. Mansoor had fought under Haqqani when they defeated the Soviets on this very ground, so he was confident. The harsh terrain and the inhospitable weather would surely allow him to defeat the lesser "creatures of comfort" Americans. That was Mansoor's reality, and he made it clear that he wasn't going to change his mind, no matter what his men advised. With his decision, the enemy fighters inside the Shahi Khot were also operationally incarcerated; along with their commander, they were prisoners of precedent.

18

THE BATTLE BEGINS:

STAY CALM, THINK!

Sundown, March 1

The convoy of trucks that would carry our Afghan allies into battle lined up on the road outside the Gardez safe house. I watched from my perch in the northeast watchtower as four hundred Afghans attempted to assemble into a "Westernized" version of a military formation. There was something odd about the scene. This was not how the Afghans were used to organizing themselves. After a few minutes of futility, someone screamed something in Pashto, and they all raced toward their assigned trucks. Like a circus clown car in reverse, four hundred Afghan soldiers, each with his own weapon and pack, stuffed himself into the eight dilapidated "jinga" trucks.* With the temperatures diving into the midtwenties, the Afghans likely appreciated their sardine-like predicament for the warmth it would provide during the expected

---

*Jinga trucks are flatbed vehicles about the size of a dump truck, painted with intricate patterns and bright colors. They get their name from the chimes that dangle and jingle from the base of the vehicle whenever it moves.

two-hour journey down the lunar landscape road that led to the Shahi Khot (see Map 5).

Just before midnight, one of the top-heavy jinga trucks caromed off a crater and tumbled onto its side. Seven Afghans were wounded, one critically. Men were screaming, the road was blocked, and the convoy fell behind schedule. Two more trucks would tumble before the convoy reached the valley. The insidious effects of battlefield friction were beginning to take their toll on the Afghan soldiers and their Special Forces advisors, and they had yet to encounter a single enemy.

A few ticks after midnight (it was now March 2), Goody assessed that the time was right to start moving into position. With two men in overwatch, Goody and another sniper crept forward. Goody was cautious. His concern was with the unpredictability of the human animal. You can never predict when someone will decide to get up and go out to stretch his legs, or seek out a place where he can be alone, or to find a spot to relieve himself. With this fact in mind, although still hours before he expected to initiate his assault, Goody coordinated with an AC-130 gunship flying high overhead to cover his movement. Just in case!

At exactly 4:00 A.M., just as Goody expected, the unexpected occurred. One of the enemy fighters burst out of the tent in search of a spot to relieve his bladder. As he meandered purposefully through the rocks, his path took him directly toward the stock-still snipers. Whether he caught sight of the Americans or whether his senses naturally alerted him to something unnatural, no one will ever know. Luckily for the team, his emotions betrayed his common sense: he panicked. As if on fire, he ran screaming toward the tent to alert his sleeping comrades. Goody chose to open fire, and with his feather-light touch to the trigger of his M-4, he fired the opening shots of Operation Anaconda. Within minutes, three of the five enemy were dead; two others clawed and crawled toward the valley. As Goody pulled back, the AC-130 took over and used its precision optics and lethality to stop their crawl.

Goody called me. "Mission accomplished. Position terminated with extreme prejudice."

"Good job," I responded. "Any intel?" Goody located one of the fighters' journals; inside was the fighter's commentary on the enemy's day-by-day activities leading up to the battle. It also contained an encyclopedia of terrorist tactics and tricks, which included highly detailed sketches and formulas for booby traps, bombs, and bombers. The one chapter it didn't have was how to defend against Americans who infiltrate over eleven-thousand-foot peaks.

All three AFO teams were now in position to dominate the valley.

Sitting in the Gardez TOC, I pulled out the interview article from Haqqani. *Don't believe everything you hear about Americans being creatures of comfort, Mr. Haqqani. It's not reality!*

THE ENEMY: *At midnight on Saturday, the airplane activity upon the village increased, which caused some brothers to anticipate a near attack. No sooner did the clock strike four in the morning, than the air attacks began on the area, especially the peaks surrounding the village. I asked the brothers to head for their assigned areas, behind the village, and I myself remained with the group to take care of some necessary matters and then followed them when the situation permitted me to do so. During this time, the bombardment had increased greatly and was repeated in more than one area, and no sooner had I prayed the morning Fajr prayer with the brothers who remained with me, than we began to see helicopters hovering above us. There were many of them—more than twenty aircraft in total, including the fighter planes.*

D-Day, March 2

There were no self-congratulatory high fives among AFO or anyone else in the safe house in Gardez. For the next two and a half hours, it was thirteen against 450. All AFO members were engaged in a continuous cycle of locating, marking, and destroying enemy targets inside the valley, while maintaining a hyperalert security status for enemy fighters trying to do the same to them. Minutes after Mako 31 stole their OP from the enemy fighters, our Special Forces and Afghan brethren were victims of a friendly fire incident involving the same AC-130 that supported Mako 31's assault. The toll was tragic: four U.S. and Afghan vehicles destroyed, three killed (one American, two Afghans), and seven wounded.[1]

As the remaining Special Forces and Afghan soldiers loaded their dead and wounded on an evacuation helicopter, enemy mortars fired from the top of Tergal Ghar slammed into the earth around them like explosive exclamation points (see Map 5). Demoralized from three vehicle rollovers and the AC-130 friendly fire incident, many of the Afghans simply dropped their weapons and began walking north, on the road back to Gardez. Exposing themselves to enemy fire, Chris H. and his men attempted to herd individual Afghans into groups where they could coax and coddle them to hang in there and stay the course, but the Afghans had collectively had enough. Chris called me to share his fatalistic assessment: "We've tried everything. They say they're done." A minute later Chris added, "We're heading back to the Gardez safe house."

The hammer was broken.

On the other side of Tergal Ghar, the first CH-47s began touching down on the snow-carpeted valley floor. As the men ran out the backs of the helicopters they were greeted by a hailstorm of enemy mortar and machine-gun fire. Between twelve and seventeen soldiers were wounded within the first few minutes of landing. The anvil was getting hammered.

Jimmy called and informed me that General Hagenbeck and his staff had decided to call off the second wave of helicopters. The combination of enemy mortar and machine-gun fire, worsening weather, and the need to evacuate the wounded drove their decision. Just a few hours into the start of Operation Anaconda, General Hagenbeck and his staff were forced to focus all available resources toward evacuating the wounded and moving the few troops who had made it into the valley out of the enemy's kill zone.

The Chinese symbol for crisis is "danger-opportunity,"* which roughly translates to "without the danger there cannot arise the opportunity."[2] In the midst of the 10th Mountain crisis, pinned down on the valley floor, and in danger of destruction from an enemy who outnumbered and outpositioned them, a bountiful opportunity arose for AFO.

THE ENEMY: *The fact was that the village of Shahi Khot—despite having expanses of land on all sides—was completely surrounded by a group of high mountains, which brought the element of coldness to the area, and so was very rarely bare of snow.*

After about an hour of continuous circling over the village and its surroundings, the American troops were dropped by parachute from the planes on three locations. The first drop was on the primary area that fell on the peaks of the overlooking mountains at the entrance of the valley that leads to the rear bases, where they were faced by the brothers who had left us. They were about ten Arab brothers under the command of Brother Ghazi, who affiliated with two groups that were centralized on one of the peaks that was opposite that of the airdrop. The two groups were composed of Uzbek and Afghan brothers.

We had some rear bases that had been established to protect the village and that were reached via a long valley surrounded by the lofty mountains. These bases are the ones that we used when we encircled the American airdrops from behind, such that the enemy fell in the clutches of those who surrounded them on one hand, and those who were stationed in the village on the other. By the Grace of Allah alone, we were able to inflict great losses on the enemy ranks through these tactics.

The enemy forces around the valley likely could not believe their good fortune. The Americans had landed their helicopters on the val-

*(危機)

ley floor and in full view of the fighters dug in on the high ground surrounding the valley. However, as was so often the case during the battle, distance mattered. The Shahi Khot Valley is expansive. The maximum effective range of the enemy's AK-47 rifles was three hundred to four hundred meters. To kill the vulnerable Americans on the valley floor, they had to get close enough to hit them. To do so, the over-eager enemy spilled out of their well-protected and well-concealed nests and unknowingly exposed themselves to the targeting lasers and predatory eyes of the AFO teams perched above them.

Enemy mortar crews were vaporized, command and control sites ceased to do either, and enemy fighters moving between positions to re-arm and reinforce never showed up. The three AFO teams were engaged in a continuous cycle of describing targets, vectoring attack aircraft, making corrections, and then moving on to new targets. At times the only limiting factor was the speed with which they could speak into their headsets:

- Corkscrew 5-0, this is Juliet 1, enemy command and control site, located at grid 15119100, position marked with laser.
- Juliet 1, this is Corkscrew 5-0, I have two 1,000-pound JDAMs. I tally your laser at grid 15119100.
- Corkscrew 5–0, you're cleared hot.
- Roger, bombs away, 33 seconds until impact.
  (33 seconds later)
- Corkscrew 5-0, nice work. Target neutralized.[3]

Inside the TOC in Gardez, I wondered out loud why the enemy didn't seem to recognize the pattern of ever-growing numbers of their comrades who were no longer answering radios or showing up for their rendezvous.

"It's 'cause they don't talk to each other," was Glenn's insightful response. "Remember what the Taliban informer told us: the Al Qaeda fighters don't allow the Afghan Taliban to talk to them."

Glenn hit it on the head: the enemy didn't understand what was going on around them because they weren't talking to each other. Their rigidly hierarchical caste system prevented them from sharing mission-critical information.

Along with their eagle-eyed view of the battlefield, one of the biggest advantages the AFO teams had was their boundaryless communications. Each team maintained continuous communication with their fellow AFO teams, the aircraft flying overhead, and with the 10th Mountain troops on the valley floor. The multiple radios at each OP empowered the teams to ask questions, listen to each other's insights, and understand the friendly and enemy activity going on around them.

Even though the enemy fire began to slacken, there just wasn't a lot the 10th Mountain soldiers could do on the valley floor except lie low and search for cover from the oppressive enemy fire. They were in dire straits.

Jimmy called and updated all of AFO on General Hagenbeck's current thought process. "If they can stabilize their wounded and get the rest of their forces inserted, they might be able to turn the tide; they want to know if we can buy them some time." All three AFO teams had the same response: "As long as they need."

Although none of us verbalized it, we recognized that the law of unintended consequences was on our side. The dire straits of the 10th Mountain troops, exposed and vulnerable on the valley floor, was the bait that continued to lure the enemy fighters out of their protective positions, where AFO could target and destroy them. *Without the danger there cannot arise the opportunity.*

In the late afternoon, the 101st ground force commander, whose helicopter landed just below the OP that Goody now occupied, assessed the enemy situation and the status of his forces in the valley. With the Afghans in retreat, there was no hammer. The portion of his forces that made it into the valley was pinned down and out of position, so by proxy, there was no anvil. He decided it was time to flush the plan. He attempted to call General Hagenbeck and report his prognosis, but discovered that his radio had "gone to shit." Since Goody was only a stone's throw away, the 101st commander asked to borrow Goody's radio and made his call on the AFO satellite radio net. Jimmy answered and handed the headset to General Hagenbeck. The 101st commander's tone was urgent. "Recommend we exfiltrate all forces from the valley at nightfall." General Hagenbeck listened to his commander on the ground, paused, and then agreed. All of AFO was listening.

After hearing the sit-rep from the Special Forces a few hours earlier, I now realized that the three main American forces on the Shahi Khot battlefield had three distinctly different pictures of how the battle was going. In combat, when it comes to understanding the reality of the situation and seeing the battlefield, geography and psychology are inexorably linked.

The Special Forces and Afghans were on the outside of the valley. Demoralized by battlefield friction and by their inability to get in, they were forced to withdraw to the safe house in Gardez to fight another day. The 10th Mountain forces were inside the valley. Pinned down and exposed on the valley floor, they assessed their situation as hopeless, and decided their best option was to withdraw back to Bagram, to fly again another day. The three AFO teams occupied the key terrain* that dominated the ground inside and outside the valley. From their eagle-eye perches, the three teams had superb situational awareness, which they continued to translate with devastating lethality on the unwitting enemy.

Seconds after General Hagenbeck got off the radio, I got on.

"Jimmy, pass this sit-rep to the commander [General Hagenbeck]."

Key terrain is terrain that provides a decisive advantage to whichever side holds it in battle.

Unbeknownst to me, Jimmy put me on the speakerphone. General Hagenbeck and his two deputy generals were standing behind him listening to everything I said.

"I believe that pulling out would be a huge mistake; the AFO teams are decimating the enemy and continue to hold almost all of the key terrain around the valley."

I also shared what we had on deck for the next twenty-four hours.

"We'll continue to bomb the key enemy positions on Tergal Ghar. We've identified the enemy's key trail networks behind the mountains, which we'll bomb and cut off tonight. We have a resupply scheduled for tonight that will allow the teams to stay in position and support the 10th Mountain forces while continuing to destroy the enemy for another four days." I paused, then summarized:

"We believe this is the battlefield opportunity of a lifetime. AFO is going to stay in position and keep on killing until there's no more killing to be done."

I wasn't trying to engage in histrionics, nor was I trying to criticize anyone's decision to pull out, I simply recognized the same lesson we had learned from the warlord in Orgun: the best way to create an accurate portrayal of reality is to share information. On this account, I also felt complicit.

As Jimmy described it later: "General Hagenbeck huddled with his key leaders in the corner of the 10th Mountain's Bagram TOC." He had had no idea how successful the overall battle had actually been up to that point; all he knew was that it hadn't gone according to the plan. Once he fully understood the AFO reality, he had a completely different picture; he could see the battlefield and he knew what the right thing was to do.

General Hagenbeck then did something that should provide a salutary lesson for all future leaders in every profession: he changed his mind! He did this based on the reality-correcting context of the guy on the ground. Despite having stated his previous decision over a satellite radio heard by his superiors and subordinates all across the globe, General Hagenbeck pushed aside his ego and did the right thing. It would turn out to be the right decision for the mission, the right decision for his men, and the right decision for General Hagenbeck.

In the chaos of the moments that followed, the 10th Mountain warriors went entrepreneurial. They innovated, they adapted, they were audacious, and in the end, they were victorious.

19

TAKUR GHAR:

WHEN ALL THE LAUGHTER DIED IN SORROW

Sundown, March 2 (fourteen hours after Goody initiated the battle)

THE ENEMY: *We spent our night alert and on guard, to deter any more airdrops throughout the night, as was expected. Before performing the morning Fajr prayer, we divided the brothers into three groups: the first joined the group of Maulawi Saif-ur-Rahman Mansoor, for he needed more people; the second took position where the Shillika ZSU-23 antiaircraft cannon was situated, at the entrance to the valley; which left myself along with three other brothers as support for any of the groups that needed more men. To begin with, we headed toward the location of the Shillika and took our positions in the rear, to help curb the aerial bombardment, which had increased significantly. During the entire period, the enemy did not cease to spray the mountain peaks and valleys with the lava of bombs and missiles, while machine guns sprayed their bullets in every direction. The martyrs were too many to count. Many of the Afghans were now martyrs. One brother tried to hide in a trench from the bombs, but the trench was full to the top with dead Uzbeks.*

The DCG was monitoring the battle from his TOC at Bagram. Congratulatory phone calls for what AFO had accomplished were streaming in from high-ranking leaders across the globe. Many of the high-ranking leaders, along with their staffs, let the DCG know that they planned to stay glued to their satellite radios for the remainder of the battle.

My secure satellite phone rang inside the safe house in Gardez. It was the DCG.[1] "Pete, wonderful job. Look, we can't ask you guys to continue this; you're not set for that. What I want to do is turn this over to the SEALs. Let them command it, and let them continue prosecuting the fight. You and AFO need to be out looking for the next battlefield. I want to send some SEALs down and I want you to get these guys in there as quick as possible."

When he called, all three AFO teams were engaging enemy fighters in the valley, and all three had various issues and requests that required my immediate attention and facilitation, so while the DCG's bizarre suggestion definitely met my criteria for red-alert status, my men were my priority, and I needed to get back on the radio and get my mind back into the battle.

I responded with rapidity: "Sir, my teams are fine for at least another forty-eight hours; I recommend that any team going into the valley goes through the same routine as the three teams already in the valley. Before they infiltrate they need to spend some time at Gardez so they can acclimate to the altitude and study the terrain and the history of the Shahi Khot. They need to talk to the CIA, the Special Forces, and the Afghan militiamen who have been working in the area." I threw in what I thought would be the clincher: "Sir, sending those teams in without any time to prepare for the environment doesn't make sense; it's setting them up for failure."

Glenn, whose bloodshot eyes and tangled hair from forty-eight hours of no sleep had earned him the nickname "the mad professor," shook his head with resigned frustration. "I knew it; they have no idea how much preparation we put in to ensure those teams could operate in this environment."

To those in Bagram, Masirah, and North Carolina monitoring the battle over the satellite radio and watching the sporadic images beamed back to earth from unmanned aerial aircraft, it probably seemed simple enough: put a team on the high ground with a radio and let them call in precision air strikes on the enemy. But as would happen so many times in the next hundred hours, those leaders were making decisions based on a false reality: they had no context.

Sunrise, March 3

As sunrise approached, a wintry haze settled over the Shahi Khot Valley, preventing the AFO teams and, by proxy, everyone else from seeing the battlefield for at least a few more hours. I had been up for almost fifty-five hours. Everyone has their psychological or visual cues that tell them they need to sleep. With me, it's all visual. I remember looking out the window at a large rock and thinking it looked very much like a cartoonish apparition of a washing machine. *"What is that washing machine doing out there?"* I took my headset off and headed for our tent.

Two hours later, my watch alarm went off. Not yet lucid, I grabbed my pistol from under my pillow, tucked it into my belt, and stumbled out into the courtyard to relieve myself and brush my teeth. The sky above was presidential blue, and it was noticeably warmer. *The snow will be melting and we'll need to adjust our camouflage pattern,* I thought. I could smell beans and rice, and someone was listening to the song "Kashmir" by Led Zeppelin in one of the tents. I had always loved that song. I headed back to the TOC to get an update on what had occurred while I was asleep.

Walking through the muddy courtyard, I noticed at least two new vehicles and a bunch of unfamiliar faces scurrying about. Glenn ran up to me; he was frustrated and talking fast: "Two teams of SEALs drove into the compound an hour ago. The officer in charge of them is waiting for you in the TOC."

Sometimes when I'm sleep deprived, I don't wake up real well; this was one of those mornings. *Why did they come down here without calling us first?* I thought. The Afghans operating our checkpoints were on high alert; they believed in shooting first and asking questions later.

The new arrivals included two SEAL teams code named Mako 30 and Mako 21.[2]

"What are you doing here?" I asked the SEAL officer, whose name was Vic. He told me that the DCG ordered him "to C2 [command and control] the SEALs," and that he had orders to infiltrate the two SEAL teams into the Shahi Khot as soon as possible to support the fight.[3]

I grabbed the satellite phone and walked outside to call the DCG.

"What's going on, sir?" I asked incredulously. "Same thing I told you," the DCG replied. "I want these guys in the fight. Vic is in charge of the Blue guys (Blue is a nickname some use to refer to SEALs, referring to the color of water), you just stay in charge of the AFO guys, and when do you think you can turn them over to Blue?"

"Sir, there's no need to shove these guys into the fight. I don't need to put two more teams in tonight, we control the valley, not them—" He cut me off. "Pete, put both SEAL teams into the fight tonight. That's an order."[4] He hung up. The operational sweetspot was shutting down.

In a few hours I was scheduled to accompany Spider and the Special Forces teams back to the valley to reinsert the Afghans. The number of military units now on the battlefield would make this a complex maneuver. We believed it was critical that all three leaders—Spider, Chris H., and I—move forward with the Afghans. Our proximity would allow us to see the battlefield together, make face-to-face coordinations and decisions, and do everything we could to reduce the risk of friendly-fire incidents. The reinsertion of the four hundred Afghans would finally allow us to seal the entire valley. We could then move into the valley, capture the remaining enemy, collect fresh clues, and follow any and all leads to potentially deliver the deathblow to Al Qaeda forces in Afghanistan.

Inside the now bustling Gardez TOC, SEALs, AFO, and Special

Forces members scrutinized maps and prepared for the night's operations.

One of the recently arrived SEAL team leaders was a good friend of mine whom I had worked closely with during numerous other real-world missions around the globe. His name was Slab. Built like a marathon runner, he was quiet and introspective, and never wasted words. I was glad to have Slab at Gardez; he was one of a handful of guys I would pick for any team or any mission; I trusted him inherently. I grabbed him in the TOC and walked outside to talk in the courtyard.

"Slab, I'm really uncomfortable with you guys going right in," I told him. "I want to make sure you get all the advantages that the other guys had."

"I totally agree," Slab replied. "But I do what I'm told, and we're being told to go in tonight."[5]

A few hours later the SEAL teams briefed their plans. One of the SEAL teams (Mako 21) would fly into the valley on a CH-47, land on the valley floor near a secure 10th Mountain–occupied position, then move by foot to link with Juliet team, drop off much-needed supplies for Juliet, then continue moving east to their OP on the eastern ridge of the valley. Simultaneously a second CH-47, with Slab and Mako 30 onboard, would fly to a landing zone 1,300 meters northeast of Takur Ghar, called LZ 1 (see Map 6). From Landing Zone 1, Mako 30 would hike up to the top of Takur Ghar and establish their OP. An AC-130 would fly over both landing zones before the helicopters landed, to ensure they were free of enemy.

Both plans would break our unofficial no-helicopter rule, but at this point there was no other alternative. The DCG had ordered them in that night and the time/distance reality meant there was no other way.

To make it to his OP on top of Takur Ghar before daylight, Slab deduced that he and his team had to be inserted as early in the cycle of darkness as possible. Slab estimated it would take a minimum of four hours to make the ascent.

On the road in front of the safe house, a new and improved truck convoy lined up to ferry the Afghans back to the battlefield. My vehicle was positioned in the middle of the column. My vehicle was outfitted with a sat-com radio as well as a more dependable line-of-sight radio. It also had a ruggedized mini-laptop computer to send and receive digital messages. The vehicle was rigged to provide me with the same communications capabilities that I had in the Gardez TOC. Tera and I worked feverishly to test and install the equipment and to make sure everything was ergonomically positioned to allow me to operate in the dark, while driving, or while under fire.

At 10:00 P.M., thirty minutes before the SEAL teams' helicopters were scheduled to arrive, Vic approached me and, after engaging in small talk about my vehicle, began discussing the concept of switching Mako 30's helicopter landing zone from LZ 1 to the top of Takur Ghar Mountain. He had brought the same idea up hours earlier, but both Slab and I had dismissed the concept for tactical reasons. Fully aware that Mako 30 was only thirty minutes away from moving to their landing zone, I cut right to the chase. "There's nothing on the ground cueing us to make a change, so it doesn't make sense to change it." I added that even if we wanted to adjust the landing zone location the helicopter pilots would never consider any change at the eleventh hour; it was against their standard operation procedure. Finally, I told him that Jimmy had already coordinated Mako 30's mission with all other units on the battlefield. "No problem," he responded, not pressing the issue. We talked for a few more minutes about coordination for the night's operations, during which I reinforced to him that I would be running things from my vehicle near the fishhook and that if he had any questions or issues, he should call me immediately.

"You got it," he replied as he walked away into the dark.

Why would he ask to change the helicopter landing zone thirty minutes before take off? I wondered. *It didn't make sense.*

Somewhere around 10:30 P.M., both SEAL teams moved to the Gardez landing zone, a few hundred meters behind the safe house.

At 11:23 P.M., two Chinook helicopters arrived.[6] After a series of airspace-related delays, both helicopters developed engine problems. The pilots radioed back to the TF 11 TOC at Bagram for guidance, then informed Slab that the earliest they could get him and his team into his designated landing zone was 2:30 A.M. With sunrise at 6:00 A.M., Slab instantly recognized that he would not have enough cover of darkness to climb to the top of the mountain. His recommendation was to delay the mission twenty-four hours.[7] Vic then decided to call the TF 11 TOC at Bagram on the satellite radio and discuss the situation with the next-higher-ranking officer in his chain of command. "The earliest infiltration time possible is now 2:45 to 3:00 A.M.," Vic told the officer. "Mako 30 [Slab] requests to delay twenty-four hours. What would you like to tell the team?" The message that the TF 11 TOC sent back: "We really need you to get in there tonight."[8] With that de facto order, Vic resurrected the concept of flying Mako 30 directly to the top of Takur Ghar. He began by discussing the particulars of his plan with the MH-47 pilot in charge.

The pilot calculated the effect of flying a couple of thousand feet higher than the original landing zone. "I can get you there, but I don't know that there's a suitable landing zone at your OP." (He was referring to the top of the mountain.)

"It should be no problem," Vic advised, then added. "I've seen [satellite] imagery." The mission was back on again, the helicopter pilots agreed to insert Mako 30 directly on top of the Takur Ghar peak.

On the frozen blackness of the Gardez landing zone, Vic had made a decision about a mission he was unsure of, against an enemy he was unaware of, on a battlefield he had never stepped foot on. In the chaos of the moment, when the mission and his men were counting on him to look, listen, and ask questions about what was going on around him, he disregarded the reality-revealing context of the man standing next to him (Slab), and the guys on the ground a few hundred meters away (AFO), and decided to defer to his military hierarchy instead.

The hierarchical decision-making process implies that the leader at every level of the pyramid is the person in charge of deciding and directing everything below him. By proxy, the highest-ranking individual is the one who always has the best answers, the deepest understanding, and the best solutions. The unstated "right" of Vic, and the TF 11 leaders in the Bagram TOC to override Slab and make the Takur Ghar decision was both a prime example of how deeply entrenched the process is in the military, and of its unsuitability to ever produce optimized decisions in fast-moving and complex situations.

Rigid adherence to the hierarchy is enforced on the modern-day battlefield by the satellite radio, the VTC, and hubris. Although Slab knew exactly what the right thing was to do, his officer in charge, Vic, standing right next to him, was the one discussing the decision on the satellite radio back to the TOC at Bagram. On the other end of the radio were Vic's Navy superiors at Bagram, who were in turn, getting guidance from their superior, the DCG (an Air Force general), who was deferring to the guidance he was getting via daily VTCs from the commanding general (an Army helicopter pilot) in North Carolina.[9] Each leader in the precarious chain likely felt the implied cultural pressure to provide "the answer," and in the process, to display his deep understanding of the situation at hand. Ironically, one of the most contributive ways to show that deep understanding is not to answer at all, and instead to conduct a reality check.

All anyone at any level of the TF 11 multilayered hierarchy had to do was make a perfunctory call to Slab, Jimmy, or me, and ask a simple question: "What's your recommendation?" Our reality was that there was no mission-critical requirement to get a team on top of that mountain that night, and there may not have been the next night either. The enemy was already teetering on their last legs—we controlled the valley, not the enemy. Slab recommended a twenty-four-hour delay to provide him with adequate time to move to the top of the mountain under the cover of darkness. If someone had asked either Jimmy or me, we would have asked or deferred to Slab. *Always listen to the guy on the ground.*

No one in AFO was privy to the discussions or the decisions made by Vic and the TF 11 TOC concerning Takur Ghar until many hours later. The life-and-death decision the hierarchy produced that night certainly wasn't optimal, but the decision itself was not fatal. The decision not to share it would be.

> THE ENEMY: *With the first signs of night, [A]C-130 planes arrived that carried machine guns similar in caliber to the DShk (12.7mm), although they were also able to fire missiles, and had night vision, which would allow vision for a distance of up to six kilometers away. We could do nothing but raise our hands and pray to Allah. Our brothers had dispersed, and were motionlessly positioned in trenches, for the enemy's weapons could detect any movement. Since the brothers had been engaged in battle until night, the planes found us to be easy night targets and on that night, about twenty mujahideen were killed by their planes. Seven of them were Arabs, these being: Abul-Baraa Al-Maghribi (Morocco), Abul-Baraa Ash-Shami (Syria), Abu Bakr Al-Maghribi (Morocco), Abul-Hasan As-Somali (Somalia), Khalid Al-Islambooli Al-Ghamidi (Arabian Peninsula), Abu Bakr Azzam Al-Urduni (Jordan), and Abdus-Salam Ghazi Al-Misri (Egypt).*

Takur Ghar Mountain, 2:40 A.M.

While Slab and Mako 30 loaded their engine-roaring helicopter in the freezing blackness of the safe house landing zone, a lone AC-130 prowled the sky over the 10,469-foot snowcapped peak of Takur Ghar.[10] The AC-130 had been trolling the valley for enemy fighters all night. Up to this point, when the AC-130 was sent to a location to look for enemy, they searched for living, breathing, fighting humans. When they found them, they destroyed them. The sensor suite on the AC-130 consists of television and infrared sensors, and radar.[11] These sensors enable the gunship to identify enemy targets either visually or electronically, day or night, and in virtually any weather conditions. The air force personnel inside the AC-130 scanned the Takur Ghar peak with their sensors. The sensors worked fine, but the individuals looking through the sensors didn't know why they were scanning the mountaintop. No one had shared with them that they were supposed to be scanning the mountain in preparation for a helicopter full of SEALs to land on top of it. Despite a spiderweb of footprints in the snow, as well as a trench encircled DShK tripod-mounted machine gun standing guard on the western edge of the peak, the officer manning the sensors didn't see any enemy, so he pronounced the mountain secure.

At approximately 3:00 A.M., the MH-47 carrying Mako 30 braked, flared, and hovered before attempting to touch down in a small depression near the top of the peak. An intense firestorm of RPG and machine-gun fire enveloped the aircraft.[12] Seven Uzbek fighters fired everything they could load. Three RPG rounds slammed into the aircraft, taking out one of the two engines, the entire electric system, and the hydraulic systems that controlled the aircraft's steering. The aircraft bucked like a wounded bronco, causing one of the SEALs who had positioned himself to disembark, to tumble out the back of the aircraft onto the snow-covered peak below. The pilot managed to regain control of the aircraft as it disappeared over the backside of the peak. Violently shaking like an "unbalanced washing machine," the aircraft descended rapidly. In a brilliant display of airmanship, the pilot and crew finagled the helicopter to an upright landing on the valley floor. Miraculously no one inside the aircraft was seriously injured.[13]

My convoy had just pulled into the western edge of the fishhook (see Map 6), when my radio crackled to life; it was Slab.

He was more excited than usual, but still calm and collected. Slab told me his aircraft had crash-landed on the valley floor and that one man (Neil Roberts) had fallen out of the helicopter on top of the mountain. I instantly realized what that meant: *They tried to land on top of the mountain!*

I asked Slab for his location. He paused while he got a reading from his GPS, and then recited the grid coordinates back to me. Slab and the disabled MH-47 were located in the 18-92 grid square (see Map 6). At this point in the battle I didn't need to look at a map to recognize what part of the valley a specific grid was in—I had received and passed so many Shahi Khot grid coordinates over the past seventy-two hours that the map was etched inside my head; I could see the battlefield. The helicopter was sitting within close proximity to 10th Mountain forces and almost directly in front of Juliet team's OP (see Map 6). I also understood the brutal reality of the fallen SEAL's predicament. I knew that Uzbek and Chechen mujahideen did not take prisoners. We had to rescue him immediately, or the fallen SEAL would soon be dead—if he wasn't already.

Huddled together with Chris H. and Spider inside the crumbled remains of an ancient Afghan fort, the first thing we did was to shit-can the plan to infiltrate the Afghans. Our priority was to understand what was going on around us. I immediately contacted the three AFO teams and asked them for a sit-rep. From their dominating perch on the eastern ridgeline, Juliet team could see both the top of Takur Ghar and the spot where the helicopter crash-landed on the valley floor. They quickly confirmed everything that Slab had just reported. I used my line-of-sight radio to talk with the AC-130 flying over the valley at the time, and kept my satellite radio clear for the teams who continued to call in missions on other pockets of enemy fighters around the valley. The AC-130 was flying directly over Takur Ghar. I requested the crew to describe everything they saw as vividly and with the greatest detail possible.

The AC-130 reported seeing an infrared strobe light flashing, and a growing number of individuals surrounding the strobe light. "How many?" I asked. "A lot," he replied. A few seconds later, the AC-130 reported that the strobe no longer blinked.[14] Then in an excited tone, he blurted, "Five to ten enemy, they're moving around now, it's hard to keep track."

As each TOC inside the country and out learned of the incident, frantic requests for information began to overwhelm and clog the AFO satellite net. A cacophonic duel erupted between TOCs as each successive call "stepped on" or interrupted the previous call. The situation went from bad to worse as each caller asked the other to repeat what they were saying before they were stepped on.[15]

Slab had only one thought: to return to the peak and rescue his teammate. After being ferried back to the Gardez landing zone, he and his team jumped back on the CH-47, and within minutes, Mako 30 was lifting off to return to Takur Ghar. Shortly thereafter, a Predator arrived in the sky above the peak and immediately began relaying its images back to the TOCs at Bagram and Masirah.[16] Jimmy fed me the information as he gleaned it. It complemented what the AC-130 was telling me.

The enemy on top of Takur Ghar were milling around the peak. Exposed and bunched up, they were extremely vulnerable. Slab and I discussed the situation and agreed on a rescue concept. I shared the concept with the AC-130.

"When Mako 30's helicopter is between one and three minutes out, I want you to fire your 105 mm weapon as close as possible to the enemy fighters on top of the mountain, then watch to see if any one individual breaks away from the group. You'll need to use your best judgment. If you think it may be the fallen SEAL [Roberts], then use all of your weapons to protect him. You are cleared hot to destroy everyone else."

"Roger, understand," the AC-130 radio operator responded. I continued, "Understand that you must suppress the enemy on the mountain before the helicopter arrives. Kill as many as possible while they are in the open and vulnerable. Do not let the helicopter land if you haven't suppressed the enemy." "Roger, understand," the AC-130 repeated. Then Jimmy weighed in from Bagram. "The enemy is in the open; they're still milling around and bunched up on top of the mountain."

Juliet team could also see the enemy on top of the mountain; they injected their affirmation of the concept. We had multiple "guys on the ground," each with a different piece of the puzzle; together we had a shared reality and I felt like we were starting to understand what was going on around us.

Slab's helicopter was less than five minutes from the peak. Jimmy got back on the net. Watching the Predator image of the enemy from the 10th Mountain TOC, Jimmy's intent was to keep all of us in the valley updated with everything he knew. "The enemy is still bunched up on top of the mountain," he reported in a quick, calm, and concise manner.

"We don't need you getting all worked up on the radio," the emotion-strained voice of the DCG barked over the radio. "Get off the net; we've got it." The DCG's condescending rebuke made it sound like Jimmy was some random outsider who was interfering with the DCG and his TOC's organizational right to issue orders and control the battle. But Jimmy wasn't trying to tell people what to do; he was trying to share with people what he knew.

From his vastly networked seat in the 10th Mountain TOC, Jimmy had used his skills as a connector to gather and share key pieces of the battlefield puzzle. He knew where all the AFO and 10th Mountain forces were, he had a visceral understanding of the enemy situation and the mission, and he had a live bird's-eye view of the mountaintop from the Predator feed. The DCG had the Predator image and he had his rank.

With Spider at my side, I checked my watch; Mako 30's helicopter was only two minutes away from the mountaintop. I stared at the top of the mountain, adjusting my night vision goggles in expectation of the flashes and fireballs from the AC-130's lethal weapons buffet that I was certain were soon to follow.

Inside the *Star Wars*–like TOCs at Masirah and Bagram, the staffs were going beehive.[17] Like most staffs, their first instincts were likely that they had to do something; they had to start planning and issuing orders. Arrayed like a college lecture hall, the staff officers watched and listened to the battle while sitting in their tiered tables and seats, transfixed by the grainy images from the Predator feed, which instructed their reality from the gigantic plasma screen mounted in the front of each room.

The Predator above Takur Ghar was flying at 17,000 feet above sea level—more than a mile above the 10,200-foot mountaintop.[18] Its images were fed through a satellite in outer space that digitally secured the signal before sending it back to earth. The resulting human images were of blurry, black Gumby-like figures with barely recognizable objects in their hands. Perhaps most misleading of all, the Predator view is narrow angle, described metaphorically as "looking at the world through a soda straw." Through the soda straw you're never sure what is really going on around your image.

At some point the DCG and his staff in Masirah began to believe that their access to the satellite radio nets and especially the Predator feeds gave them as much understanding of events in the Shahi Khot Valley as they needed to take over the operation and run things from their location.[19] Perhaps in response to the heavy traffic that had subsumed the AFO satellite net immediately after Mako 30's first attempt to land on the mountain, someone in the TF 11 chain of command decided it would be a good idea to switch the satellite radio frequency. From a higher headquarters perspective, the radio is a means to issue orders and provide direction to subordinates; changing the frequency would make it easier for them to do that. For AFO and the men on the ground, the radio was our primary method of networking ideas and sharing information; as such, it was our lifeline.

Communication short-circuits like this seem innocuous enough when they occur, but as time continues to march on, they turn into decision-making errors that slowly begin to accrue, compounding one on top of the other, indiscernibly snowballing toward critical mass. The snowball was starting to roll.

After switching to the new frequency, the staff at Masirah (1,100 miles and one time zone away) began directing all forces and all aircraft involved in the rescue of the fallen SEAL, Neil Roberts. The one-dimensional allure of the Predator feed was informing their decision-making reality. Precisely because it was one-dimensional, it could never be correct, and because it wasn't shared, it could never be corrected. Like the warlord and the intelligence analyst in Orgun, the

DCG had grossly overestimated the omnipotence of technology. He failed to understand that the reality of the situation could only be fully understood and accessed through the collective omniscience of the guys on the ground.

With a sense of urgency fueled by the knowledge that a fallen comrade's life was hanging in the balance, the MH-47 pilots flying Mako 30 from Gardez, flew their aircraft at full throttle toward the Takur Ghar peak. The orbiting AC-130 sighted its guns and cameras on the "sitting duck" enemy fighters who were still milling around below them. The crew of the AC-130 knew that somewhere down below them a lone SEAL was potentially fighting for his life. As they readied to fire, the friendly-fire incident from the opening moments of the battle was still fresh on their minds. They had to be sure, so the AC-130 called on the recently changed sat-com frequency to request permission from the ground force commander to commence firing. Unbeknownst to the crew of the AC-130, the switch in satellite nets meant that they were actually talking to a TF 11 staff officer.

The man talking to the AC-130 crew was sitting in a tent in Oman Masirah (see Map 3). A well-meaning officer, he still didn't understand that Roberts had fallen out of the helicopter on top of Takur Ghar. Instead, he believed Roberts had fallen on the valley floor, where 10th Mountain soldiers were in close proximity. Watching events unfold through the soda straw lens of the Predator feed, he seemed sure of only one thing: that he was confused.

"Are we cleared to fire?" the officer on board the AC-130 pleaded in frustration as the enemy milled about below him, and Mako 30's helicopter rapidly closed with the peak.

The staff officer in Masirah responded:

"Waste everyone." Then before the AC-130 could reply, "Negative, do not fire; there may be friendlies down there," followed a few seconds later by, "Don't worry, our good guy has been picked up by a friendly team."[20]

I never heard the AC-130's final request for permission to fire, nor did I hear the contradictory guidance given by the bewildered staff officer at Masirah, and was thus powerless to provide the corrective context from my guys on the ground.

The designated time for Mako 30's landing had come and gone. I hadn't seen or heard any fire from the AC-130; they never received permission.

As I gazed up at the top of the mountain, I had no sense of the calamity unfolding in front of me; I couldn't see it. Staring a hole in the top of the peak, I pleaded to myself, *Why hasn't the AC-130 fired? Something isn't right . . .*

THE ENEMY: *Just then, I received news on the wireless from the Uzbek brothers stationed at Mount Abdul-Malik that they had brought down an American helicopter on the peak opposite to them, but that a large number of their soldiers were still alive. [Note: The helicopter in question was a "Chinook" CH-47 and the Uzbek Mujahideen shot it down with the ZSU-23 antiaircraft cannon.] Therefore, they asked us to hurry to Mount Abdul-Malik, because there were only seven brothers stationed there, out of whom three had already been killed. We did not possess advanced defensive weapons that were able to fight the aircraft. But, by the Grace of Allah the Almighty, we discovered that some of our weapons, despite their simplicity and oldness, were very effective at handling the aircraft.*

The second CH-47 landing on Takur Ghar fared little better than the first. As the helicopter attempted to land, machine-gun bullets chewed the skin of the aircraft like it was papier-mâché. Slab only had one mission on his mind: his men. With no thought for his own safety, he charged off the back of the helicopter, leading his team of six brave warriors through knee-deep snow, directly toward the belly of the bunker-encased beast. Despite having its hull splayed open by well-aimed machine-gun fire, the CH-47 was still airworthy enough to lift up and accelerate off the mountain.

The completely frustrated crew of the AC-130 finally realized they were talking to the wrong guy on the ground and immediately re-established communications with me on the line-of-sight radio. They narrated what they saw below. Slab and his team continued to fire and maneuver up the slope to close with and destroy the enemy in the bunker. The AC-130 could still see all the enemy fighters below them, and could have almost certainly had a decisive effect during the opening moments of the firefight, but there were no communications between Mako 30 and the AC-130. The AC-130 crew all but begged for someone, *anyone*, on the mountain below to talk to them and give them permission to make a difference. There were no answers to their calls. The radio, to which they were calling, lay on the back of Mako 30's communication specialist, Air Force Tech Sergeant John A. Chapman, who lay mortally wounded in front of the enemy bunker. The rest of Mako 30 was caught in a vicious crossfire. With one man dead and another seriously wounded, Slab directed Mako 30 to take cover on the side of the mountain. A few minutes later, Slab contacted me and the AC-130 on his handheld radio. Again, the old-fashioned line-of-sight radio proved a lifesaver. With communications reestablished, Slab directed the AC-130 to begin pounding the enemy on top of the mountain. But the enemy, having taken cover during the opening moments of the gunfight with Mako 30, was now much less vulnerable.

The image on the screen in the Masirah and Bagram TOCs at that moment portrayed the real-time life-and-death struggle on top of Takur Ghar between the enemy and the brave warriors of Mako 30. In a video game, when your guy gets shot, you hear a jingle and your guy gets to start the game over. In real life, when you see your guy get shot on the Predator image, you better do a reality check, or your guys are gonna die.

Bagram, 3:45 A.M.

At Bagram, the DCG alerted the Ranger quick reaction force (QRF). Believing that time was their enemy, the QRF rushed out to their pre-positioned helicopters on the Bagram airstrip. When the young captain in charge of the QRF asked a senior staff officer, "What's our mission?" the staff officer replied, "We've got to get you guys in the air and get you down to that vicinity. When you get down to Gardez, come up on the satellite net. We'll give you further instructions."[21] The staff officer believed that the priority of the moment was to get the rescue force down to the safe house in Gardez, where they would be less than ten minutes from the mountain. In theory, a logical concept but for one small detail: the QRF helicopters weren't equipped with working satellite radios, so there was no way to communicate or share information between the rescue force helicopters and the TOCs in Bagram and Masirah. Forced to launch in the midst of mayhem and confusion, the Ranger QRF had no idea what their mission was and no idea what had happened to the men of Mako 30. More damning still, the pilots were never told not to land on the same "lava hot" landing zone on which Mako 30 had now landed and been pummeled twice.

Slivers of daylight began highlighting the peaks. To ensure continuous communications with Slab, I had to make sure I kept a clear line of sight between my radio and his. Slab was stationary and couldn't move, so with Spider at my side and my radio on my back, I nomadically wandered the scrub desert floor around the fishhook.

"Get down!" Spider screamed, as he disappeared into the dusty depression of a dry creekbed. "What are you doing?" I yelled back to him. "They're firing rockets at us. Get down," he repeated. "I can't; I'll lose comms with Slab," I explained as an object whooshed over our heads and splashed in the sand a hundred or so meters to our right. "Better to lose comms than lose your friggin' head," Spider lectured. But Slab was up there fighting for his life; his lifeline was his line-of-sight radio connectivity back to me. If I hit the ground, I'd lose the line of sight. Luckily, I also recognized the distinctive whoosh and landing pattern of the rockets as that of a Soviet-made BM-21, which history has proven to be notoriously inaccurate and ineffective. "It's a

BM-21, fuck it!" I yelled to Spider as I continued walking and talking to Slab. Spider stood back up and brushed himself off. "If you think I'm gonna lie here digging trenches with my buttonholes while you walk around looking all fearless and shit, you got another thing coming." Inside I smiled; outside I imagined what Slab and his team might need next as I continued to walk and talk.

After Slab updated me on the status of his wounded teammate, who was stable, the AC-130 called to inform me that they would likely have to return to their base soon, due to the increased risk profile of flying during daylight.

He then added that he might not be able to stay long enough to cover the arrival of the Ranger QRF.

"Ranger QRF? What are you talking about" I asked.

That was when it hit me; now it all made sense. Someone else was making decisions and issuing orders; everything I thought I knew about the rescue situation had turned out to be something other than what it seemed.

I called Jimmy and asked him to find out the status of the QRF and give me a sit-rep as quickly as possible. Then I called the AC-130 back to make sure he understood how critical it was that he didn't leave his protective perch above the mountain before the QRF arrived.

"I'm checking on the status of the QRF right now; in the meantime you have to stay in position," I told the AC-130.

The AC-130 responded: "Roger, we'll try, but we're being told by our higher headquarters in Uzbekistan that we have to depart the area before daylight."

"You can tell your higher headquarters in the rear that this is a direct order from the AFO commander on the ground. You are not to depart this area; if you leave now, the QRF helicopters will be blown out of the sky. Acknowledge, over."

The AC-130 didn't respond, it was already leaving its protective perch and, in the process, the Ranger QRF completely vulnerable to the waiting enemy.

Captain Nate Self and his Ranger rescue force, along with the brave but oblivious crews on board two helicopters, were barreling at breakneck speed toward Takur Ghar. As the QRF helicopters bore down on the mountain, staff officers at both Bagram and Masirah TOCs frantically attempted to get through to them and share a simple message: "Don't land on top of the mountain." But they had no communications with the helicopters, so onward the helicopters flew.

Although the satellite radios on board the QRF helicopters did not work, I later learned from Captain Self that he could hear me talking on his own line-of-sight radio as his helicopter approached the Shahi Khot Valley.[22] My heart sank when I realized the implications of his comment. "Why didn't you check in with me and ask me for an update?" I asked as compassionately as I could.

"Because" he replied, "you weren't in my chain of command; I was waiting for my own chain of command at Bagram to give me guidance." Once again, the invisible boundary inferred by an administrative organizational structure and hierarchy, combined to prevent someone, in this case the young Ranger captain, from accessing his last best shot at the lifesaving context of the guys on the ground. As a result, in the chaos of the moment he wasn't able to go entrepreneurial. *How would we organize if we didn't know how we were supposed to organize?*

By the time the Rangers landed on the top of Takur Ghar, most everyone monitoring the battle realized that the mountaintop was too hot to land on—except the Rangers themselves. The snowball effect of bad decisions caused by a lack of shared reality was now turning avalanche.

At 6:10 A.M., as the two CH-47's carrying the QRF attempted to land on the peak, the lead helicopter was immediately disabled by the reinforced and reinvigorated Uzbek fighters, who were fending off their third helicopter assault in less than six hours.

"Today I feel like a Ranger!" shouted a brave young warrior who was killed the minute the lead CH-47 touched down. Captain Self waved off the second CH-47 and then hit the ground with his men. His unstated mission instantly transitioned from rescue to survival.

Over the next few hours, the Rangers fought a desperate battle against a tenacious band of Uzbek fighters. The Uzbeks had a distinct advantage over the Rangers: most had been living up there for many days; they knew every nook and cranny of the boulder-encrusted peak. The Uzbeks used their backyard knowledge to fire and maneuver from all sides of the mountain. But the Uzbeks were unaware that Juliet team had their backs. As they had done hours earlier for the 10th Mountain soldiers on the valley floor, Juliet team seized the opportunity, and began relaying and reporting the positions of the unwitting enemy to the Rangers, while simultaneously providing targeting guidance to the attack aircraft flying overhead. The turning point came around 10:00 A.M., when Juliet team pinpointed and then provided terminal guidance for the precision-fired missile that neutralized the last of the enemy fighters firing from the bunker.

After reuniting with their teammates who landed uncontested on a secure patch of ground on the eastern side of the mountain, the Rangers were able to secure the entire mountain peak, link with Mako 30, and recover the bodies of both the missing SEAL (Neil Roberts) and his air force teammate (John Chapman). Counting the two members of Mako 30, seven brave warriors from army, navy, and air force special operations units died on top of Takur Ghar. Eleven others were seriously wounded.

After the Rangers and SEALs were evacuated back to Bagram, the three AFO teams, consisting of army, navy, and air force operators, remained undetected in their OPs, and continued to decimate the last vestiges of enemy fighters in the valley.

THE ENEMY: *Brother Abu Ali Talha Al-Uzbeki even contacted me over the wireless to make me firm, strengthen me, and console me, and he swore that victory was ours. While I was deep in thought over his call, little did I know that these words were his last words, as he bade farewell to the mujahideen to join the martyrs, after sustaining heavy injuries from the aerial bombardment. We begged our commander, Saif-ur-Rahman*

Mansoor, to allow the brothers to leave the valley. This was the way of the mujahideen, move away from an enemy that outnumbers and possesses superior weapons. We had no water, my mouth was bleeding, and the sores prevented me from eating my bread. All the Uzbeks were now martyred; the Afghans were all gone.

Then I received word that our commander was martyred and I began to cry. We tried to get to his body to carry him away but the bombs were too many and the enemy were now everywhere.

I asked all our brothers to retreat, except the ones manning the PK machine gun and RPG-7 rocket launcher. Brother Abu Talib As-Saudi insisted upon staying and said to me, "I feel ashamed in front of Allah to retreat from the Americans." Due to the heavy bombardment, a large portion of his head was missing, but he joined us as we began our retreat.

The brothers all dispersed in different directions. I traveled with ten Arab brothers. Due to the increased number of Coalition forces blocking the area as well as the aerial channels the enemy had, we were forced to travel for three days and nights in conditions that were extremely harsh. We had nothing to eat with us, except a case of green tea and a pot in which to boil snow. After this long journey, enduring the cold and the snow, and traveling over mountain peaks and through valleys, we finally reached a village where we received a great welcome, such that it made us forget all that we had suffered and endured, and All Praise belongs to Allah Alone.

We had to delay the reinsertion of our Afghan allies due to the Takur Ghar firefight, but as the battle on top of the mountain raged, our presence around the fishhook allowed us to finally seal off the western side of the valley. On the third attempt to insert the Afghans into the valley, we made sure they were allowed to organize and fight the way they knew best—as Afghans. Released at the fishhook, they starburst into the valley in teams of three or four men, moving like mountain goats up, over, and across the ridges, and always, eventually, gravitating to the high ground. Within a few short hours they controlled the entire valley.

Using the grid coordinates of enemy positions reported by the AFO teams during the battle, we crisscrossed the valley to examine remains and collect intelligence. There were a lot of both.

We came across the body of one of the known enemy leaders, Saif Rahman Mansoor. He too had recorded his thoughts and decisions in a journal, which we read while standing over his catatonic carcass. Mr. Mansoor had ignored repeated pleas from his fighters to withdraw from the valley. He had defeated a massive Soviet heliborne assault force on the very same terrain; he was sure the pattern would repeat itself against the Americans. But even as his men died all around him, and the 10th Mountain closed in on all sides, he refused to accept the brutal reality of his situation. He had made up his mind to stay, and he wasn't going to change it. He died while incarcerated in the prison of precedence.

In the dry creekbeds, right where the Russian lessons-learned report said they would be, were five D-30 122-millimeter howitzers. They had survived undetected from our high-tech surveillance satellites by using good old-fashioned low-tech guile; they were covered with tan tarps and leafless shrubbery. Blood trails and other battlefield litter were strewn about, forming what we called the enemy's trail of tears. The trail pointed eastward, like an arrow, straight toward Pakistan, the same sanctuary the enemy used in the 1980s. After studying the terrain and recognizing that there were only a handful of routes the enemy could take to get through the mountains, India team (now beefed up with five additional Delta operators) parted company with the rest of AFO and headed into the mountains to cut off the enemy retreat and destroy them before they made it to the border.

Patterns of thinking, patterns of decision-making, and patterns of history. Once you recognize the patterns that inform the behavior of your enemy, you can adapt to them, and your enemy is toast. AFO was able to successfully recognize many of the enemy's patterns in the Shahi Khot, but it wasn't their patterns—creatures of habit, historical hubris, and fighting from high-ground—from which the lessons of Operation Anaconda should be focused: rather, it was the use of the guiding principles that enabled us to detect the patterns that provide the truly meaningful lessons:

- The mission, the men, and me
- Don't get treed by a chihuahua
- When in doubt, develop the situation
- Imagine the unimaginable; humor your imagination
- Always listen to the guy on the ground

As artisans of the art of war, these were the paints that, when combined and applied, revealed the key friendly and enemy patterns as they unfolded in front of us. Yet, when we stepped back to assess whether we created a masterpiece or a piece of you-know-what, we discovered that Operation Anaconda revealed a broader, more overarching lesson about patterns. It was this: No matter how many patterns you recognize—or think you recognize—they won't do you any good unless they're shared.

GUIDING-PRINCIPLE LESSON:

It's Not Reality Unless It's Shared!

How do perfectly smart people make bad decisions? In an organizational context, it's almost always the result of a lack of shared reality. "It's not reality unless it's shared" isn't just a guiding principle for how to think and make decisions, as the lessons from AFO and Operation Anaconda revealed; it's also a guiding principle for how to operationalize those thoughts and decisions; specifically how to organize, communicate with, and lead an organization.

Organizing

Organize for the mission. Forget the line and block diagrams; their only true function is administrative. They create boundaries to sharing information and accomplishing your mission. Throw them out with every new mission you undertake. Imagine a natural-disaster scenario: What would you do if your people were cut off from all their different headquarters and all their institutional histories? Constantly ask yourself and your organization this question: How would we organize if we didn't know how we were supposed to organize? Then do it!

Communicating

Communicate with one central philosophy: boundarylessness. Boundaryless means no borders, and in all directions. Openness is good; compartmentalization and secrecy are not. Sharing information is how we create an accurate portrayal of reality. It not only makes the whole wiser than the individual parts, it also serves as an effective system of checks and balances to correct misinterpretations by individuals who don't have all the pieces of the puzzle.

"Need to share" is the most important stamp any information file or insight can have. It shouldn't be lost on anyone that most of the key clues that enabled AFO to recognize the enemy's patterns and find their redoubt in Shahi Khot came from unclassified documents and sources. The Ali Mohamed document, the Afghan general's advice, the books on the Soviet-mujahideen war, the Haqqani interview article, the Soviet officer's battle report, and finally, the spindly finger on the end of the shepherd's hand. Today, the key information we have on the enemy's reality during the battle comes from the mother of all openness: the Internet, which underscores a key point concerning information openness; databases and the Internet don't download themselves! You have to take action to make action. You have to take time to search, read, contextualize, and save; you have to take time to saturate, incubate, and illuminate.

Leading

How do you ensure that you and your organization establish and maintain a shared reality? The answer is common sense.

Let common sense guide your thinking, your decision making, and the way you operationalize both. The single best thinking and decision-making tool a leader has is to consistently conduct reality checks by asking a profoundly simple question: "What's your recommendation?" I asked Ali Mohamed; I asked the Afghan general; I asked the warlord; I asked Kris; I asked Speedy; I asked Goody; I asked Slab, and what I got in return was pure, unadulterated tacit knowledge—knowing how to obtain desired end states, knowing what to do in order to obtain them, and knowing when and where to actually act on them. The power of the question goes beyond just the context-rich tacit knowledge it reveals; it also has a potent intrinsic effect on the responders. It lets them know that you respect their input, and as a leader, you respect the primacy of the guy on the ground!

Whether you're working in an organization such as the U.S. government, a billion-dollar business, or even a personal relationship, your reality isn't real unless it's shared. You have to share your straight-from-the-ground thoughts with others (preferably in a face-to-face setting) or your reality will fester and decay, and eventually the decision not to share may be fatal.

NOTES

INTRODUCTION

1. Michael R. Gordon and Bernard E. Trainor, *Cobra II* (New York: Pantheon Books, 2006), 443.

2. Ibid., 327.

3. http://www.defenselink.mil/home/features/2006/Iraqi-Freedom-Day-2006/index.html.

4. Gordon and Trainor, 443.

5. Ibid.

6. Ibid.

7. Ibid., 444.

8. Ibid., 443.

9. Fred Barnes, "The Commander: How Tommy Franks Won the Iraq War," *Weekly Standard*, June 2, 2003.

10. Gordon and Trainor, map: "Delta Force Route and Engagements," xiii.

11. Ibid., 443.

12. Ibid., 331.

13. Kevin Woods, Michael R Pease, Mark E Stout, Williamson Murray, and James G. Lacey, "A View of Operation Iraqi Freedom from Saddam's Senior Leadership," *Iraqi Perspectives Project*, 131. "The impression of these reports was that a large

American armored force was driving from Jordan and across the western desert. This impression would have profound implications later in the war. Over time, these and other reports helped to fix in Saddam's mind the idea that the main co-alition attack was coming out of Jordan."

14. "Team Tank: Armor in Support of Special Operations," *Veritas: Journal of Army Special Force History* (Winter 2005), 69–73.

15. Ibid.

16. Ibid.

17. Gordon and Trainor, 443.

18. Ibid.

19. Ibid.

20. Ibid., 442.

21. Ibid., 444.

22. Ibid.

23. Ibid., 443.

24. Ibid., 444.

25. Woods, Pease, Stout, Murray, and Lacey, 131.

26. General Patton was one of the first military leaders to recognize and describe this historical incongruity between that which is actually recorded as history and those who actually make it.

CHAPTER 1

1. See Holloway Commission Report, http://www.gwu.edu/~nsarchiv/NSAEBB/NSAEBB63/doc8.pdf.

CHAPTER 2

1. Eric Haney, *Inside Delta Force* (New York: Delacorte Press, 2002), 104.

2. Ibid.

3. Ibid.

4. William G. Boykin, *Never Surrender* (New York: FaithWords, 2008), 74.

5. http://en.wikipedia.org/wiki/Delta_Force.

CHAPTER 3

1. Boykin, 297.

2. http://www.nato.int/sfor/organisation/mission.htm.

3. Ibid.

4. Richard J. Newman, "The first account of secret U.S. missions in Bosnia," *US News and World Report*, June, 28, 1998. http://www.usnews.com/usnews/news/articles/980706/archive_004280.htm.

5. Boykin, 303.

6. Mark Bowden, *Blackhawk Down* (New York: Atlantic Monthly Press, 1999), 23.

7. http://www.un.org/icty/cases-e/index-e.htm.

8. Sean Naylor, *Not a Good Day to Die* (New York: Berkley Caliber, 2005), 106.

9. Haney, 164.

10. www.bigfootencounters.com.htm "While traveling in remote parts of Montenegro collecting stories and beliefs from the local people, he came across a man who had actually claimed to have seen hairy human-like creature many years ago in the nearby mountains. The man's name was Bozo Radoviæ who was a peasant and a sheep watcher."

11. Edward de Bono, *Lateral Thinking* (New York: Harper and Row, 1970), 11.

CHAPTER 4

1. National Commission on Terrorists Attacks, *The 9/11 Commission Report* (New York: W.W. Norton and Company, 2004). See On Fadl, e.g., Intelligence reports on historical background of Bin Ladin's army (Nov. 26, 1996; Apr. 18, 1997); on the structure of al Qaeda and leadership composition (Dec. 18, 1996; Dec. 19, 1996; Dec. 19, 1996); on roles and responsibilities of the organizational component (Dec. 19, 1996); on objectives and direction (Jan. 8, 1997; Jan. 27, 1997); on the financial infrastructure and networks (Dec. 30, 1996; Jan. 3, 1997); on connections and collaboration with other terrorist groups and supporters (Jan 8, 1997; Jan. 31, 1997; Jan 31, 1997; Feb. 7, 1997); on activities in Somalia (Apr. 30, 1997); on Bin Ladin's efforts to acquire WMD materials (Mar. 18, 1997). On the other walk-in source, see CIA cable, Jan. 3, 1997. Material from the Nairobi cell was introduced into evidence during the testimony of FBI Special Agent Daniel Coleman, *United States v. Usama Bin Laden*, No. S(7) 98 Cr. 1023 (S.D.N.Y.), Feb. 21, 2001 (transcript pp. 1078–1088, 1096–1102). Mike interview (Dec. 11, 2003).

2. "The Spider in the Web" *Economist*, September 20, 2001, http://www.economist.com/world/na/displayStory.cfm?Story_ID=788472.

3. National Commission on Terrorists Attacks, *The 9/11 Commission Report*, 111.

4. Ibid.

5. Steve Coll, *Ghost Wars* (New York: Penguin Books, 2004), 414.

6. *The 9/11 Commission Report*, 110.

7. Ibid.

8. Coll, 391.

9. *The 9/11 Commission Report*, 110.

10. Ibid.

11. *The 9/11 Commission Report*, 111.

12. Ibid.

13. Coll, 342.

14. Ibid., 391.

15. http://usmilitary.about.com/library/milinfo/navyfacts/bltomahawk.htm.

16. In *Undaunted Courage*, Stephen Ambrose's bestselling account of the Lewis and Clark expedition, there is no chapter on planning; instead, chapter Seven is titled "Preparing for the Expedition."

17. While reading the 9/11 Commission report in 2004, I discovered that the CIA actually landed on one of the same dry lake beds in 1997 to exfiltrate Mir Amal Kasi, the Pakistani migrant worker who had shot up the entrance to the CIA Headquarters in 1993.

18. *The 9/11 Commission Report*, 113 (I was never aware of any other "Unit" involvement in the UBL mission until I read the following passage in the 9/11 Commission report in 2004): "Military officers reviewed the capture plan" and, according to "Mike," "found no showstoppers." The commander of Delta Force felt "uncomfortable" with having the tribals hold Bin Ladin captive for so long, and the commander of Joint Special Operations Forces, Lieutenant General Michael Canavan, was worried about the safety of the tribals inside Tarnak Farms. General Canavan said he had actually thought the operation too complicated for the CIA—"out of their league"—and an effort to get results "on the cheap."

CHAPTER 5

1. "Bombings of the U.S. Embassies in Nairobi, Kenya and Dar es Salaam, Tanzania on August 7, 1998." U.S. State Department Report of the Accountability Review Boards.

2. "Chronology of Planning," DOD memo, December 14, 1998.

3. Osama bin laden FAQ, www.msnbc.com, September 15, 2001.

4. Washingtonpost.comTerrorist Data.htm.

5. *The 9/11 Commission Report*, 130.

6. Sandy Berger's testimony before the Joint Inquiry Committee, September, 19, 2002.

7. NSC e-mail, Clarke to Berger, August 8, 1998; Samuel Berger interview (January 14, 2004); CIA memo,"Khowst and the Meeting of Islamic Extremist Leaders on August 17, 1998."

8. NSC notes, checklist re military strikes, August 14, 1998 (author appears to be Clarke). On the military plans see "Chronology of Planning," DOD memo, December 14, 1998.

9. For a time line of the decision-making events, see NSC memo to Steinberg et al., August. 17, 1999. The list of concurrences is drawn from talking points prepared for Berger's use with the main four leaders of the House and Senate; the list explicitly mentions the attorney general. NSC e-mail, Clarke to Berger, August 19, 1998. Reno told the 9/11 commission she did not mention her concerns to the president but discussed them with Berger, Tenet, White House Counsel Charles Ruff, and DOJ staff. Janet Reno interview (December 16, 2003).

10. *The 9/11 Commission Report*, 189.

11. Ibid., 117.

12. Robert Dorr, "Battles Domestic and Military Heat Up," *Washington Watch* (October, 1998): 8.

13. *The 9/11 Commission Report*, 145.

14. Ibid., 140.

15. Richard H. Shultz Jr., "Showstoppers: Nine reasons why we never sent our Special Operations Forces after al Qaeda before 9/11." *The Weekly Standard* (January 26, 2004).

CHAPTER 6

1. Coll, 442.

2. "Showstoppers: Nine reasons why we never sent our Special Operations Forces after al Qaeda before 9/11."

3. Timothy Roche, Brian Bennett, Anne Berryman, Hilary Hylton, Siobhan Morrissey, and Amany Radwan, "The Making of John Walker Lindh," Time.com (September 29, 2002).

4. *United States of America v. John Phillip Walker Lindh, a/k/a "Suleyman al-Faris," a/k/a "Abdul Hamid,"* In the United States District Court for the Eastern District of Virginia, Alexandria Division.

5. http://www.merip.org/mer/mer224/224_aidi.html, www.newsindia-times.com/ 2002/02/15/after9-us.html, http://www.yaleherald.com/article.php?Article=185, http:// www.foxnews.com/story/0,2933,121040,00.html.

CHAPTER 7

1. Haney, 104.

2. Boykin, 174.

CHAPTER 8

1. Gallaway, J. Carlton, "The Complete Microwave Oven Service Handbook," http://www.gallawa.com/microtech/microwave_repair_handbook.html.

2. Gunther Greulich, "Who invented GPS?" *GPS World* (January 2007).

CHAPTER 10

1. "Operation Enduring Freedom–Order of Battle." http://www.globalsecurity. org/military/ops/enduring-freedom_orbat-02.htm.

2. Naylor, 32. See also: "A Nation Challenged: Strategy; Shifting Missions Come with Rising Risks," *New York Times* (December 9, 2001).

3. Robert S. Tripp, Kristin F. Lynch, and John G. Drew. "Supporting air and space expeditionary forces: lessons from Operation Enduring Freedom," Rand Corporation, 2004.

4. Boykin, 16, 251.

5. Bob Woodward, *Bush at War* (New York: Simon & Schuster, 2002), 165. "Special Operations early were not possible," Rumsfeld said. "Can't do it in the north, haven't really got good targets yet in the south."

6. Ibid., 248.

7. Ibid., 249.

8. "Deployed commanders now use secure VTC routinely for situational awareness in status briefing updates" http://www.mit-kmi.com/print_article.cfm?DocID=505.

9. "The Americans have left it too late to send in ground troops before winter," *The Independent* (November 6, 2001). Available at: http://independent.co.uk, accessed on November 7, 2007.

CHAPTER 11

1. Naylor, 76.

2. J. M. Berger, *Ali Mohamed Sourcebook* (More than 400 pages of analysis, court and intelligence documents about al Qaeda's most dangerous sleeper agent).

3. *Luke Harding, Julian Borger,* and *Richard Norton-Taylor,* "The fierce Taliban response to the Delta Force raid led to a review of similar planned operations, and to questioning of the leadership of the war's US commander, General Tommy Franks." *The Guardian* (November 6, 2001).

4. http://www.globalsecurity.org/security/profiles/abu_musab_al-zarqawi.htm.

5. Woodward, 314.

6. Naylor, 28.

CHAPTER 12

1. http://www.cooperativeresearch.org/timeline.jsp?other_al-qaeda_operatives=ali Mohamed&timeline=complete_911_timeline.

2. Joseph Neff, and John Sullivan, "Al-Qaeda terrorist duped FBI, Army," *Raleigh News & Observer* (October 24, 2001).

3. See exclusive, never-before-published material included in this wire-bound collection, selected and compiled by INTELWIRE.com's *J. M. Berger,* lead researcher of the cable TV documentary on Ali Mohamed, *National Geographic Presents: Triple Cross: Bin Laden's Spy in America.* Preview *Introduction and Table of Contents.* See also: http://www.aim.org/aim-column/bin-ladens-military-mole.

4. U.S. State Department Report of the Accountability Review Boards. "Bombings of the U.S. Embassies in Nairobi, Kenya and Dar es Salaam, Tanzania on August 7, 1998."

5. Guilty plea of Ali Mohamed. *United States v Ali Mohamed,* October 20, 2000.

6. *Raleigh News and Observer,* October 24, 2001.

7. Larry C. Johnson, a former deputy director of the Office of Counterterrorism at the State Department who had previously worked for the CIA, confirms it at least in part. He told the *San Francisco Chronicle* that the CIA had a brief relationship with Ali Mohamed after he offered in 1984 to provide information about terrorist groups in the Middle East. http://www.aim.org/aim-column/bin-ladens-military-mole.

8. *Raleigh News and Observer,* October 24, 2001.

9. Lance Williams and Erin McCormick, "Bin Laden's man in Silicon Valley, Mohamed the American orchestrated terrorist acts while living a quiet suburban life in Santa Clara," *San Francisco Chronicle* (September 21, 2001).

10. US Immigrant Veterans New Battle, http://english.aljazeera.net/NR/exeres/BAECBE58-5596-4BCA-AFA0-6A7B2B4B2807.htm.

11. George Crile, *Charlie Wilson's War: The Extraordinary Story of the Largest Covert Operation in History* (New York: Atlantic Monthly Press, 2003), 126.

12. *Raleigh News and Observer*, October 24, 2001.

13. http://www.aim.org/aim-column/bin-ladens-military-mole.

14. "Anatomy of a Terrorist Attack: An In-Depth Investigation into the 1998 Bombings of the U.S Embassies in Kenya and Tanzania," Matthew B. Ridgway Center for International Security Studies at the University of Pittsburgh.

15. *Raleigh News and Observer*, October 24, 2001.

16. According to 1999 court testimony from Khaled Abu el-Dahab, the other known member of Mohamed's Santa Clara, California, Al-Qaeda cell. *New York Times*, November 21, 2001.

17. Guilty plea of Ali Mohamed, *United States v Ali Mohamed*, October 20, 2000.

18. Phoenix Consulting:http://www.intellpros.com/traininginfo_fullcatalog.php?offset=15&pagenumber=4.

19. Naylor, 76.

20. Interviews with Colonel John Mulholland and General Tommy Franks for PBS documentary. http://www.pbs.org/wgbh/pages/frontline/shows/campaign/ground/torabora.html.

CHAPTER 13

1. Woodward, 313.

2. Ibid., 314.

CHAPTER 14

1. A paper written by Col. Andrew Milani of the 160th Special Operations Aviation Regiment, entitled "Pitfalls of Technology: A Case Study of the Battle of Takur Ghar" outlined the entire force structure of Special Operations forces in country at the time. This unclassified paper is now one of the main references used by Wikipedia for Operation Anaconda. http://en.wikipedia.org/wiki/Operation_Anaconda.

2. Naylor, 34

3. Executive summary of the Battle of Takur Ghar, released through the Department of Defense, May 24, 2002, http://www.defenselink.mil/news/May2002/d20020524takurghar.pdf.

4. General Tommy Franks, *American Soldier* (New York: HarperCollins, 2004), 251, 261.

5. Malcolm Gladwell, *The Tipping Point* (New York: Little, Brown and Company, 2000), 41.

6. Naylor, 23.

7. Executive summary of the Battle of Takur Ghar, released through the Department of Defense, May 24, 2002, http://www.defenselink.mil/news/May2002/d20020524takurghar.pdf.

8. Naylor, 39.

9. The story of our encounter with the warlord was told by Deputy Secretary of Defense Paul Wolfowitz during a public speech in Washington, D.C., in 2005.

CHAPTER 15

1. Naylor, 8.

2. Ibid., 9.

3. Ibid.

4. Ibid.

5. Ibid., 10.

6. Ibid.

7. Ibid., 39.

CHAPTER 16

1. Jay Solomon, "Failed Courtship of Warlord Trips Up U.S. in Afghanistan," *Wall Street Journal*, November 8, 2007. "Mr. Haqqani is now one of the major rebel leaders roiling Afghanistan. But back in autumn 2002, he secretly sent word that he could ally with the new U.S.-friendly Afghan government. The warlord had once been a partner of the Central Intelligence Agency, and later closely collaborated with Osama bin Laden and the ruling Taliban."

2. Richard S. Ehrlich, "Afghanistan: An American Graveyard?" *The Laissez Faire City Times*, October 29, 2001.

3. http://www.time.com/time/magazine/article/0,9171,1101030407-438861,00.html. The *Time* article describes that the Iraqi military circulated copies of the movie *Black Hawk Down* before the war, as a manual for defeating the Americans.

4. Naylor, 32.

5. Ibid.

6. Ibid.

7. Franks, 493.

8. Naylor, 80.

9. Although specifically forbidden in the USSOCOM Public Affairs Guidance from providing off-record interviews, it is obvious from a close reading of *Not a Good Day to Die* that a number of key TF 11 high-level leaders talked to Sean Naylor "off the record."

10. Naylor, 81.

11. Ibid.

12. Ibid., 39.

CHAPTER 17

1. The Battle of Shahi Koht of March 2002, described and analyzed by one of the participants, Abdul-'Adheem Article ID: 1055 | 2516 reads *Translated by Azzam Publications*. The original form of this enemy account was published in 2003 on the Taliban website (www.azam.com) The website had a similar interactive protocol as Wikipedia. As I checked on site over the many months that followed, the account continuously transmogrified from its original content into the propaganda-inspired mess that is posted today. There were at least three enemy first-person accounts written by enemy fighters during and after the battle. I was able to read all three in their original untouched format and corroborate much of what they said by cross-referencing each account with both friendly and enemy sources of information. The number of enemy that was in the valley is a topic of much debate among both historians and participants of the battle. The number used in this book comes from an aggregation of the three accounts I read.

2. Naylor, 141.

3. Ibid., 142.

4. Ibid., 144.

5. Ibid., 156.

6. Ibid., 157.

7. Ibid., 169.

8. Ibid.

9. Ibid.

10. Ibid., 176.

CHAPTER 18

1. See Centcom report available at http://www.globalsecurity.org/military/library/news/2002/11/mil-021108-centcom01.htm.

2. Chinese Recorder, vol. 69, no. 1 (January 1938): 2.

3. Joint Publication 3-09.3 *Joint Tactics, Techniques, and Procedures for Close Air Support.* See chapter 5, fig. V-9, example of standard brevity terms required to vector attack aircraft using lasers, http://www.globalsecurity.org/military/library/policy/dod/doctrine/jp3_09_3.pdf.

CHAPTER 19

1. Naylor, 286.

2. Ibid.

3. Ibid.

4. Ibid., 302.

5. Ibid., 303.

6. Ibid., 307.

7. Ibid., 309.

8. Ibid.

9. Ibid.

10. Executive summary of the Battle of Takur Ghar, released through the Department of Defense, May 24, 2002, http://www.defenselink.mil/news/May2002/d20020524takurghar.pdf.

11. http://en.wikipedia.org/wiki/Lockheed_AC-130.

12. Executive summary of the Battle of Takur Ghar.

13. Ibid.

14. Naylor, 318.

15. Nate Self, *Two Wars: One Hero's Fight on Two Fronts—Abroad and Within* (Wheaton, Illinois: Tyndale House Publishers, 2008), 216.

16. Ibid.

17. Ibid.

18. http://science.howstuffworks.com/predator.htm.

19. Naylor, 322.

20. Ibid.

21. Ibid., 328.

22. Self, 146. "I recognized the voice on the radio, it was Pete Blaber, a man with a long history with the Rangers and Delta Force . . . I trusted him, if he's in control here, everything will be fine."

INDEX

Page numbers followed by "n" indicate notes.

Abdullah, Fazul, 181
Abu Jihad, 181
Abu Zarqawi, 173
Abu Zubeida, 173
AC-130s, 83, 221, 263, 265, 276, 280–281, 282, 283, 286–287, 288, 290
"actionable intelligence," 89, 91, 92
action (taking) to make action, 158–159
action vs. interaction, 14
activity patterns of UBL, 73–74
adaptable mind-set of AFO men, 205
additional men, request for, 233, 234
advanced force operations (AFO). See also battle begins (stay calm, think!); organizing for combat (dealing with a natural disaster); reality; Takur Ghar
adaptable mind-set of AFO men, 205
defined, 203
exploring the frontier (recognizing enemy patterns), 221, 222, 238, 239
headquarters of, 229–230
mujahideen fighters destroyed by, 266, 267–268, 269, 270
adventurer, Ali Mohamed, 184, 194, 195
Afghan general (ex) for on-the-ground knowledge, 159–162, 163, 168, 296
Afghanistan. See also Al Qaeda; battle begins (stay calm, think!); exploring the frontier (recognizing enemy patterns); mujahideen fighters; organizing for combat (dealing with a

natural disaster); reality; Takur Ghar
Afghan soldiers, Operation Anaconda, 262–263, 265, 269, 275, 277, 293–294
daughter of Afghan warlord as face of future of, 210–212
hatred of UBL and Al Qaeda, 157, 163, 211
homes in, 220
intelligence on, 65–66, 68, 69
mountainous terrain of, 109–110
on the ground in (riding the edge of chaos), 203–213
resistance fighters, Ali Mohamed volunteering for, 185
Soviet war in, learning from, 223, 296
"too risky," infiltrations into, 94
warlords, establishing relationships with, 206–212
Afghanistan-Pakistan border, 81
AFO. See advanced force operations
Aideed, Mohamed Farrah, 139
Aimes, Aldrich, 194
air assault (helicopter), 239–241
AK-47s, 267
Albright, Madeleine (Secretary of State), 87
Alexander the Great, 211
Al Farooq mosque (New Jersey), 188
Al Farooq terrorist training camp and Lindh, 99–100
Al-Iman University and Lindh, 97

all-terrain vehicles (ATVs) used by Juliet team, 247, 251, 254
Al Qaeda. *See also* Afghanistan; embassy bombings (only failure is a failure to try); Taliban
  Afghan warlord's hatred of, 211
  Ali Mohamed falling-outs with, 189
  caste system, 246, 267–268
  embassy bombings and, 88
  infiltration of Al Qaeda (discovering the art of the possible), 94–105
  John Walker Lindh and, 99–100
  leaders' vulnerability in Kandahar, 173
  Osama bin Laden (UBL), 63–85
  trained by Ali Mohamed, 181–182, 188, 194
altitude, acclimation to, 226
always listen to the guy on the ground (guiding-principle lesson), 15, 128, 129–131, 168, 279, 295. *See also* guy on the ground
Ambrose, Stephen, 82
Americans as "creatures of comfort," 224, 261, 264
Amin, Idi, 139
"anvil and hammer," 250, 265, 268
Apocalypse Now (film), 75, 233
Appalachian Mountains, Delta Force selection process, 31, 32
Aqil's infiltration of Al Qaeda, 101
armored division, 9
arrest of Ali Mohamed, 189
art of the possible, discovering the (infiltration of Al Qaeda), 94–105
"Art of the Possible, The," 145, 176
Atef, Mohammed and Ali Mohamed, 188–189
athleticism of Blaber, 22, 30, 32
ATVs (all-terrain vehicles) used by Juliet team, 247, 251, 254
audacity, principle of war, 234
"aye, aye," 258, 258n

backpackers vs. military, 111
backpacking, forty-pound standard, 114–115, 118
"backside" support, 117
Baghdad, 9
Bagram Air Base, 179, 204, 219, 230, 231, 232, 238, 273, 284, 288, 291
battle begins (stay calm, think!), 262–271

battlefield chaos and genius, Special Forces, 201–202
Battle of LZ X-ray, 240
Bear Went over the Mountain, The (Grau and Jalali), 223
Beirut, 106
Berger, Sandy (National Security Advisor), 87, 88, 89
BGM-109C/D Tomahawk Block III cruise missiles, 90
Bill (Unit commander), 2–3, 7–8, 11–12
bin Laden, Osama (UBL), 63–85. *See also* Afghanistan; Al Qaeda; mujahideen fighters; Taliban
Blaber, Pete. *See also* guiding-principle lessons; Special Forces Operational Detachment (Delta, Delta Force, the Unit)
  Ali Mohamed (counterfeit double agent), 180–197
  battle begins (stay calm, think!), 262–271
  Bob Marshall Wilderness Area, "the Bob" (Montana), 106–131
  calm before the storm (Man-Huntin' Project), 135–143, 150–151, 215
  embassy bombings (only failure is a failure to try), 86–93
  exploring the frontier (recognizing enemy patterns), 220–241
  gorilla warfare (Bosnia-Herzegovina), 40–59
  imagining everyone's potential as the guy on the ground, 148–163
  imagining how to seek out the guy on the ground, 164–179
  infiltration of Al Qaeda, 94–105
  natural selection (getting into Delta Force), 31–39
  9/11 (four-inch knife blade), 144–147
  on the ground in Afghanistan (riding the edge of chaos), 203–213
  organizing for combat (dealing with a natural disaster), 214–219
  Osama bin Laden (UBL), 63–85
  patterns of hindsight, 19–30
  Takur Ghar, 272–297
  Task Force Wolverine, cloverleaf incident (Tikrit, Iraq), 1–13
Blackhawk Down (film), 75
Blade (Unit reconnaissance expert), 53
blending in anywhere, Special Forces, 36, 107

BM-21, 289
Bob (Unit operator), 235–236, 252
Bob Marshall Wilderness Area, "the Bob"
    (Montana), 106–131
body movements and deception, 190
Bogotá, 106
bombing cars, 20–22, 38
Bosnia-Herzegovina (gorilla warfare), 40–59
Bosniaks (Muslims), 42
boundaryless, 218–219, 243, 268, 296–297
boundary-spanning, 158, 159–163
box (rank-and-file) formations, Civil War,
    28
brainstorming
    gorilla warfare (Bosnia-Herzegovina),
        48–54, 59
    imagining everyone's potential as the guy
        on the ground, 155–158, 174
    imagining how to seek out the guy on the
        ground, 174–176
broken-down vehicle idea, 48, 51
Bruiser (Unit operator), 48, 53, 54
burkhas, 166n, 166–167
Bush, George W. (President), 98, 171
Bush at War (Woodward), 151

C-17s, 6
calm before the storm (Man-Huntin'
    Project), 135–143, 150–151, 215
camera, taking on mission, 249–250, 256
capture recommendations for UBL, 64, 65,
    81–82, 83–84
cardboard cow idea, 50–51, 52–53, 59
Casanova (Unit operator), 119, 121, 122,
    123–124
caste system of Al Qaeda, 246, 267–268
casualties, Operation Anaconda, 265, 266,
    288, 292
CG (commanding general) vs. Blaber, 8,
    9–10, 11–12, 13, 233, 243–244, 245
CH-47s, 75n, 250, 250n
challenges, 32
Chamberlain, Joshua, 11
Chapman, John A. (SEAL), 288, 292
Cheney, Dick (Vice President), 162
childhood of Blaber, 19–22
Chris H. (Special Forces commander), 215,
    216, 222, 265, 275, 282
CIA
    Ali Mohamed and, 182–183, 194
    exploring the frontier (recognizing enemy
        patterns), 221, 222, 222n

imagining how to seek out the guy on the
    ground, 173, 179
on the ground in Afghanistan (riding the
    edge of chaos), 202, 205, 206, 208,
    209
organizing for combat (dealing with a
    natural disaster), 214, 215, 218
reality check (what's your
    recommendation?), 244, 245
civilian defense contractors and military,
    collaboration between, 135–136
civilians, avoiding contact with, 247
Civil War battlefield trip, 27–28
Clarke, Richard (National Security
    Council), 87, 89
Clinton, Bill (President), 91, 94
clothing, thermo-regulating, 114
cloverleaf incident (Task Force Wolverine,
    Tikrit, Iraq), 1–13
cognitive science, 58
Cohen, William (Secretary of Defense), 87,
    91–92
cold weather environment skills, Special
    Forces, 107
Colombia, 108, 110, 117, 158
Colombian drug cartel kingpins, 139
combat experience of AFO men, 205
combat troops to support troops ratio
    (tooth to tail), 6
"coming off one's base," 190
commanding general (CG) vs. Blaber, 8,
    9–10, 11–12, 13, 233, 243–244, 245
commando costume, Blaber, 25
common sense
    derailers of, 122, 124–125, 130–131
    essence of global war against terrorisms,
        175
    providing context, 38–39
Common Sense (Paine), 175
communication (boundaryless) and shared
    reality, 296–297
communication short-circuits and decision-
    making errors, 285–286, 289, 291
communications specialists, pushing to
    pilot teams, 218
compartmentalized nature of planning and
    intelligence, 71, 90, 91, 93, 296
computer whiz in NWFP, Lindh as, 98
concussion grenade idea, 48–50
congratulations to terrorists about embassy
    bombings from UBL, 88
connector skills, importance of, 204–205

conspiracy, U.S. government incapable of planning big, 149

context

common sense, context as, 38, 39

don't get treed by a chihuahua: decision-making without context (guiding-principle lesson), 15, 38–39, 75, 93, 295

recognizing patterns and, 145

Continental Divide, crossing, 110n, 110–111, 112, 114, 125, 127–128

conventional vs. guerrilla army, Vietnam, 26

counter-elicitation, 189–190, 192, 193

counterfeit double agent (imagining how), 180–197

courage, 252

"creatures of comfort" Americans, 224, 261, 264

creatures of habit, mujahideen fighters as, 223, 224

credibility, assessing, 67, 160

creekbeds for artillery and lines of communication, mujahideen fighters, 224

Croatians (Catholic Christians), 42

cruise missiles

Osama bin Laden (UBL), 74, 75, 77–78

Small Group recommendation, 89–90, 90–91, 94, 105

cultural dynamics of Bosnia, 47–48

curiosity and human nature, 52–53

D-30 122-mm howitzers, 294

"danger-opportunity," 266, 266n, 268, 270

Danno (AFO member), 207

daughter of Afghan warlord as face of future of Afghanistan, 210–212

daughter of PIFWC, 45, 52

Dayton Peace Agreement, 42

DCG. See deputy commanding general

D-Day, 201–202

dealing with a natural disaster (organizing for combat), 214–219

decision-making

poor by government agencies and military, 26, 27, 28, 29, 30

without context: don't get treed by a chihuahua (guiding-principle lesson), 15, 38–39, 75, 93, 295

decisive point for capture operation, 55

Dee (Unit intelligence analyst), 64–65, 66, 67, 68, 69, 71, 73, 74, 77, 78, 81, 83, 85

Deer Hunter, The (film), 25

defense acquisition reforms, 137–138

defense contractors, collaboration with military, 135–136, 137

Deliverance (film), 116

Delta/Delta Force. See Special Forces Operational Detachment

Department of Defense, 230

deputy commanding general (DCG)

exploring the frontier (recognizing enemy patterns), 230–231, 232

Takur Ghar, 273, 274, 275, 276, 279, 284, 285, 288

desert environment skills, Special Forces, 107

Desert Island, Persian Gulf, 148–163

Desert One Hostage Rescue Mission, 28–30

developing the situation. See when in doubt, develop the situation (guiding-principle lesson)

disclosure agreements, ix–xi

discovering the art of the possible (infiltration of Al Qaeda), 94–105

disguises, deception, diversions to confuse and confound enemy (Special Forces), 5, 6, 7, 13, 43, 84

Dolly Varden Creek, 124

don't get treed by a chihuahua: decision-making without context (guiding-principle lesson), 15, 38–39, 75, 93, 295

dots (facts and events) prior to 9/11, connecting, 145–147

Drago (Unit operator), 47n, 47–48

drag queen Afghan security guard, 207, 208

DShK machine gun, 281

east side, Shahi Khot Valley (Juliet team), 247, 251–252, 253–254, 256, 259

effects-based warfare, 177

ego, powerful pull on humans, 23

Egypt Air, 182

Eid ul-Fitr (Id-Ul-Fitr), 255, 255n

emailing mother from NWFP, Lindh, 98

embassy bombings (only failure is a failure to try), 86–93. See also Al Qaeda

emotional intelligence, respect for, 111

empty target raids, 150, 151, 152–153, 155, 156, 157, 168, 171–172, 173, 227
enabling vs. end-state objective, 55
enemy
    always having a vote, 43, 57
    defining, 156–157, 162–163
    patterns, recognizing (exploring the frontier), 220–241
environment, organizing according to, 218
environmental reconnaissance
    Bosnia-Herzegovina, 46–47
    exploring the frontier (recognizing enemy patterns), 228–229
    Shahi Khot Valley, 235, 236–237
environmental training, Special Forces, 107–108
ethnic cleansing, 42
experimentation by reconnaissance teams, 236
exploring the frontier (recognizing enemy patterns), 220–241
"eyes on the target," 227

face-to-face meetings
    Blaber and Ali Mohamed, 180, 189, 191–195
    UBL and Lindh, 100, 101
facts and events (dots) prior to 9/11, connecting, 145–147
failure (only) is a failure to try (embassy bombings), 86–93
Falconview mapping software, 46–47
false reality of leaders, 274
"fanatic" label, 185, 186, 195
FARC guerrillas of Colombia, 110
fatwah, 66, 66n
FBI and Ali Mohamed, 187, 188, 189, 194
feet (navigating with), Delta Force selection process, 37
5th Special Forces Group. See also Special Forces Operational Detachment (Delta, Delta Force, the Unit)
    imagining how to seek out the guy on the ground, 173, 179
    on the ground in Afghanistan (riding the edge of chaos), 205, 206, 208, 209, 212
    organizing for combat (dealing with a natural disaster), 214, 215, 218
50/10 technique, 119
5307th Composite Unit (Provisional), "Merrill's Marauders," 1n

filming of raids, 152, 153, 171, 172
finding missions, Blaber, 20
finger, Shahi Khot Valley (Mako 31 team), 247–248, 252, 253, 255, 256
firearms and walking the Bob, 115–116
1st Battalion, 87th Regiment (I-87) of the 10th Mountain Division, 238
first-aid bags, 117
fishhook, Shahi Khot Valley (India team), 247, 252–253, 259
Flathead River, 119–200
food (scarcity), Blaber's childhood, 19–20
footprint paradox, 75–77
foreign intelligence sources, 44
Fort Bragg (North Carolina), 40–41
forty-pound standard for backpacking, 114–115, 118
Foster, Jodie, 146–147
four-inch knife blade
    Ali Mohamed as, 187, 188
    9/11, 144–147
Franks, Tommy (General, Commander in Chief of U.S. Central Command), 204, 205, 238
Fredericksburg, 28
freedom of choice, 104, 131
Friedman, Thomas, 174–175, 176
friendly fire incident, 265
Frosty (intelligence operative), 164–165
future, preparing for, 16
future of Afghanistan, daughter of Afghan warlord as face of, 210–212

Gahahn, Adam's infiltration of Al Qaeda, 102
Gardez safe house, 167, 211, 216, 220–221, 233, 239
Gettysburg, 27–28
Ghazni, 167
Gladwell, Malcolm, 204
Glenn (Unit intelligence analyst), 44, 45, 239, 273–274
Goody (SEAL), 238, 249–250, 253, 255, 256–257, 258, 259, 263, 269
Google maps, 47
Gore-Tex, 114
gorilla suit idea, 53–55, 56–57, 58, 59
gorilla warfare (Bosnia-Herzegovina), 40–59
government databases, 67, 71
GPS navigation system, 136
Grau, Lester, 223

Green Berets, Ali Mohamed as member of, 182, 183–187
Grenada, 106
grizzly bears in Bob Marshall Wilderness Area, 109, 116, 123, 126, 127, 128, 129
ground infiltrations behind enemy lines (longest), 5
guiding-principle lessons. *See also* patterns; when in doubt, develop the situation (guiding-principle lesson)
 always listen to the guy on the ground, 15, 128, 129–131, 168, 279, 295
 don't get treed by a chihuahua (decision-making without context), 15, 38–39, 75, 93, 295
 imagining the unimaginable, humor your imagination, 58–59, 146, 295
 it's not reality unless it's shared, 295–297
 patterns, recognizing as, 14–15, 294–295
 3Ms (the Mission, the Men, and Me), 10–16, 244–245, 258, 295
guy on the ground. *See also* on-the-ground knowledge
 always listen to the guy on the ground (guiding-principle lesson), 15, 128, 129–131, 168, 279, 295
 Bob Marshall Wilderness Area, "the Bob" (Montana), 129
 imagining everyone's potential as the, 148–163
 imagining how (counterfeit double agent), 180–197
 imagining how to seek out the, 164–179
 9/11 (four-inch knife blade) and, 146–147
 Takur Ghar, 283
 understanding, 219

Hagenbeck, Buster (Major General)
 battle begins (stay calm, think!), 260, 265, 268, 269, 270–271
 exploring the frontier (recognizing enemy patterns), 238–239
 reality check (what's your recommendation), 243, 245, 257, 259
"hammer and anvil," 250, 265, 268
"hand-cannon, the" (Smith & Wesson 44 Magnum), 115–116
handrailing, 120
Haqqani, Jalaluddin (mujahideen commander), 223, 224–225, 260, 264, 296

hatred of UBL and Al Qaeda, Afghanistan, 157, 163, 211
Hayat, Khizar and Lindh, 97–98, 99
head-on assaults and mission failures, 228
hedging options, 104
helicopter air assault, 239–241
 longest in history, 153
 mujahideen fighters, shooting of, 281–282, 287, 291
 no-helicopters policy, 227–228
 Operation Anaconda, 239–241, 250, 250n, 255, 259–260, 265, 266–267
 Osama bin Laden (UBL), 74, 75n, 75–76
 Task Force Wolverine, cloverleaf incident (Tikrit, Iraq), 4, 9
helicopter crash (false), 178
helicopter insertion of SEALs, 276, 277–278, 281
Hersch, Seymour M., 171–172, 174
H-hour, 254, 255, 257
hiding places of UBL, 167–168, 195
hierarchical decision-making process, 278–280, 291
"highly coveted employee," 187
high-probability countries for operations, 108
high school years of Blaber, 22–24
high-value targets (HVTs), 229
hijacked plane as WMD, 145–146
Hitler, Adolf, 139
Hollywood portrayal of Special Forces, x, 75–76
homes in Afghanistan, 220
Homer (SEAL), 237–238
hostile wilderness of Bob Marshall Wilderness Area, 109, 117
hot-spots, feet, 119
hubris, derailer of person's common sense, 122, 124–125, 130–131
human intelligence, 66–67
humility (valued over self-aggrandizement), Special Forces, 15
humor your imagination, imagining the unimaginable (guiding-principle lesson), 58–59, 146, 295
Hussein, Saddam, 1, 2, 5, 6, 7, 13
HVTs (high-value targets), 229
hypothermia potential, 114

ICTY (International Criminal Tribunal for the former Yugoslavia), 42
Id-Ul-Fitr (Eid ul-Fitr), 255, 255n

illumination thinking phase, 70, 80, 103, 297

imagining everyone's potential as the guy on the ground, 148–163

imagining how (counterfeit double agent), 180–197

imagining how to seek out the guy on the ground, 164–179

imagining the unimaginable, humor your imagination (guiding-principle lesson), 58–59, 146, 295

"impenetrable" Al Qaeda, 100

incubation thinking phase, 70, 80, 103, 297

India team, 235, 247, 252–253, 259, 294

individual skills (maintaining), Special Forces, 107

infiltrating
Afghanistan, 166
Al Qaeda (discovering the art of the possible), 94–105
Kandahar and Kabul, 166–167

information as currency of spies, 216

integrating CIA and Special Forces into pilot teams, 218

intelligence analysts, pushing to pilot teams, 218

intelligence captured, Operation Anaconda, 264, 294

intelligence on Afghanistan, 151–152

interaction vs. action, 14

interagency unity of effort and success, 214, 215

intercepted phone calls (signal intelligence), 66, 67

International Criminal Tribunal for the former Yugoslavia (ICTY), 42

International Criminal Tribunal in The Hague, 57

Internet, 136, 296–297

Iran, 227

iridium satellite phone, 125

Islam, Yusuf (Lindh), 96

Islamic fundamentalism, Lindh, 95, 96–97

Islamic Movement of Uzbekistan, 242

it's not reality unless it's shared (guiding-principle lesson), 295–297

Jalalabad, 71, 167

Jalali, Ali Ahmad, 223

Jama'at, Tablighi and Lindh, 97

Jan, Qari Muhammad Tahir, 242

Jawad, Maulawi, 242

Jeff (Al Qaeda supervisor), 86, 88, 182. See also Mohamed, Ali (counterfeit double agent)

Jefferson, Thomas, 82, 83

Jimmy (AFO member), 204–205, 215, 216, 217, 218, 219, 239, 255, 257, 259, 268, 269, 270, 283–284, 290

Jinga trucks, 262, 262n

John (CIA), 215, 216

Joint Operations Center (JOC), 150

Juliet team, 235, 247, 251–252, 253–254, 256, 259, 292

jungle environment skills, Special Forces, 107

Kabul, 214, 239–240

Kahane, Meier, 188

Kalispell (Montana), 110, 117

Kandahar, 65, 67, 68, 72, 83, 151, 153, 161–162, 163, 173

Kap (Unit operator), 119

Kashmir, 108, 108n

"Kashmir" (Led Zeppelin), 274

Kelty backpacks, 115

Kennedy, John (President), 26

key terrain occupied by AFO teams, 269, 269n, 270

Kherchtou, L'Houssaine, 188

Khowst, 71, 72, 73, 89, 167

Kim Il Sung, 139

Knob Creek Kentucky Whiskey, 128

Korean War, 10

Kris K. (Unit operator), 235, 247, 252, 254

Kuwait, 106

Landing Zone 1, Takur Ghar, 276, 277

"last supper," 117

law of unintended consequences, 268

leading and shared reality, 297

Lecter, Hannibal, 147

Led Zeppelin, 22, 274

Lee, Robert E. (General), 27, 28

lessons from key events, unlearned, 13–14. See also guiding-principle lessons

Lewis and Clark scenario
Bob Marshall Wilderness Area, "the Bob" (Montana), 113, 114
calm before the storm (Man-Huntin' Project), 141–142
imagining everyone's potential as the guy on the ground, 166

Lewis and Clark scenario (*cont.*)
  imagining how to seek out the guy on the
    ground, 175, 176–177, 178–179
  infiltration of Al Qaeda, 102, 104, 105
  Osama bin Laden (UBL), 82–83, 84
LexisNexis, 156, 174
Librettos (mini-laptop computers), 46–47
life experiences of terrorists, 146–147
Life magazine, 26
Lindh, John Walker's infiltration of Al
    Qaeda, xii, 94–100, 102, 104, 105
Lindh, Suleyman al- (Lindh), 96
line-of-sight radio, 288, 289, 291
listening to the guy on the ground, always
    (guiding-principle lesson), 15, 128,
    129–131, 168, 279, 295. *See also* guy
    on the ground
"living laboratory" for operational
    breakthroughs, Bosnia-Herzegovina,
    47
locals, listening to
  Bob Marshall Wilderness Area, "the
    Bob" (Montana), 110–113
  exploring the frontier (recognizing enemy
    patterns), 220, 236
logistics (Special Forces), awesome
    capability of, 149–150
Longstreet, James (General), 28

M-4 rifles (checking chambers) and
    changing mind-set, 209
madrassa, 98, 98n
Mako 21 team, 275, 276
Mako 30 team, 275, 276, 277, 278, 280,
    281, 283, 284, 286, 288, 289
Mako 31 team, 237–238, 247–248, 252,
    253, 255, 256–258, 264, 265
man-ape creature sightings in Balkan
    Mountains, 58
Manassas, 28
Man-Huntin' Project (calm before the
    storm), 135–143, 150–151, 215
Mansoor, Maulawi Saif-ur-Rahman
    (mujahideen commander), 242,
    260–261, 293, 294
Mao Tse-tung, 220
marauding mission, success of, 1, 5–7, 13
Masirah, 232, 233, 257, 284, 288, 291
maverick, Ali Mohamed as, 184, 194,
    195
maximum-security prison, 190–191
McNamara, Robert, 26

MDMP (Military Decision-Making
    Process), 79–80, 240–241
"meat-eaters," 111
Medal of Honor recipient, 11
Menewar, 251
Merrill, Frank D., 1n
"Merrill's Marauders" (5307th Composite
    Unit, Provisional), 1n
MICE (money, ideology, coercion,
    excitement), 193–194
microwave oven, 136
Military Decision-Making Process
    (MDMP), 79–80, 240–241
Mill Valley mosque (California) and Lindh,
    95, 97
mind set of terrorists, 146–147
minefield planted by Al Qaeda, 242, 251
Ministry of Dirty Tricks, 177–178
mission, organizing according to, 218
Mission, the Men, and Me (3Ms), guiding-
    principle lesson, 10–16, 244–245, 258,
    295. *See also* Blaber, Pete
"modern-day warfare," models of, 139
Mogadishu (Somalia), 7, 106
Mohamed, Ali (counterfeit double agent),
    180–197, 296
money, ideology, coercion, excitement
    (MICE), 193–194
Moore's Law, 47, 256, 256n
"moral flexibility" of Ali Mohamed, 194,
    195
Motel Hell (film), 51
mountain environmental recons, 228–229
Mountain House freeze-dried meals, 115
mountainous terrain, Afghanistan,
    109–110
mountain training, 108–109. *See also* Bob
    Marshall Wilderness Area, "the Bob"
    (Montana)
moving targets and cruise missiles, 77–78
mujahideen fighters. *See also* Afghanistan;
    Al Qaeda; Taliban
  battle begins (stay calm, think!), 264,
    266
  destroyed by AFO, 266, 267–268, 269,
    270
  patterns of, 71, 185–186, 223–224
  reality check (what's your
    recommendation), 242, 254–255,
    260–261
  situational awareness trumped by
    precedent, 260–261

Takur Ghar, 272, 280, 287, 292–293
U.S. support of, 185–186
multisource corroboration of intelligence,
    66–67

Nairobi (Kenya) U.S. Embassy bombing,
    86–87, 88, 164, 181, 188, 189
National Forest Service, 110
National Park Service forest ranger (Sue),
    120–124, 128, 129, 130
natural disaster, dealing with (organizing
    for combat), 214–219
natural selection (getting into Delta Force),
    31–39
Navy SEALs
    helicopter insertion, Takur Ghar, 276,
        277–278, 281
    Mako 21 team, 275, 276
    Mako 30 team, 275, 276, 277, 278, 280,
        281, 283, 284, 286, 288, 289
    Mako 31 team, 237–238, 247–248, 252,
        253, 255, 256–258, 264, 265
    ordered by DCG, Takur Ghar, 273, 274,
        275, 276, 277
Naylor, Sean, 229–230, 231–232, 233, 236
"need to share," 296
negative reflections on individuals and
    learning lessons, 13
New Yorker, 171–172
nimble, getting, 218
9/11 (four-inch knife blade), 144–147
Nixon, Richard (President), 26
nondisclosure agreements, ix–xi
Noreiga, Manuel, 139
Northern Alliance, 179, 214
Northwest Frontier Province (NWFP), 98,
    102
Nosair, Al Said, 188
Not a Good Day to Die (Naylor),
    229–230
nuclear material for WMD, Al Qaeda
    attempts to obtain, 66
NWFP (Northwest Frontier Province), 98,
    102

OBL, 64n. See also bin Laden, Osama
    (UBL)
Officer Candidate School, 30
olfactory sense of grizzly bears, 109, 123
Omar, Mullah, 151, 172, 173
101st Airborne Division, 238, 239–240,
    250

on the ground in Afghanistan (riding the
    edge of chaos), 203–213
on-the-ground knowledge. See also guy on
    the ground
    Bosnia-Herzegovina area, 45–46
    technology vs., 255–257
operational insights, Ali Mohamed,
    164–168, 169, 170, 171, 176, 177, 296
operationally incarcerated in prison of plan,
    260–261
operational needs (difficult-to-solve),
    finding solutions to, 135, 136
operational security, ix–xi
operational sweet spots, 201–202
Operation Anaconda, 222n, 229–230,
    238–239. See also battle begins;
    exploring the frontier (recognizing
    enemy patterns); reality; Takur Ghar
Operation Infinite Reach, 90–91
opportunities lost
    Ali Mohamed, 181
    cancellation of capture mission, UBL,
        84–85
    imagining how to seek out the guy on the
        ground, 173
    video teleconference (VTC), 155
organizing for combat (dealing with a
    natural disaster), 214–219
organizing for the mission and shared
    reality, 296
Orgun AFO team, 206, 207–212, 217
Other Side of the Mountain, The (Grau and
    Jalali), 223
out-of-the box creative options, 228
outrageousness as barrier buster, 59
Owhail, Mohamed Rashed Daoud al, 88

Padilla, José's infiltration of Al Qaeda,
    101
pain and fooling your brain, 33, 37
Paine, Thomas, 175
Panama, 106
Panther (Unit commander), 1. See also
    Blaber, Pete
Pappas, Billy, 22, 23
parachute (phantom) operations around
    Kandahar, 177–178, 202
paranoia of UBL, 72, 73, 74, 91
Pashtuns, 71
patriot, Ali Mohamed as, 184
patterns. See also guiding-principle lessons
    Blaber (patterns of hindsight), 19–30

patterns (*cont.*)
  recognizing as guiding-principle lessons, 14–15, 294–295
  recognizing enemy patterns (exploring the frontier), 220–241
Patton, George, 234
Pearl, Daniel, 101
pepper spray for grizzly bears, 115, 116
permission to fire, request by AC-130, 286–287
Persian Gulf tactical operations center, 231
Persons Indicted for War Crimes (PIFWCs), 42, 43, 44–45, 47, 52, 56, 57, 139
Peshawar terrorist training camp and Lindh, 99
physical fitness responsibilities of Unit operators, 40
Pickett, George (General), 27
Pickett's Charge, 27–28
PIFWCs (Persons Indicted for War Crimes), 42, 43, 44–45, 47, 52, 56, 57, 139
pig/bear incident, Delta Force selection process, 33–35, 38, 39
pilot teams, 206
Polartec fleece, 114
Popular Science, 78
post-holing, 112, 112n, 122, 127
Pot, Pol, 139–140
potential as the guy on the ground, imagining everyone's, 148–163
Powell, Colin, 158–159
precedence, prison of, 294
Predator (Unit operator), 48–50, 54, 107–108, 116
Predator drone, images from, 283, 284–285, 286, 288
preparation, importance of, 113
press, value of, 172
pride, derailer of person's common sense, 122, 124–125, 130–131
proficiency, higher state of (Special Forces), 106
project design teams, 136, 139
prom night prank, Blaber, 22–24
psychological impact of helicopter assault, 240
psychological objectives, 152, 153, 173
psychologist ("the psyche"), 69–71, 80, 103

QRF (Ranger quick reaction force), 288–289, 290–292
questioning everything, 39

"Rakkasans" (3rd Brigade of the 101st Airborne Division), 239
Ranger quick reaction force (QRF), 288–289, 290–292
rank-and-file (box) formations, Civil War, 28
Rashid, Ahmed, 157
readiness, higher state of (Special Forces), 106
reading terrain, 127
reality. *See also* shared reality
  correcting context of guy on the ground, 270–271
  it's not reality unless it's shared (guiding-principle lesson), 295–297
  reality check (what's your recommendation?), 242–261
"real-world-mission scenarios," 141
Recognition-Primed Decision Model, 79n
recognizing enemy patterns (exploring the frontier), 220–241
reconnaissance missions, Shahi Khot Valley, 234–238
Red Dawn (film), 5
red not found in nature (RNFN), Bosnian women's hair, 46
religiously defined factions within Bosnia-Herzegovina, 42, 43
rendezvous point (RV), 32
requests for information (RFI), 67, 71
"required reading" table, 223
rescue mission, Takur Ghar, 283–292
Rex (AFO team leader), 206, 207, 208, 209, 210, 212
RFI (requests for information), 67, 71
riding the edge of chaos (on the ground in Afghanistan), 203–213
"ring of fire" (tanks and antiaircraft guns), Kandahar, 151, 161–162, 163
risk aversion of modern-day military, 75–77, 104–105
RNFN (red not found in nature), Bosnian women's hair, 46
Rob (Unit operator), 148, 149, 177
Roberts, Neil (SEAL), 281, 282, 283, 292
ROE (rules of engagement) flexibility, 45
"Roger," 258n
Roy (Unit operator), 119, 121–122, 123, 125–126, 127, 128
rucksack, 31, 32, 33
rules of engagement (ROE) flexibility, 45
RV (rendezvous point), 32

SA. *See* situational awareness
sacrifice of men (senseless) by government
    agencies and military, 26, 27, 28, 29,
    30
Sadat, Anwar, 185
sailor's guiding principles, 13, 14, 15
Sana'a (Yemen), 95–96
Santayana, George, 13, 14
Sarajevo, 106
satellite cell phone, UBL stopping usage of,
    91
satellite for detecting a person's genetic
    code, 140
satellite net (overwhelmed), Takur Ghar,
    282–283
satellite radio frequency, switched by DCG,
    285, 286
saturation thinking phase, 70, 80, 103,
    297
Schaefer Meadows, 119, 200
SEALs. *See* Navy SEALS
seeking out the guy on the ground,
    imagining how, 164–179
Self, Nate (Ranger), 290–291
September 11 (four-inch knife blade),
    144–147
Serbs (Orthodox Christians), 42, 43
SFORs in Bosnia, 42–43
Shahi Khot Valley
    Ali Mohamed, hiding place of UBL, 167
    east side, Juliet team, 247, 251–252,
        253–254, 256, 259
    exploring the frontier (recognizing enemy
        patterns), 223–224, 225–227, 232,
        234–237, 296
    finger, Mako 31 team, 247–248, 252,
        253, 255, 256
    fishhook, India team, 247, 252–253, 259
    organizing for combat (dealing with a
        natural disaster), 216
shared reality. *See also* reality
    communication (boundaryless) and,
        296–297
    exploring the frontier (recognizing enemy
        patterns), 238, 239–240
    it's not reality unless it's shared (guiding-
        principle lesson), 295–297
    leading and, 297
    on the ground in Afghanistan (riding the
        edge of chaos), 212–213
    organizing for combat (dealing with a
        natural disaster), 214, 218

organizing for the mission and, 296
Takur Ghar and, 283, 291
Sharif, Nawaz (Pakistani Prime Minister),
    94
Shawnee National Forest, 24–25
Shelton, Henry (General, Chairman of the
    Joint Chiefs of Staff), 87, 89, 91
shepherd (Afghan) and Shahi Khot,
    225–226, 296
Shillika ZSU-23 antiaircraft cannon, 272
shock and awe (thunder run) vs. marauding
    mission, 9–10, 11
signal intelligence (intercepted phone calls),
    66, 67
Silence of the Lambs (film), 146–147
Silver Star recipient, 113
Simpson, O. J., 190
sit-rep, 7, 7n, 238
situational awareness (SA). *See also* when in
    doubt, develop the situation (guiding-
    principle lesson)
    enemy (situational awareness of),
        reducing, 177
    falsely increased by VTC, 154–155
    maximum-security prison and, 191
    Osama bin Laden (UBL), 78–79, 80
    trumped by precedent (mujahideen
        fighters), 260–261
    trumped by tyranny of the plan, 171,
        259–260
six-hundred-dollar toilet seat, 137–138
skepticism of locals about walking the Bob,
    110–111, 113
Slab (SEAL), 276, 277, 278, 279, 280, 281,
    282, 283, 284, 287, 288, 289, 290
sleeper cells, 170
Small Group and embassy bombings, 87,
    88–90, 91, 92–93
Smith & Wesson .44 Magnum, "the
    hand-cannon," 115–116
"snain," 56
sniper and meetings with warlords, 207
snowshoes, 112, 118, 127
solution-focused collaboration between
    military and civilian defense
    contractors, 135–136
Somalia, 66, 181, 227
Southern Illinois University (SIU), 24–30
Soviet war in Afghanistan, learning from,
    223, 296
Special Forces (Green Berets), Ali Mohamed
    as member of, 182, 183–187

Special Forces Operational Detachment
(Delta, Delta Force, the Unit), x. *See
also* advanced force operations (AFO);
Blaber, Pete; CIA; 5th Special Forces
Group; Navy SEALs
   battlefield chaos and genius, 201–202
   blending in anywhere, 36, 107
   Bob Marshall Wilderness Area, "the
      Bob" (Montana), 106–131
   Desert One Hostage Rescue Mission,
      28–30
   disguises, deception, diversions to
      confuse and confound enemy, 5, 6, 7,
      13, 43, 84
   environmental training, 107–108
   exploring the frontier (recognizing enemy
      patterns), 221, 222
   Hollywood portrayal of, x, 75–76
   humility , valued over self-
      aggrandizement, 15
   individual skills, maintaining, 107
   logistics forces, 149–150
   "meat-eaters," 111
   operational sweet spots, 201–202
   physical fitness responsibilities, 40
   proficiency, higher state of, 106
   psychologist ("the psyche"), 69–71, 80,
      103
   readiness, higher state of, 106
   selection process, 31–39
   success (past), counting for nothing, 106
   warrior hug, no-touch, 204
speed, illogic of, 119
Speedy (Unit operator), 235–236, 243,
   248–249
Spider (CIA), 222, 234, 242–243, 246, 275,
   282, 284, 289, 290
spike mat (tire-puncturing device), 55–56,
   56n, 57, 59
Stan (Vietnam veteran, defense contractor),
   137–138, 139–140
stationary targets and cruise missiles, 77
stay calm, think! (battle begins), 262–271
stealth technology, 137
Stevens, Cat, 96
strategic reconnaissance skills of AFO,
   205
Stress Phase, Delta Force selection process,
   31–38
Stu (Unit operator), 119, 122, 124–125,
   130
"students of knowledge," 95

success (past), counting for nothing (Special
   Forces), 106
Sue (National Park Service forest ranger),
   120–124, 128, 129, 130
supplies and preparation, walking the Bob,
   113, 114, 115
switchbacks, 123, 125–126

tacit knowledge, 129–130, 155, 192–193,
   297
tactical operations center (TOC), 221–222,
   236
taking action to make action, 158–159
Takur Ghar, 272–297
Taliban. *See also* Afghanistan; Al Qaeda;
      mujahideen fighters
   dogma and Lindh, 98–99
   research on, 156–157, 160, 161
   squad leader, sharing information, 246
Taliban (Rashid), 157
tanks, Task Force Wolverine, 2, 3, 4, 6, 7, 9
tanks and antiaircraft guns ("ring of fire"),
   Kandahar, 151, 161–162, 163
Tanzania U.S. Embassy bombing, 87, 164,
   181, 188, 189
target folder, 63n, 63–64, 65
Tarnak Farms, 66, 67–68, 71, 73, 74, 83,
   84
Task Force 11, 229–230, 231–232, 239,
   243, 278, 279, 285, 286
Task Force Sword, 229. *See also* Task Force
   11
Task Force Wolverine, cloverleaf incident
   (Tikrit, Iraq), 1–13
technology
   on-the-ground knowledge vs., 255–257
   supremacy, military's faith in, 169–170,
      285–286
Tenet, George (CIA Director), 87, 89
10th Mountain Division, 238, 239, 242,
   244, 245, 248, 250, 260, 265,
   266–267, 268, 269, 271
Tera (Unit communications specialist),
   50–51, 52–53, 57
Tergal Ghar, 252, 253, 270
terrain, reading, 127
terrain and preparation, walking the Bob,
   113–114
terrorism, 65, 66. *See also* Al Qaeda
thermo-regulating clothing, 114
thinking, making time for, 236
thinking phases, 70, 80, 103, 297

3rd Brigade ("Rakkasans") of the 101st Airborne Division, 238

3Ms (the Mission, the Men, and Me), guiding-principle lesson, 10–16, 244–245, 258, 295

thunder run (shock and awe) vs. marauding mission, 9–10, 11

Tikrit, Iraq (Task Force Wolverine cloverleaf incident), 1–13

time/distance estimates
Bob Marshall Wilderness Area, "the Bob" (Montana), 113–114, 122
exploring the frontier (recognizing enemy patterns), 237

time-lapse images of Tarnak Farms, 68

time to recognize patterns, 145

tire-puncturing device (spike mat), 55–56, 56n, 57, 59

TOC (tactical operations center), 221–222, 236

toilet seat, six-hundred-dollar, 137–138

Tomahawk (BGM-109C/D) Block III cruise missiles, 90

"too risky," infiltrations into Afghanistan, 94

tooth to tail (ratio of combat troops to support troops), 6

Tora Bora, 167, 195, 230

Torres, Hiram's (Mohamed Salman) infiltration of Al Qaeda, 101–102

Toyota Land Cruisers used by UBL, 72, 73–74, 83, 84, 91

tracers, 2, 4

trapped tank, Task Force Wolverine, 3–4, 8, 11

travel by UBL, 72–73, 73–74

travel window of wanted PIFWC, 44, 45, 56, 57

treed by a chihuahua, don't get: decision-making without context (guiding-principle lesson), 15, 38–39, 75, 93, 295

"tribals, the," 71

Trojan horse technique, 5, 6, 9

Tuzla safe house, 43–44, 55

UBL. See bin Laden, Osama

UH-60 helicopters, 75n

Undaunted Courage (Ambrose), 82

unimaginable (imagining the), humor your imagination (guiding-principle lesson), 58–59, 146, 295

Unit, the. See Special Forces Operational Detachment

United Nations, 42, 44

unlearned lessons from key events, 13–14. See also guiding-principle lessons

urban environment skills, Special Forces, 107

U.S. embassy bombings (only failure is a failure to try), 86–93
Ali Mohamed and, 181, 182, 188, 189

U.S. Forest Service, 109

U.S. News and World Report, 101–102

U.S. secret agent, Ali Mohamed's desire to become, 194–195

U.S. support of mujahideen fighters, 185–186

USS Cole, 98

Uzbek fighters, Takur Ghar, 292

Val (Unit operator), 68, 69, 73, 74, 77–79, 82, 151, 152

values and psychotic terrorists, 146

vehicle reconnaissance missions, Shahi Khot Valley, 234–235

Vic (SEAL commander), 275, 277, 278, 279

video teleconference (VTC), 154–155, 170, 232–233

Viet Cong
Blaber's respect for, 26–27
mujahideen fighters vs., 223

Vietnam War
Battle of LZ X-ray, 240
Blaber's interest in, 26–27, 28
helicopters and failed missions in, 227

VTC (video teleconference), 154–155, 170, 232–233

wadis, 4

walking the bob (Bob Marshall Wilderness Area, "the Bob," Montana), 106–131

Walter (Vietnam veteran, Special Forces), 111–113, 118, 128, 129, 130

warlords (local), establishing relationships with, 206–212

warrior hug, no-touch (Special Forces), 204

"warrior's cocktail," 21

warrior seed in every boy, 20, 22

warriors' sharing of lessons learned, 13–14. See also guiding-principle lessons

weather
Afghanistan, on-the-ground knowledge, 162, 163

weather (*cont.*)
  best time to attack, bad weather, 228
  preparation, Bob Marshall Wilderness
    Area, "the Bob" (Montana), 113, 114
Welch, Jack, 133
Westmoreland, William, 26
We Were Soldiers Once...and Young (film),
  75, 240
what's your recommendation? (reality
  check), 242–261. *See also* shared
  reality
when in doubt, develop the situation
  (guiding-principle lesson), 15, 295. *See
  also* guiding-principle lessons;
  situational awareness (SA)
  adaptation advantage, 103–104
  audacity advantage, 103, 104–105
  embassy bombings (only failure is a
    failure to try), 92
  exploring the frontier (recognizing enemy
    patterns), 222, 234, 236
  imagining everyone's potential as the guy
    on the ground, 153
  imagining how to seek out the guy on the
    ground, 176, 202
  infiltration of Al Qaeda, 100, 102–105
    innovation advantage, 103
    on the ground in Afghanistan (riding the
      edge of chaos), 205, 213
    organizing for combat (dealing with a
      natural disaster), 218
    Osama bin Laden (UBL), 78, 80, 81–82
    reality check (what's your
      recommendation?), 260
    traditional planning vs., 102–103
withdrawal recommendation, Operation
    Anaconda, 268–269, 270
Wolverine Task Force, cloverleaf incident
    (Tikrit, Iraq), 1–13
Woodward, Bob, 151, 162
World Front for Jihad against Jews and
    Crusaders, 66
World War II Manhattan Project, 175
Worldwide Most Wanted List, 173

Yemen, attack on U.S. Troops, 66
Yemen Language Center and Lindh,
    95–96

"zero-defect operations," 76
Zindani, Sheikh al- and Lindh, 96–97
Zubaida, Abu, 102